39TH CONGRESS, 1st Session. } HOUSE OF REPRESENTATIVES. { Ex. Doc. No. 34.

REVENUE SYSTEM OF THE UNITED STATES

10753695

LETTER

FROM THE

SECRETARY OF THE TREASURY,

TRANSMITTING

The report of a commission appointed for the revision of the revenue system of the United States.

JANUARY 29, 1866.—Referred to the Committee of Ways and Means and ordered to be printed.

TREASURY DEPARTMENT, *January* 29, 1866.

SIR: Herewith I have the honor to present to you a report from Messrs. David A. Wells, Stephen Colwell, and S. S. Hayes, appointed a commission for the revision of the revenue system of the United States, in accordance with the provisions of the 19th section of the amendatory act of Congress, approved March 3, 1865.

In presenting this report, it may be proper for me to remark that, with the single exception, perhaps, of the one in regard to the time at which the payment of the principal of the national debt should be commenced, the recommendations of the commission have my hearty approval. The very important work devolved upon the commission, as far as it has been prosecuted, has been most admirably performed. I earnestly ask that the report may receive the early and careful consideration of Congress.

I am, very truly, your obedient servant,

HUGH McCULLOCH,
Secretary of the Treasury.

Hon. SCHUYLER COLFAX,
Speaker of the House of Representatives.

REPORT OF THE UNITED STATES REVENUE COMMISSION.

TREASURY DEPARTMENT,
Office of the U. S. Revenue Commission, January, 1866.

SIR: The undersigned, members of the commission appointed by the Secretary of the Treasury in accordance with the provisions of section 19 of the amendatory act of March 3, 1865, "To provide internal revenue," &c., have the honor to submit the following report:

The following are the provisions of the act, above referred to, constituting this commission:

"That the Secretary of the Treasury is hereby authorized to appoint a commission, consisting of three persons, to inquire and report at the earliest practicable moment upon the subject of raising by taxation such revenue as may be necessary in order to supply the wants of the government, having regard to and including the sources from which such revenue should be drawn, and the best and most efficient mode of raising the same, and to report the form of a bill; and that such commission have power to inquire into the manner and efficiency of the present and past methods of collecting the internal revenue, and to take testimony in such manner and under such regulations as may be prescribed by the Secretary of the Treasury."

The commission, thus authorized, became fully organized in June, 1865, by the appointment of the following members: David A. Wells, of New York; Stephen Colwell, of Pennsylvania; and Samuel Snowden Hayes, of Illinois—with E. B. Elliott, of Massachusetts, as secretary; and has, since then, been constantly engaged in the discharge of the duties assigned to it.

The creation of a commission charged with the investigation of important public questions with reference to future legislation, and, at the same time, consisting of other than members of the National Legislature, was undoubtedly a novelty in American experience. It finds, however, frequent precedents both in Great Britain and in France, and is believed to present some obvious advantages over the methods, ordinarily followed, of conducting such investigations through congressional committees.

In the present instance, a more unrestricted opportunity has been afforded to the commission for personally inquiring into and making themselves practically acquainted with the nature and character of some of the great sources of national revenue, and of observing the operation of the revenue laws in respect to the same, than could have been well enjoyed by a congressional committee, upon the members of which would have rested, at the same time, the onerous and responsible duties of legislation, the many and varied claims of constituents, and also, to a greater or less extent, the claims of important private interests. The commission, therefore, in view of these advantages, confidently anticipate that the first result of their labors, as now presented, may receive the unbiased judgment of the Congress to which they are to be submitted.

Previous to the year 1861 the United States stood before the world in the anomalous position of a great nation with, substantially, no national debt. Since then the measures required for the maintenance of the national existence have entailed upon the nation a debt rivalling or exceeding in magnitude the accumulated deficits of any of the old states of Europe, and rendering necessary the collection of an annual revenue which, though at present somewhat indefinite, may be safely stated as unparalleled by the collections of any other nations, with the exception of France and Great Britain. The question of the hour, then, is, "In what manner shall this debt be treated, the payment of its interest be provided for immediately and recurringly, and the payment of its principal gradually, without impairing the strength and resources of the nation, or of arresting its progress and development?" To endeavor to answer this question in part, is the business with which the commission find themselves charged by the appointment of the Secretary of the Treasury and the authority of Congress.

The same exigency which created the debt, has also rendered it expedient that the nation should thus far avail itself of every means in its power to raise, by direct and indirect taxation, the largest possible revenue in the least possible time, without much regard to acknowledged politico-economic laws or precedents; so that, at the present time, the sources of national revenue may be said to be commensurate and co-extensive with every department or sub-department of trade or industry in the country, as well as of every form of fixed or circulating capital.

It accordingly became apparent to the commission, at the outset, that any attempt to embrace in their investigations, prior to the time of the presentation of a first report, the whole field of inquiry assigned to them, would not only be impracticable, but, also, that any effort with this object in view would, from its necessary diffuseness, lead to no practical or satisfactory results. They therefore, in default of any specific instructions, either from Congress or the Secretary of the Treasury, other than were contained in the act authorizing the commission, adopted the plan of taking up specifically, for investigation, those sources of revenue which our own experience and the experience of other countries have indicated as likely to be most productive under taxation, and most capable of sustaining its burdens. The result of these investigations the commission propose to submit in the form of independent and special reports.

In carrying out this plan, they have sought to make themselves practically acquainted with each subject of inquiry by personal inspection, (when the investigation related to a specific branch of industry,) and by putting themselves in all cases into direct and frequent communication with revenue officials, and with representative business men from every section of the country. The commission have also, in most cases, caused the information communicated to them to be received in the form of testimony, under oath, and to be faithfully reported; and they express the hope that Congress will consider it expedient to order this record to be preserved in printed form. Representing, as it does, the experience and matured opinions of the best business men of the country, each speaking about his own profession, and often revealing facts which, in daily life, are screened from the public eye, this testimony cannot but be of great value for future reference; and in laying it before Congress and the people of the country, the commission feel that they will have rendered an important service, whether their specific recommendations shall be adopted or not. The parliamentary archives of Great Britain contain many such repertories of evidence, to the value of which the public men of England, and the scientific inquiries of all countries, have again and again testified.

It is evident that the work of the commission, prosecuted in the manner described, must necessarily be protracted and laborious. The six months during which they have been occupied have scarcely been sufficient for becoming acquainted with the requirements of their work, and for the gathering of materials to serve as the basis of investigation; and the *unconsidered* statements and memorials touching the relation of the business interests of our country to our revenue system, which have thus far accumulated in their hands, will require at least six months for their proper examination and discussion. They accordingly offer no apologies, if in this their present report the extent of their investigatons should seem too limited for the time during which they have been occupied.

One of the greatest difficulties encountered from the outset has been to obtain exact and comprehensive information; and the commission, as the result of their experience, feel warranted in asserting that no full and reliable statistics concerning any branch of trade or industry in the United States, with possibly a few exceptions, are now or have ever been available.

The census of 1860, only made available for detailed reference some four or five years after its enumeration, has been to the commission of but little service. Nor do the statistics which have been furnished from time to time by the Treasury Department afford the knowledge of those facts which are so essential as a groundwork for the labors of the commission.

On the 9th day of August, 1865, in response to a call for information relative to the importation of spirits distilled from grain, and the duties accruing therefrom, the following returns were sent:

Statement (submitted August 9) exhibiting the quantity of spirits distilled from grain imported into the United States, with rates of duty and imposts accruing thereon, during the fiscal years ending on the 30th of June, 1862 to 1864, inclusive.

Year ending—	Gallons imported.	Duty per gallon.	Duties accruing.
June 30, 1862	1,137,082	$0 50	568,541
June 30. 1863	1,064,576	1 00	1,064,576
June 30, 1864	667,163	1 00	667,163

Subsequently the commission, finding that the above returns did not, in any degree, correspond with the statements of the New York trade, called for a re-examination of the same, and, in answer to their call, were furnished with a re-statement of the foregoing returns, as follows:

Statement (submitted November 2) exhibiting the duties collected upon the importations of spirits distilled from grain, at Boston, New York, Philadelphia, Baltimore and San Francisco, during the fiscal years ending June 30, 1862, 1863, and 1864.*

Year ending—	Gallons.	Duty per gallon.	Duties.
Jnne 30, 1862......................	30,190	$0 40 to 50	$14,534
June 30, 1863......................	45,393	1 00	45,363
Jnne 30, 1864......................	175,144	1 00	175,144

In further illustration, they also submit copies of the returns sent to the commission, under dates of September 12 and November 2, 1865, respecting the imports and duties accruing on chiccory.

Statement (submitted September 12) exhibiting the quantity and value of chiccory imported into the United States, with rates of duty and imposts accruing thereon, for the following years:

	Pounds imported.	Duties accruing.
Year ending June 30, 1862....................	7,451,771	$215,842
Year ending June 30, 1863....................	10,641,350	305,983
Year ending June 30, 1864....................	5,243,760	107,033

Statement (submitted November 2, 1865) exhibiting the duties collected on the importations of chiccory, &c., at Boston, New York, Philadelphia, Baltimore, and San Francisco, for the following years:*

Year ending—	Pounds.	Duty per pound.	Duties.
June 30, 1862..................	7,069,186	1 to 2 cents.	$102,600 30
Juno 30, 1863..................	5,215,105	2 to 3 "	140,402 98
Jnne 30, 1864..................	5,825,346	3 to 4 "	†160,750 83

* Returns from San Francisco received only up to April 30, 1864.

† Although the latter table embraced ***only the five principal ports***, yet it will be observed that the *quantity* and *value* of chiccory imported in the year 1864, as given therein, exceed in amount those given in the former table, which purported to include the returns from ***all the ports*** in the United States.

Subsequently the commission called for a statement of imports, exports, and values of various articles for the fiscal year 1864–'65, and under date of December 19, 1865, they received the following statement, with others, respecting the coffee trade of that year:

Imports:	
Quantity, pounds	104,316,581
Value	$10,966,541
Exports:	
Quantity, pounds	21,962,943
Value	$5,687,856
Estimated consumption:	
Quantity, pounds	82,353,638
Value	$5,278,685

The duties received on the above quantity consumed were, at five cents per pound, $4,117,681.

It will be seen from the above statement that the value of all the coffee imported during the year was returned at ten and a half cents per pound, when the actual fact was that the average invoice price of the coffee imported in the United States during the year 1865 was not less than thirteen cents, and was probably in excess of that figure. Looking next at the treasury statement of the exports of coffee, we find that the 21,962,943 pounds sent out of the country during the same year had *the extraordinary value of nearly twenty-six cents per pound;* while the 82,353,638 pounds retained for consumption had a *value of only six and four-tenths cents per pound;* and finally, the value of the quantity retained for consumption, $5,278,685, paid, at the duty of five cents per pound, an aggregate of $4,117,681, *being seventy-eight per cent of the whole value.*

The truth is, that until of late no occasion has existed to call for the preparation by the Treasury Department of correct statistical data concerning the commerce of the country, and consequently but little attention has been paid to this matter. The changed state of affairs, the present difficulties experienced by this commission, and the future difficulties which in many ways must occur from the want of correct and detailed commercial statistics, will, it is hoped, induce Congress to make careful provision for their preparation and publication.

In the Bureau of Internal Revenue a better system prevails, and the published returns of revenue and the amounts received from specific sources are believed to be substantially correct. Overburdened, however, as this bureau was with work, and delayed by a want of promptness on the part of district collectors,* many of whom are destitute of business experience, it was unable to furnish the commission with any detailed statement of its specific sources of revenue for the fiscal year ending June 30, 1865, until nearly six months thereafter.

Another great source of difficulty experienced by the commission in conducting their investigations, with a view of arriving at any correct estimates of the future revenue of the country, has been the abnormal and disturbed condition of every branch of trade and industry since 1861, owing to the effects of the war, the frequent alterations of the tariff, and the inauguration of the internal revenue system. Many branches of trade and industry have been curtailed during this period from *thirty* to *seventy-five per centum,* and some few have been entirely destroyed.* Every advance made in the tariff and in the excise has,

* By a circular of the Commissioner of Internal Revenue, dated December 29, 1865, it appears that during the previous four months alone over three hundred and fifty errors in the returns of district collectors, in sums varying in amount from a few cents to nearly *sixty thousand dollars,* were detected.

* See Special Report on Distilled Spirits.

moreover, been anticipated to such an extent by every class of importers, dealers, manufacturers, and speculators, that it cannot be said as yet that the government has fully tested the capacity of any one of what may be considered as its great and legitimate sources of revenue. Thus, for example, the commission estimate that on the 1st of July, 1864, the date when the advance in the tax on distilled spirits, of from sixty cents to one dollar and fifty cents per gallon, took effect, *there were made and stored*, in anticipation of this advance, *at least forty millions of gallons*, or a quantity sufficient to supply the wants of the country for at least a year in advance. Since July 1, 1864, therefore, the receipts of the government from distilled spirits have, from this cause, necessarily been inconsiderable. Of cigars, in like manner, it is estimated that from seventy to eighty millions were manufactured and stored in the city of New York alone, in anticipation of the tax. The stock of spices imported into the country, previous to the advance of the tariff, was also probably equal to nearly two years' supply; while in the case of the insignificant article of matches, on which the tax is only one cent per bunch, the stock accumulated in anticipation of the tax was so large, that it has not, even at the present date, (January, 1866,) been entirely exhausted.

This abnormal condition of things, coupled with the fact that the excise has been levied, to a great extent, on a basis of greatly inflated values, renders it extremely difficult to predicate anything with certainty concerning the future from the immediate past.

Before entering into any discussion on the working of our present revenue system, and of the changes which it may be expedient to make in it, the commission would ask attention to a brief *résumé* of the revenue systems of the two countries of Europe which are most akin to the United States in population, resources, and development—France and Great Britain. In both of these countries the necessity of large taxation, extending over a period of many years, has induced a thorough investigation of the subject, and the record of their experience cannot be profitably ignored in the framing of a permanent system for the United States.

REVENUE SYSTEM OF GREAT BRITAIN.

The close of the great European war, in 1815, found Great Britain with a complex system of taxation, the growth of her necessities at a period when vast military and naval expenditures, and the burden of an increasing debt, had tasked the ingenuity of ministers to devise new sources of revenue. "The love of imposts was omniscient; it seized on every article which by any possibility an Englishman could want." More than a thousand different kinds of foreign produce paid tribute at the custom-house, while the heavy hand of the exciseman was laid on many articles of home production and of indispensable domestic use.

Navigation laws—long before adopted to control the carrying trade between Great Britain and her colonies and the rest of the world—had operated to repel foreign commerce; and corn laws, enacted in the interest of the landed aristocracy, had carried the food of the people to starvation prices. The law of 1815 wholly prohibited the importation of foreign wheat till the home price reached eighty shillings a quarter, or about $2 50 a bushel. Under the operation of this law the price of wheat rose from sixty-four shillings a quarter in 1815 to an average of ninety-four shillings in 1817, and in June of that year reached the frightful figure of one hundred and twelve shillings and eightpence, or $3 50 a bushel. Trade languished, the people were starving, and bread riots disturbed the peace and menaced the safety of the kingdom. This state of things gave birth to the struggle between the landed proprietors and the manufacturers, which ended thirty years afterwards in the repeal of the corn laws and the triumph of free trade. The workmen clamored for cheaper food, while their employers petitioned Parliament to extend their markets. The war, with its restrictions on foreign intercourse, had made England the chief manufacturer of the world. A dense population, colonies planted in every clime, a great mercantile marine, and the possession of abundant coal and iron, and of much private capital, supplied conditions to cheap production and a wide diffusion of products such as set the competition of other nations at defiance.

These natural and acquired advantages were, however, in a measure neutralized by unwise commercial restrictions and burdensome taxes, but with the restoration of peace these burdens began gradually to be removed. The commerce of the East had been set free from the monopoly of the East India Company in 1814. The treaty of reciprocity with the United States in 1815, which was followed by similar treaties with the European powers, and alterations made in the navigation laws in 1822, opened the British islands more freely to foreign commerce, and at the same time enlarged the carrying trade of British ships. Heavy duties on raw materials, and materials partly wrought, entering into domestic manufactures, were repealed or greatly lessened; and though the duties on foreign fabrics were also lowered, the importation of some of them seriously interfered with the home manufacturer. In silks alone the French were superior, and against that superiority the British manufacturer was protected by restrictive duties, down to the ratification of the treaty with France in 1860, when, for the sake of advantages to be gained in the export to France of coal, iron, machinery, and other British products, the silk duties were repealed.

From 1815 to 1840 the condition of the manufacturer was steadily improving; but great ameliorations were still needed before the productive capacity of the country could obtain its full development. Foreign competition in the home market had long ceased to be feared, and the only hindrances now lay in domestic restrictions. A parliamentary report in 1840 showed that out of a customs revenue of £22,000,000, £20,000,000 was derived from duties on raw materials and on food; and it disclosed the still more remarkable fact that ninety-four and a half per cent. of this revenue was levied on seventeen articles, while more than eleven hundred articles contributed to make up the residue of five and a half per cent., being the insignificant sum of £1,250,000. In the more numerous category were included all foreign manufactures except of silk.

It thus appeared that the duties on the foreign imports of Great Britain were a direct tax on the home producer; the high price both of raw materials and of food helping to swell the cost of manufactures, and thus benefiting the foreign competitor. "A nation of manufacturers can only subsist as they sell their produce, and they can sell their produce only as they sell it cheap. But the ability to sell their produce cheaply implies a cheap command of the raw material and of the workman's food; to tax these is to decree the nation's ruin and involve all classes alike in bankruptcy and pauperism."

This was the argument of the Manchester party in 1840, and it speedily came to be the creed of the nation. The policy of protection to agriculture yielded at last, and the revenue system was subordinated to the more important end of creating national wealth. All duties burdensome to the manufacturer were repealed, both in the nature of customs and excise, the policy being to enable the British producer to apply the largest amount of home labor to the smallest value in foreign staples, under conditions which enable him to put his product into foreign markets at the lowest possible cost.

This principle is the key to British free trade, and it is claimed to be of universal applicability; but it may be gravely questioned whether it is not protection in a more subtle form. Such is the opinion of M. Block, a modern French economist of eminence, who classes under protective measures the freeing of raw materials and of food from customs duties.

Having described the influences which have determined the present revenue system of Great Britain, we proceed to give the details of the modern budget.

The gross revenues of the United Kingdom for the year ending March 31, 1865, were as follows:

Customs	$115, 023, 808
Excise	97, 048, 180
Stamps	47, 659, 870
Land and assessed taxes	16, 439, 670
Income and property taxes	39, 928, 865
Post office	20, 852, 197
Crown lands	2, 212, 000
Miscellaneous	14, 967, 183
Total	354, 131, 773

Of the *customs revenue* ($115,023,808) twenty-five specified articles yielded $112,819,781, while all other articles (not specified) yielded only $49,431. The balance, appearing under the head of customs, was derived from the duty on British spirits collected at the custom-house, ($1,468,445,) and from sundry petty sources.

The chief portion of this class of revenue was derived from the following twelve articles:

Coffee and chiccory	$2, 604, 803
Corn-meal and flour	2, 839, 979
Currants and raisins	1, 825, 626
Spirits	16, 522, 249
Sugar and molasses	27, 113, 370
Tea	22, 355, 431
Tobacco and snuff	30, 579, 989
Wine	6, 597, 023
Wood and timber	1, 389, 450
	111, 827, 920

Of the *excise* ($97,141,618) the sum of $97,048,180 was derived from nine specified articles, viz:

Chiccory	$52, 315
Hackney carriages	513, 235
Licenses, including game licenses	10, 722, 015
Malt	31, 972, 765
Race-horses	38, 730
Railways	2, 196, 660
Stage-carriages	645, 890
Spirits	50, 883, 655
Sugar	22, 915
	97, 048, 180
All other articles	93, 438
	97, 141, 618

Of the *stamp duties* ($47,659,870) the greatest portion was collected under the following heads:

Deeds and other instruments	$8, 183, 920
Probate of wills and letters of administration	7, 555, 805
Bills of exchange	3, 846, 555

Commutation on bank notes	645, 015
Receipts, drafts, and other 1*d.* stamps	2, 501, 245
Marine insurances	1, 993, 840
Licenses and certificates	655, 920
Newspapers	587, 735
Legacies and successions	11, 689, 970
Fire insurances	7, 861, 980
Probate court fee stamps	674, 300
Patents for inventions	567, 895
Sundry minor classes	895, 690
	47, 659, 870

The *land tax* yielded $5, 619, 600

The *assessed taxes* were mainly under the following heads:

Inhabited houses	$4, 584, 030
Servants	1, 056, 220
Carriages	1, 794, 005
Riding horses	1, 256, 785
Other horses and mules	690, 000
Dogs	1, 051, 650
Armorial bearings	307, 495
Unenumerated	79, 885
	10, 820, 070

The following are about the percentages yielded by each item to the revenue: customs, 32; excise, 28; stamps, 13½; land and assessed taxes, 5; income and property taxes, 11; post office, 5½; miscellaneous, 5.

Of the *customs* revenue, ninety-one per cent. was derived from five articles: spirits, sugar, tea, tobacco, and wine.

Of the *excise*, ninety-seven per cent. was derived from licenses, malt, and domestic spirits.

Intoxicating beverages and tobacco yielded nearly forty per cent. of the total revenue.

The most productive *stamp duties* were those on the conveyance and transmission of property, deeds, probate of wills, and legacies and successions. Next to these stood stamps on policies of insurance.

The *direct tax on land* seems very small, being only about one and a half per cent. of the total revenue; but estates and interest in land are reached through the income tax, of which nearly sixty per cent. (under schedules A and B) is assessed on real property and the profits of occupying it.

The *income tax* is at present six pence in the pound, or more than four per cent. on the assessed valuation. This tax originally created by Mr. Pitt, in 1798, as a war tax, was repealed in 1815, when it yielded $75,000,000. It was re-imposed by Sir Robert Peel, in 1842, to enable him to make his reductions of the tariff. It has varied from five pence to one shilling and four pence, (during the Crimean war,) and, though long treated by the chancellor of the exchequer as a temporary expedient, has been found too useful to be dispensed with, and it is likely in future to have a permanent place in the Budget.

Such are the leading features of the British revenue system. Having always a regard to the exemption of home industry from burdens, Great Britain thus raises her taxes: 1. From articles of necessary and large consumption, as tea, sugar, and coffee. 2. From articles of indulgence, as spirits, beer, (malt,) tobacco, and wine. 3. From licenses and other taxes on occupations. 4. From stamps on legal documents, the conveyance and descent of property, and instruments of business. 5. From occupied houses, and the luxuries of living, servants, horses, dogs, and carriages. 6. From incomes derived from realized property and professional and other earnings. 7. From the post office.

REVENUE SYSTEM OF FRANCE.

The ordinary revenue of France, according to the Budget of 1865, was derivable from the following sources:

Direct taxes	$63,072,280
Registration, stamps, and public domains	81,537,883
Royal forests	8,051,300
Customs duties and salt	29,485,000
Indirect taxes	115,600,400
Post office	14,482,000
Sundry revenues	26,441,989
Produce of miscellaneous taxes	11,736,360
Total	350,407,212

To understand the foregoing table, it will be necessary to analyze the several items, and finally to rearrange them, arbitrarily, with a view to a more intelligible classification.

The *direct taxes* are made up as follows:

Land tax	$33,660,000
Tax on persons and on tenant occupancy	9,687,600
Doors and windows	7,272,240
Licenses ("patentes")	11,801,440
Pleasure horses and carriages	540,000
First warning to newspapers	111,000
Total	63,072,280

The *land tax* is assessed, not on the real value of the land, but on the net rental or income, receipts and expenditures being estimated on an average of ten years. If there are buildings, they are separately assessed on the same principle, the land on which they stand being valued as if for cultivation.

The tax on *persons* is in the nature of a poll-tax, and is estimated at the value of three days' labor, according to the average price paid in the commune.

The tax on *tenant occupancy* ("contribution mobilière") is imposed on all occupants of rented dwellings, and is usually nine or ten per cent. of the rental.

The tax on *doors and windows* is according to a fixed scale; it is levied only on occupied houses, and is usually paid by the tenant.

The *license tax* ("patente") is a tax on trades and occupations, and on certain of the liberal professions. The amount of it is regulated by the nature of the occupation, having regard to the population of the city or town where it is exercised, and by the rental of the premises in which it is carried on. So indispensable is this license, that without it the person of whom it is required cannot sue in a court of justice, have the benefit of any judicial decision, or receive any magisterial certificate.

The revenue from *registration, stamps,* and *public domains* is thus distributed:

Registration, mortgages, &c.	$63, 844, 400
Stamps	15, 255, 600
Sales from and income of public domains, &c	2, 437, 883
	81, 537, 883

Registration is the necessary mode of authenticating various private acts and events, and it is imposed chiefly with a view to revenue. All judicial and magisterial acts are required to be recorded for this purpose, as well as for perpetuating evidence.

Stamps are of two sorts—the one, impressions stamped by government officers on paper, which is required to be used for certain classes of documents; and the other, movable stamps, like the revenue stamps of the United states, which are used and cancelled in the same manner.

The receipts for sale of property and other income from the *public domains* are of a miscellaneous character, and of small amount, and need not be specified.

The chief produce of the *royal forests* is wood and timber, the sale of which yielded the considerable sum of eight millions of dollars.

Customs duties and salt.—This head of the revenue is divided into import duties on—

Miscellaneous merchandise	$14, 439, 200
Colonial sugar	7, 058, 600
Foreign sugars	2, 285, 000
	23, 782, 800
Export duties	82, 000
Navigation dues	832, 600
Sundry customs duties	278, 000
Duty on the consumption of salt, collected through the custom-house	4, 509, 600
	29, 485, 000

Indirect taxes are thus distributed:

Duties on beverages	$42, 685, 400
Duties on consumption of salt, not collected at the custom-house	1, 683, 000
Duties on domestic sugar	11, 786, 000
Produce of government sale of tobacco	45, 295, 600
Produce of government sale of gunpowder	2, 550, 800
Sundry and miscellaneous duties	11, 599, 600
	115, 600, 400

Under the head of *sundry revenues* are the following:

Revenue from the universities	$571, 700
Revenue from Algeria	3, 850, 000
Sums reserved and saved from civil pensions	2, 915, 740
Increase of sinking fund	19, 104, 549
	26, 441, 989

Among the *miscellaneous taxes* ($11,736,360) are taxes on estates in mortmain; on patents for inventions; on telegraphs; profits in new issue of bronze currency; revenues from prisons and houses of correction, &c., &c.

The following classification seems to us to present the sources of revenue more clearly than that adopted in the French budget:

Direct taxes, ownership and use of land and buildings, poll-taxes, licenses, &c.		$63, 072, 280
Registration, stamps, &c.		81, 537, 883
Royal forests (wood and timber sold)		8, 051, 300
Customs duties on foreign merchandise		14, 439, 200
Exports, navigation, and other miscellaneous customs duties		1, 192, 600
Sugar, import duties on colonial	$7, 058, 000	
Sugar, import duties on foreign	2, 285, 000	
Sugar, excise duties on domestic	11, 786, 000	
		21, 129, 600
Salt, collected through custom-house	4, 509, 600	
Salt, collected elsewhere than custom-house	1, 683, 000	
		6, 192, 600
Beverages		42, 685, 400
Tobacco, sale of		45, 295, 400
Gunpowder, sale of		2, 550, 800
Sundry indirect taxes (not enumerated)		11, 599, 600
Post office		14, 482, 000
Revenue from Algeria		3, 850, 000
Income of sinking fund		19, 104, 549
Miscellaneous		15, 223, 800
Total		350, 407, 212

It will be seen by the foregoing analysis that direct taxes, registration, stamps, customs duties, sugar, beverages, and tobacco, yielded more than seventy-six per cent. of the whole revenue, in the following proportions: direct taxes, eighteen per cent.; registration and stamps, twenty-three per cent.; customs duties, (excluding sugar,) four and a half per cent.; sugar, six per cent.; beverages, twelve per cent.; and tobacco, thirteen per cent. The deficit in the French budget for 1864 is reported at about 50,000,000 francs.

Comparing the French with the English revenue system, we observe the same exemption from taxation of home industry, especially of those manufactures which find a market in foreign countries. Land is subjected to heavier burdens in France than in England, and the freedom of occupation and action is restrained by heavier exactions in the way of licenses, stamps, and registrations. The revenue derived from foreign imports is trifling in comparison with the customs revenue of Great Britain. The appetites and indulgences of the people are reached alike in both countries by heavy taxes on sugar, beverages, and tobacco, and in both the post office is made to contribute a large revenue.

Of the two systems, the nature and details of which we have thus briefly sketched, the English is the only one which especially commends itself to the attention of the American investigator; and this system, the result of a long experience in the economy of taxation and national development, and for the perfecting of which the best efforts of British statesmen for at least the last quarter of a century have been assiduously given, affords, in the opinion of the commission, some indications for determining what ought to be the future revenue policy of the United States. And in saying this the commission do not wish to be understood as recommending any servile imitation of details, for nothing seems more evident than that a revenue system for a particular country cannot be framed theoretically or copied from any other, but must in every case be adapted to the resources of the country for which it is designed, and the fiscal aptitudes and capacity of its people.

Thus, upon no one point are writers on the theory of taxation better agreed than that taxation of raw materials is to be avoided as far as possible; but yet, with the experience and practice of the government of British India in respect to opium, saltpetre, and shellac, of Holland in respect to the coffee, spices, and sugar of Java and Sumatra, of China with her tea, Portugal with her wines, and Peru with her guano, it would be hardly the part of wisdom and sound policy for the United States to legislate on general principles only in respect to articles of which they, like the nations referred to, have also a virtual monopoly, and for the supply of which other territories than their own are dependent.

THE NATIONAL REVENUE SYSTEM.

The diffuseness of the present revenue system of the United States is doubtless one of its greatest imperfections, and under it the exemption of any article from taxation is the exception rather than the rule. To assert this, however, is no reflection on the judgment or skill of its authors. The system was framed under circumstances of such pressing necessity as to afford but little opportunity for any careful and accurate investigation of the sources of revenue; but it has most certainly accomplished the attainment of the end designed, namely, the raising of revenue, and the country to-day is undoubtedly receiving by taxation far more revenue than is necessary for its legitimate expenditures. As a success, therefore, our present revenue system is a most honorable testimonial not only to the wisdom of its authors, but to the patriotism of the people, who not only *endured* but *welcomed* the burdens it imposed upon them.

A system of taxation, however, so diffuse as the present one, necessarily entails a system of duplication of taxes, which in turn leads to an undue enhancement of prices, a decrease both of production and consumption, and consequently of wealth, a restriction of exportations and of foreign commerce, and a large increase in the machinery and expense of the revenue collection.

In respect to the injurious influence of this duplication of taxes upon the industry of the country the commission cannot speak too strongly. Its effect has already been most injurious. It threatens the very existence—even with the protection of inflated prices and a high tariff—of many branches of industry; and, with a return of the trade and currency of the country to anything approximating its normal condition, it must, by checking development, prove highly disastrous.

The influence of the duplication of taxes in sustaining prices is also, in the opinion of the commission, far greater than those not conversant with the subject generally estimate; and were the price of gold and of the national currency made at once to approximate, and the present revenue system to continue unchanged, it would be impossible for the prices of most products of manufacturing industry to return to anything like their former level. In proof of this the commission ask attention to the following illustrations:

By section 94 of the act of June 30, 1864, a tax of five per cent. (or its equivalent in specific duties) was imposed upon the sale of most of the industrial products of the country; lumber, breadstuffs, maple and sorghum syrups and sugar, whale and fish oils, and a few other articles, excepted.

By the amended act of March 3, 1865, an increase of twenty per cent. was made to the above rates, making the present *general* manufacturing excise tax six per cent. *ad valorem* on the sale prices of the product.

Under the operation of this law the government now levies and collects from eight to fifteen per cent. (and even in some instances twenty per centum) on almost every finished industrial product. In order to fully understand the reason of such conclusions, it must be borne in mind that but comparatively few products of manufacturing industry come to the consumer as the result of one process, but that the finished product is almost always an aggregate of several distinct and separate manufacturing processes.

A good illustration of this principle, and of the working of the revenue laws in respect to the same, drawn from one of the many statements of experience submitted to the commission, is presented in the manufacture of umbrellas and parasols, as carried on in the cities of New York and Philadelphia. It was formerly the practice of umbrella-makers to manufacture the main constituents of their product as one business; but now the business of an umbrella manufacturer is rather to assemble the various constituents of an umbrella or parasol, which are made separately and in different parts of the country. Thus, for example, the sticks, when of wood, are made in Philadelphia and in Connecticut, part of native and part of foreign wood, on which last a duty may have been paid. If the supporting-rod is of iron or steel, it is the product of still another establishment. In like manner the handles of carved wood, bone, or ivory, the brass runners, the tips, the elastic band, the rubber of which the band is composed, the silk tassels, the buttons, and the cover of silk, gingham, or alpaca, are all distinct products of manufacture; and each of these constituents, if of domestic production, pays a tax when sold of six per cent. *ad valorem*, or its equivalent. The umbrella manufacturer now aggregates all these constituent parts, previously taxed, into a finished product, and *then pays six per centum on the whole.* It is therefore evident that under the present excise system all the parts of the umbrella are taxed *at least twice*, and in some instances *three times*, thus adding from twelve to fifteen per cent. to the cost of the umbrella direct; while we may feel certain, moreover, that each separate manufacturer makes the payment of the six per cent. tax on his special product an occasion for adding from one to three per centum additional to its cost price. In some instances known to the commission this addition, thus made by the manufacturer, by reason of the payment of his general manufacturing tax, has amounted to over six per cent.

Again, in the case of books, pamphlets, &c., a tax imposed on which, being a tax upon knowledge, can only be justified on the grounds of imperative necessity, it is claimed that, including licenses and income tax, the finished book, and its constituent materials, pay from twelve to fifteen distinct taxes before it reaches the reader. Every separate item that enters into the book—paper, cloth, boards, glue, thread, gold-leaf, leather, and type material—pays from three to six per cent. in the first instance, and then five per cent. on the whole combined; and this not upon the *cost* of the manufactured article, but upon the price at which it is sold.

On cotton fabrics the tax now levied and collected ranges, according to the quality of the goods, from *nine* to *fourteen* cents per pound.

On refined sugars, the tax on gross sales, by reason of an inequality of adjustment between the tariff and the excise, is now claimed to be nearly equivalent to all the additional value conferred upon them in refining by all the labor employed therein. Other articles, such as wagons, locomotives, &c., might equally well be cited as illustrations.

Such a system as this violates all the fundamental principles of taxation, inasmuch as the taxes are neither definite in amount, equal in application, nor convenient of collection. While this system prevails, furthermore, it seems useless to talk of reducing prices to anything like their former level, by a reduction or contraction of the currency.

A similar duplication of taxation to that above described must, in the opinion of the commission, also attend the adoption of a tax on sales, which at present seems to find much favor throughout the country. Local taxes on industrial circulation in every State, county, township, and village of the Union would be confessedly calamitous; but they could not be as bad as a frontier drawn around each individual in the nation, over which nothing could pass in or out, not smitten with a tax—repeated at each border.

Another matter of more serious importance, in its bearing upon the industry of the country, than the duplication of taxes, is the lack of equalization or adjustment between the tariff and the excise.

This subject, which the commission, from lack of time, have not been able to investigate as fully as they desired, but upon which they propose to present a special report, demands the serious and prompt attention of Congress. The nature of this inequality can be better illustrated by example than by argument.

We take as before, and as offering the most striking illustrations, the cases of the umbrella and the book industries. In the case of the umbrella and parasol manufacture, the cover, as a constituent element of construction, represents from *one-half* to *two-thirds* the entire cost of the finished article. The silk, the alpaca, and the Scotch gingham, of which the covers are made, are all imported; the former *paying a duty of sixty per cent.*, and the latter two *about fifty per cent. ad valorem;* the variation being slight on the quality of texture. The manufactured umbrella, covered with the same material, whose constituent parts are not taxed, either on the material used in their fabrication, or on their sale, are, however, admitted under the present tariff at *a duty of thirty-five per cent. ad valorem, or at a discriminating duty against the American and in favor of the foreign producer of from fifteen to twenty-five per cent.* If we make allowance for the various United States internal revenue taxes, it is claimed by the American manufacturers that *the discrimination in favor of the foreign producer is fully equal to forty per cent.* It needs hardly to be added, that during the past six months imported umbrellas have been sold at auction in New York and Boston, with the original cost, duty, freight, and charges paid in gold, for a less price than the American article can be manufactured; or that the business of making umbrellas and parasols in New York and Philadelphia, involving a capital of $2,000,000, and employing the labor of some five thousand persons, a majority of whom are females, is threatened with utter destruction. In two instances cited to the commission, umbrella manufacturers have closed their factories in the United States, and, with a view of exporting to this country, have transferred their capital and skill to Europe. In a communication submitted to the commission by a committee of umbrella manufacturers, they state that, "unless relief is speedily obtained, we can perceive no other possible course to pursue but the alternative of retiring entirely from the field, and leaving it to foreign hands."

In the case of books, the commission quote from a recent circular from a leading member of this trade:

"In England, books, papers, &c., are especially exempted from taxation. Here there is a duty of thirty-five per cent. on sized book-papers, and an internal revenue tax equal to about eleven per cent. on books, including the tax on paper and on the difference between the cost and the wholesale price, while the duty on imported books is only twenty-five per cent. With all these odds against us, the English manufacturer should be able to pay his duties and land his books in New York or Boston at about one-half the price at which we can make them here, to wit: His paper costs him only one-third what paper costs here; his labor and materials less than one-half, while we pay an amount about equal to his duties in internal revenue: even more, for he invoices his goods at cost, or nearly so, sending them to his own house here, while our tax is upon every separate item that enters into the book. * * * * An average book would, perhaps, take one pound of paper.

This in America now costs	30	cents.
Other material, say	10	"
Labor	12	"
11 per cent. internal revenue tax	7½	"
Total cost in the United States	59½	cents.

Paper in England	10 cents.
Other material	5 "
Labor	6 "
Tariff	5¼ "
Total cost of English book delivered here	26¼ cents.*

"The difference in exchange at the present time probably would make the tariff about equal to the internal revenue on the American book, still leaving the English book, landed in New York or Boston, to cost only about half as much as the American book made here. How long will it take, with this state of things existing, to transfer all the miscellaneous book publishing to London, and to cripple our paper mills, and send our skilled workmen into other channels to get a livelihood? * * * * * * *

"That a repeal or modification of the paper duty would not afford adequate relief is apparent from the fact that foreign paper can be imported now cheaper than it can be furnished of similar quality here. If this be true of what may properly be termed a raw material, so far as books are concerned, the inference is patent that the matured product should have at least equal protection with that raw material; and while the monarchical governments of Europe, especially Great Britain, make it a matter of public policy to exempt books and literature from all taxation, it is also evident that it is neither just nor equal, in a country where, above all others, the public welfare depends upon the universal diffusion of knowledge, that there should be levied upon the medium of this diffusion a higher tax in internal revenue than the foreigner who seeks our trade has to pay in duties to the customs."

The commission would add that at the present time the one article which, above all others, would seem to be a peculiar product of American industry, viz: Webster's Spelling Book, is now being printed in large quantities in London for the use of American schools.

Another striking illustration of the necessity for the equalization and adjustment of the tariff and the internal revenue act is afforded in the case of Manilla rope. By the present tariff act, *Manilla hemp* imported direct from Manilla is charged with a duty of $25 per ton; and when imported from Europe, an additional duty of 10 per cent. *ad valorem*, amounting to between $15 and $25 per ton, (according to its cost in Europe,) making, in such case, the whole duty amount to from $40 to $50 per ton. On the other hand, the duty on imported or *Manilla rope* is only 2½ cents per pound, or $56 per ton. By the internal revenue act, the tax on the manufacture of cordage is fixed at 6 per cent. on the market value, which at the present time amounts to about 1½ cent per pound, or over $33 per ton. It seems evident, therefore, that while the American manufacturers of cordage are paying a duty on hemp imported directly, of $58 per ton, (and when imported indirectly, of $73 per ton;) and while the only duty on imported rope is but $56 per ton, that not only are they without protection, but that there is a difference in the taxation against them, and in favor of foreign manufacturers, which must result most injuriously to this branch of business. We need only add that under this state of things, the importations of Manilla cordage from Europe seem to be rapidly increasing.

PROPOSED REVENUE POLICY FOR THE FUTURE.

In respect to the evils arising from excessive duplication of taxes under the internal revenue system and from a lack of equalization between the tariff and the excise, it may be urged that the remedy for the latter difficulty is most easy, viz: *by increasing the tariff*. To this, however, as a permanent measure, there are most serious objections, inasmuch as the lack of equalization is not confined to the articles specified in our illustrations, but is very general, and will be more and more extensive as the value of currency approximates to that of gold; while an increase in the tariff, sufficient to remedy all the difficulties, would render the tariff itself almost prohibitory, or at least so high as to invite continued assaults, deprive it of all elements of stability, and increase the business of the contra-

*The commission would, however, call attention to the fact that no allowance is here made for freight, insurance, and other charges of transportation, and that the cost of the English book is given in gold, the American in United States currency.

bandist. The remedy, therefore, for the difficulties above pointed out and illustrated, save in a few striking instances, which have probably resulted from oversight in the framing of the law, must, in the opinion of the commission, be sought for in *such a revision of the present internal revenue system as will look to an entire exemption of the manufacturing industry of the United States from all direct taxation*, (distilled and fermented liquors, tobacco, and possibly a few other articles, excepted.) This the commission are unhesitatingly prepared to recommend.

As, however, the revenue derived from the excise on the industrial products of the country amounted to nearly sixty per cent. of the gross internal revenue in 1863; to sixty-four and a half per cent. in 1864; and to nearly fifty per cent. in 1865, it is evident that a radical change of the kind recommended should not be made at once, but gradually, and according as experience satisfies us of our ability to substitute other and less objectionable forms of taxation adequate to produce a revenue corresponding to that relinquished.

To endeavor to remedy the difficulties growing out of the present duplication of taxation and want of equalization between the excise and the tariff, by *specific enactments of exemptions,* as has been proposed by some, would, in the opinion of the commission, be impracticable, and would crowd the statute book with such a detail of enumeration as would render the law exceedingly difficult of comprehension, and open the way for more gigantic frauds than are now practiced. The evil is radical, and the remedy must also be radical.

Looking back upon the history of the country for the last quarter of a century, we find that during the decade from 1840 to 1850 the population of the United States increased 35 per cent., while the national wealth during the same period experienced an increase of 89 per cent. During the next decade, from 1850 to 1860, the increase of population was $35\frac{5}{10}$ per cent., and of wealth over 126 per cent.* Now, without undertaking to deduce any estimates of the future from the past, the commission, nevertheless, think they are warranted in asserting that the circumstances favoring the future increase of the country, both as regards population and wealth, find no parallel in the history or experience of any other nation; and it need hardly be added that if a development in any degree approximate to the past can be maintained and continued, the extinguishment of the national debt, in a comparatively brief period, becomes a matter of no uncertainty. To secure this development, both by removing the shackles from industry, and by facilitating the means of rapid and cheap intercommunication between the different sections of the country, is to effect at the same time a solution of all the financial difficulties which now press upon us.

Until these ends are effected, it is of no avail to enumerate the natural resources of the country, or to dwell upon the energy or intelligence of our people. The experience of Great Britain and New England on the one hand, and of Mexico on the other, affords striking examples of the truth of the maxim of modern political economy, that "those countries are the richest where men are the most active, and not those where nature has been the most bountiful."

Assuming, then, that the policy indicated—which we may here restate in brief to be *the abolition or speedy reduction of all taxes which tend to check development, and the retention of all those which, like the income tax, falls chiefly upon realized wealth*—is accepted as the desirable future revenue policy of the

* "The estimated value of all the real and personal estate in the United States, belonging to individuals, in 1850, was $7,135,780,228. This included the value of 3,204,313 slaves, which, at $500 each, amounted to $1,602,156,500. This deducted from $7,135,780,228 would leave $5,533,623,728.

"The estimated value of all the real and personal estate belonging to individuals in 1860 was $16,159,616,068. This included the value of 3,953,587 slaves, which, at $500 each, amounted to $1,876,793,500. This deducted from $16,159,616,068, would leave $14,282,822,568. Thus the total capital stock of the country increased from 1850 to 1860 at the rate of 158 per cent."

country, the question next arises. In what manner and to what extent can it be carried out, and at the same time insure to the government a revenue adequate to its necessities?

SOURCES OF REVENUE.

This brings us to the consideration of the nature and capacity of the sources available to the government for revenue, and to the special department of investigation assigned to the commission.

According to the estimate of the Secretary of the Treasury, there will be required for the year ending June 30, 1867, to meet the expenditure of the government, and to provide for the interest on the public debt, a revenue of $284,317,181. Assuming this estimate as a basis, let us now examine in detail the sources whence the revenue necessary to meet this expenditure can be drawn. We would first ask attention to the revenue derivable from

IMPOSTS, OR CUSTOMS.

The following table exhibits the annual imports and exports of the United States from 1859 to 1865, inclusive:

	Value of imports.	Value of exports.	Duties received.
Fiscal year 1859..........	$338, 765, 130	$356, 789, 462	$49, 565, 824
1860..........	362, 163, 941	400, 122, 296	53, 187, 512
1861..........	350, 775, 835	410, 856, 812	39, 582, 186
1862..........	205, 819, 823	229, 790, 280	49, 056, 398
1863..........	252, 187, 587	331, 809, 459	69, 059, 642
1864..........	328, 514, 559	340, 665, 580	102, 316, 153
1865..........	234, 434, 167	336, 697, 123	84, 928, 260

For the five years prior to and including 1861, the average annual value of *imports* was in excess of three hundred and fifty millions of dollars; and for the three years next succeeding June 30, 1861, the annual average has been about two hundred and sixty-two millions.

For the five years prior to and including 1861, the average annual value of *exports* was, including gold, not far from three hundred and seventy-one millions of dollars; and for the three years next succeeding the fiscal year 1861, the annual average was a little over three hundred millions, also including gold.

With the return of at least one and a half million of men from unproductive to productive avocations, and with a renewed demand for cotton and naval stores at greatly enhanced prices, coupled with a renewed ability to supply the same, the commission think it safe to estimate the average value of our *exports* for the three years next succeeding June 30, 1866, at not less than *four hundred millions of dollars;* and as experience has shown that the demand for foreign commodities by the people of the United States is limited mainly by their capacity to purchase the same, we believe that we are further warranted in assuming that the average annual value of *importations* from abroad for the same period will *not be less than three hundred and fifty millions of dollars.*

The commerce of Great Britain is estimated to be increasing at the present time, at from eight to ten per cent. per annum. With the continuance of peace, and with the expansion of our population to thirty-eight millions in 1868—a number at least one-fifth in excess of that of Great Britain—progression, not retrogression, in American commerce, should be anticipated.

As the average of the present tariff is understood to be upwards of *forty* per cent. upon the invoiced value of those importations upon which duties are levied,* the average having been greatly increased during the past few years by the imposition of duties upon tea, coffee, and other articles previously on the free list, as well as by some additions to other articles, the commission, after making due allowance for a possible reduction of some duties, and an increase of the free list, think it safe to estimate the amount of revenue derivable from customs, for the fiscal year 1867, to be at least *one hundred and thirty millions of dollars.*†

Indeed, in view of the facts developed by the commission in their investigations, showing the enormous reduction in the consumption of some of the leading articles of importation by reason of the war, (see special reports on tea, coffee and sugar,) and the almost equally rapid increase in the consumption of the same articles since the war, they think they may safely assign a greater revenue from customs than that above given.

As will be seen by reference to these specific reports, the consumption of *coffee* in the United States decreased from the annual average of 200,000,000 pounds in 1860, to less than 80,000,000 pounds in 1863. During the same period the consumption of *sugar* decreased from thirty-one to nineteen pounds *per capita* ; and of *tea* for the whole country, about twenty-three per cent. The gain in revenue from the increased consumption of these articles in 1866, as compared with 1863–'64, will not probably be less than $200,000,000, while the aggregate revenue for that year from the same three articles will probably exceed $40,000,000. It should also be borne in mind that, by the termination of the Reciprocity treaty, many articles which are now admitted from the British provinces free of duty will hereafter be subjected to duty, and thus form another element of future increase in the customs revenue.

INTERNAL REVENUE.

We come next to the consideration of those sources of revenue referable to the excise or internal taxation.

---

* The following table, prepared for the commission by Lorain Blodget, esq., of the Philadelphia custom-house, appraiser at large, exhibits the duties paid on imports, and the average percentages of the same on the value thereof for the fiscal year 1864–'65 :

	Total imports.	Dutiable imports.	Duties paid.	Per cent. of total.	Per cent. of dutiable.
New York	$155,841,013	$143,347,382	$61,169,479	39.25	42.67
Philadelphia	8,126,085	7,265,314	3,874,815	47.67	53.33
Boston, (quarter ending March 31, 1865, only)	5,193,931	4,735,742	1,991,600	38.34	42.05
Average of the above	169,161,029	155,348,438	67,035,894	39.63	43.15

The above statement is of duties paid on merchandise entered for consumption, and on all merchandise withdrawn from warehouse for consumption for the above periods, excluding imports going into warehouse, and all estimated duties.

From this statement it appears reasonable to assume that the existing tariff levies an average of about forty per cent. on the total value of imports ; and about forty-three per cent. on the values of those paying duty.

† It is worthy of remark that the revenue derived from customs since 1861 has, in every year, exceeded the estimate of the Treasury Department. The estimate of the Secretary of the Treasury for the year 1863–'64, was $70,000,000, while the receipts were over $102,000,000 ; for 1864–'65, it was also estimated at $70,000,000, while the receipts were nearly $85,000,000. For the first quarter of the current fiscal year, the receipts from customs were over $47,000,000, and the estimate of the Secretary for the remaining three quarters was $100,000,000 ; making a probable total for the year of $147,000,000.

The aggregate receipts of internal revenue for the fiscal years 1863, 1864, and 1865, are returned as follows:

1863*	$41,003,191 93
1864	116,850,672 44
1865	211,129,529 17

The following table shows the amount derived from the principal specific sources of internal revenue in the above years, the aggregate annual amounts, and the percentage ratio of the amount derived from each specific source to the whole for the same periods:

Articles.	Receipts for fiscal year 1863.	Per cent. of the whole.	Receipts for fiscal year 1864.	Per cent. of the whole.	Receipts for fiscal year 1865.	Per cent. of the whole.
Manufactures and products:						
Books, magazines, &c	....	.....	....	.....	$354,528	.17
Boots and shoes	....	.....	....	.....	3,280,627	1.55
Bullion	....	.....	....	.....	379,518	.18
Clothing	$31,241	.07	$350,486	.30	6,820,937	3.23
Carriages	243,704	.59	320,076	.27	880,021	.41
Candles	117,133	.28	186,228	.16	326,583	.15
Chemical productions	....	.....	....	.....	317,383	.15
Cigars, cheroots, &c	476,589	1.16	1,255,424	1.07	3,087,421	1.46
Clocks, timepieces, &c	17,771	.04	39,166	.03	....	.....
Confectionery*	153,824	.37	465,793	.39	569,473	.27
Coal	318,425	.77	572,436	.40	835,994	.39
Cotton, raw	351,311	.85	1,268,412	1.09	1,772,983	.84
Cotton fabrics, yarns, threads	1,600,947	3.90	3,548,173	3.03	7,331,148	3.47
Distilled liquors	3,229,991	7.87	28,431,798	24.33	15,995,701	7.58
Fermented liquors	1,558,083	3.79	2,223,720	1.90	3,657,181	1.73
Furs	78,852	.19	113,827	.09	222,559	.10
Furniture and manufactures of wood	....	.....	1,679,940	1.43	2,733,248	1.27
Gas, illuminating	435,600	1.06	714,740	.61	1,348,324	.63
Glass, all manufactures of	138,908	.33	303,268	.26	585,430	.27
Gold manufactures, jewelry, &c	85,599	.20	218,914	.19	543,430	.26
Gunpowder	78,696	.19	155,302	.13	248,376	.11
Glue	9,048	.02	25,629	.02	44,517	.02
Gutta-percha manufactures	....	.....	5,425	.....	31,282	.014
India-rubber, manufactures of	112,700	.27	233,783	.20	635,976	.30
Iron, blooms, &c	....	.....	....	.....	52,158	.024
Iron, bar, rod, band, sheet, &c	258,536	.60	435,911	.37	807,239	.38
Iron, plate	52,221	.12	86,535	.07	150,292	.07
Iron, railroad	78,750	.19	175,838	.15	284,783	.13
Iron, railroad, re-rolled	66,336	.16	119.226	.10	376,265	.18
Iron castings	50,349	.12	242,737	.20	795,201	.37
Iron castings, (stoves and hollow-ware)	79,952	.19	123,489	.10	211,849	.10
Iron, cut nails and spikes	110,905	.27	184,500	.16	328,940	.15
Iron, pig	....	.....	....	.....	1,484,383	.70
Iron rivets, nuts, &c	6,812	.02	43,729	.037	56,498	.0 2

* The act of July, 1862, took effect September 1, and the receipts for the fiscal year 1863 are but for ten months. A discrepancy exists between these amounts and those from the office of the Secretary of the Treasury. The same receipts are not always reported and entered upon the books of the two offices on the same day. The difference is only one of account.

TABLE—Continued.

Articles.	Receipts for fiscal year 1863.	Per cent. of the whole.	Receipts for fiscal year 1864.	Per cent. of the whole.	Receipts for fiscal year 1865.	Per cent. of the whole.
Iron, miscellaneous	....	.....	....	.....	221,071	.10
Iron, manufactures of	969,082	2.36	1,891,062	1.61	3,723,310	1.76
Total iron and manufactures.	1,672,943	4.08	3,303,027	2.82	8,494,989	4.02
Lead, sheet, lead pipes, and shot	$54,614	.13	$110,527	.09	$74,460	.035
Lead, white	23,080	.056	48,564	.04	52,067	.024
Leather of all descriptions	1,982,004	4.83	4,004,047	3.43	4,337,266	2.05
Oil, coal, refined petroleum, &c.	649,962	1.58	2,255,329	1.93	3,047,213	1.44
Oil, lard, linseed, &c.	114,219	.28	217,291	.018	414,547	.19
Paper of all descriptions, binders' boards, &c.	301,472	.73	917,141	.80	1,082,476	.51
Petroleum, crude	....	.....	....	.....	229,546	.10
Pianos and other musical instruments	....	.....	....	.....	259,384	.12
Pickles, preserved fruit, vegetables, meats, &c	62.534	.15	110,791	.09	172,314	.08
Pins	15,403	.04	22,010	.02	24,802	.....
Pottery ware	22,962	.056	47,425	.04	93,221	.044
Sails, tents, shades, awnings, &c	3,771	.....	35,946	.03	78,272	.037
Salæratus, and bicarb. of soda	23,003	.057	32,974	.03	31,609	.014
Salt	118,579	.29	298,912	.25	335,349	.15
Screws, (wood)	28,760	.07	62,943	.05	122,693	.06
Ships and other vessels	1,748	.....	167,514	.14	347,218	.16
Silk, manufactures of	44,167	.107	97,653	.08	216,189	.10
Silver, manufactures of	18,372	.044	36,950	.03	59,768	.026
Snuff	34,466	.08	240,934	.20	283,352	.13
Soap of all descriptions	266,406	.65	449,001	.38	791,416	.37
Starch	15,680	.04	36,261	.03	131,232	.06
Steel	40,657	.10	91,768	.08	174,052	.08
Steel, manufactures of	149,226	.36	299,373	.25	549,767	.26
Sugar, brown or raw	134,228	.32	1,267,616	1.09	86,510	.04
Sugar, refined	220,234	.53	873,140	.79	1 957,893	.92
Tobacco, manufactured	2,576,889	6.28	7,086,685	6.32	8,017,020	3.80
Turpentine, spirits of	....	.....	....	.....	8,462	.....
Umbrellas and parasols	49,735	.12	68,770	.06	111,147	.05
Varnishes	40,131	.10	92,356	.08	149,981	.07
Water, mineral, sarsaparilla, &c	833	.....	7,014	.....	85,546	.04
Wine	8,824	.....	28,303	.02	43,216	.02
Woollen fabrics, and all manufactures of wool	1,880,029	4.58	3,655,132	3.1	7,947,094	3.79
Zinc, oxide of	15,806	.04	28,276	.02	41,641	.02
Miscellaneous articles	4,793,932	11.69	7,297,163	6.24	12,382,569	5.86
Total manufactures and productions	24,403,091	59.71	75,403,386	64.53	104,156,911	49.33
Animals slaughtered	$710,812	1.73	$695,202	.59	$1,261,357	.60
Gross receipts—						
Advertisements	$40,629	.10	$133,315	.11	$227,530	.10
Bridges and toll-roads	18,674	.045	36,354	.03	75,269	.037
Canals	....	.....	....	.....	92,421	.044
Express companies	2,680	.....	267,773	.22	529,276	.25
Ferries	20,852	.05	60,074	.05	126,133	.06

TABLE—Continued.

Articles	Receipts for fiscal year 1863.	Per cent. of the whole.	Receipts for fiscal year 1864.	Per cent. of the whole.	Receipts for fiscal year 1865.	Per cent. of the whole.
Insurance companies					805,992	.38
Lotteries					29,249	.013
Railroads			2,127,250	1.82	5,917,293	2.80
Ships, barges, &c					431,211	.20
Stage-coaches, wagons, &c					469,188	.22
Steamboats	150,620	.36	278,097	.24	638,812	.30
Telegraph companies					215,050	.10
Theatres, circuses, &c					140,442	.069
Total gross receipts	233,455	.57	2,902,863	2.48	9,697,866	4.50
Sales—						
Auction	$64,004	.15	$138,082	.12	$410,176	.19
Merchandise brokers					596,474	.28
Stock brokers					2,202,793	1.04
Gold brokers, &c					852,801	.40
Total sales	64,004	.15	138,082	.12	4,062,244	1.92
Licenses—						
Apothecaries	$27,308	.068	$29,792	.026	$32,872	.015
Auctioneers	49,092	.12	58,147	.05	80,545	.038
Bankers	90,868	.22	74,449	.06	846,686	.40
Billiards	34,120	.08	33,188	.028	54,025	.026
Brewers	70,850	.17	66,289	.06	77,747	.037
Bowling alleys	6,873		7,781		13,490	
Cattle brokers	98,090	.24	106,337	.09	207,905	.10
Commission brokers	149,869	.36	204,098	.17	213,095	.10
Produce brokers					22,954	
Pawnbrokers					13,235	
Stock brokers	105,096	.25	98,678	.08	120,912	.058
Other brokers	1,058		1,001		3,133	
Builders and contractors	6,615		73,383	.06	82,273	.039
Butchers	2,154		88,450	.07	152,421	.07
Distillers	38,632	.096	49,022	.042	42,968	.02
Hotels	255,273	.62	252,610	.21	396,768	.18
Lawyers	142,900	.35	129,186	.11	190,377	.09
Lottery-ticket dealers	10,250		3,091		43,480	.02
Manufacturers	463,630	1.13	471,091	.40	635,115	.30
Peddlers	287,456	.70	255,435	.22	459,298	.21
Photographers	44,859	.11	52,536	.045	74,608	.035
Physicians and surgeons	238,383	.58	235,583	.20	302,847	.14
Retail dealers	1,227,912	3.00	1,336,346	1.14	1,606,778	.76
Retail dealers in liquors	1,477,754	3.60	1,612,736	1.38	2,205,866	1.04
Stallions and jacks	45,985	.11	219,578	.19	277,166	.13
Wholesale dealers	1,315,118	3.20	1,229,787	1.05	3,543,105	1.68
Wholesale dealers in liquors	384,160	.93	176,765	.14	400,693	.19
Miscellaneous	249,873	.61	280,030	.24	511,116	.24
Total of licenses	6,824,178	16.64	7,145,389	6.11	12,613,478	5.96
Income	$455,741	1.11	$14,919,279	12.76	$20,567,350	9.74
Legacies and successions	56,593	.14	310,836	.27	545,807	.26
Articles in Schedule A:						
Billiard tables	$10,731	.02	$68,000	.06	$67,754	.03
Carriages and harness	243,704	.59	320,076	.28	322,720	.15
Piano-fortes					7,752	
Gold plate	46		66		126	
Silver plate	108,690	.26	130,024	.11	117,987	.056
Watches					9,139	

TABLE—Continued.

Articles.	Receipts for fiscal year 1863.	Per cent. of the whole.	Receipts for fiscal year 1864.	Per cent. of the whole.	Receipts for fiscal year 1865.	Per cent. of the whole.
Yachts	2,459	......	2,673	......	2,098	......
Other articles	....	......	....	......	252,690	.12
Total in Schedule A	365,630	.89	520,839	.44	780,266	.37
Banks, &c	$1,910,937	4.66	$7,017,547	6.00	$13,579,594	6.43
Passports	8,407	.02	11,001	......	29,535	......
Special income tax	....	......	....	......	28,929,312	13.70
Penalties, &c	27,170	.07	193,600	.16	520,362	.25
Stamps	4,140,175	10.10	5,894,945	5.04	11,162,392	5.28
Salaries	696,182	1.70	1,705,125	1.45	2,826,332	1.34
Aggregate receipts	41,003,193	......	116,850,672	......	211,129,529	......

For the current fiscal year the Commissioner of Internal Revenue, in his report, under date of November 30, 1865, estimated the receipts of internal revenue at $272,000,000. By an estimate, however, submitted to the commission, January 6, 1866, the Commissioner, from further data obtained since the publication of his report, is of the opinion that the receipts of the current fiscal year will probably reach $300,000,000. The "certificates of deposit" received at the Internal Revenue office, from June 30 to December 31, 1865, and entered upon books of the cashier, amounted to $175,556,458 02.

Distilled spirits.—Of the various sources of revenue included under the internal revenue, that of *distilled spirits* ranks first in importance. The amount of revenue derived from this source for the several fiscal years during which the internal revenue law has been in operation is as follows:

1863	$3,229,990 79
1864	28,431,797 83
1865	15,995,701 66

During the fiscal year 1863 the tax was uniformly twenty cents per gallon. For the fiscal year 1864 the tax was twenty cents until March 7, after which it was sixty cents. From July 1, 1864, until January 1, 1865, it was $1 50 per gallon, and afterwards $2. Of the receipts from excise on distilled spirits in the year 1865, $3,862,753, or nearly one-fourth of the whole amount, was from spirits previously bonded, and paying the former rate of twenty and sixty cents per gallon.

The average taxable production of distilled spirits per year, from September 1, 1862, to June 30, 1865, as returned to the department, was 40,537,371 gallons.

The amount of distilled spirits produced in the country during the year 1860 was in excess of *ninety millions of gallons.* The amount at present required to meet the consumption of the country, under the influence of the high rate of taxation imposed upon this article, is estimated by the commission at from *forty-two to forty-five millions of gallons;* and with the continuance of the present rate of excise they have no reason to believe that this amount will, for some years to come, be either largely increased or diminished.

Of the amount at present required to supply the consumption of the country, the commission estimate that probably about 39,000,000 gallons are required for drinking purposes, leaving from 3,000,000 to 6,000,000 gallons for industrial uses. This estimate does not include the amount of spirits exported, from which, by reason of the drawback, no revenue accrues. The largest amount ever exported in any one year has not, according to the official returns, exceeded 3,000,000 gallons.*

In regard to the rate of tax to be imposed upon spirituous or distilled liquors, the commission are unanimously of the opinion that the present rate of two dollars per gallon is in excess of the proper revenue standard, and that a reduction will be for the interests both of the revenue and of the country. The reasons which have led to this conclusion are presented in detail in the "Special Report (No. 5) on Distilled Spirits," to which the commission would respectfully ask attention. *They accordingly recommend that the rate of tax on distilled spirits be reduced to one dollar per gallon.*

With this rate of duty, and with the increase in the annual consumption for industrial purposes (estimated at not less than 10,000,000 gallons) which must follow, the commission are of the opinion that, making all allowances for a certain amount of illicit distillation, which, under any circumstances, will take place, an average annual revenue of *at least forty millions of dollars* from this source may be collected.

But whatever may be the rate of tax agreed upon for the future, it is clearly evident that a far more stringent and effective law than that which now exists is needed if any fair proportion of the amount which government has a right to expect from this source is to be collected, and protection at the same time extended to the honest distiller as against the competition of his illicit competitor.

The commission, therefore, present, in connexion with their special report upon this subject, a draught of a new law, which they believe will be effectual for the prevention of fraud and the securing of the revenue. This bill, which is necessarily arbitrary and restrictive, does not, in some of its essential features, meet the approval of a portion of the distilling interest of the country, and their opposition to it may be fairly expected.

The commission have, however, given a great amount of time to the investigation of this subject, and have availed themselves of the judgment of the most experienced revenue officials, distillers and dealers, from various sections of the country; and have also sought to acquaint themselves most thoroughly with the manner in which this subject is treated for revenue in the various states of Europe.

The securing of a large revenue from distilled spirits in the United States is absolutely necessary to insure the successful carrying out of any plan for simplifying the internal revenue system, and relieving the general industry of the country from a burden of taxation which must inevitably result in disaster. No industrial interest in the country can better sustain the burden of taxation than distilled spirits. The precedents of all other countries are uniform in favor of taxing spirits to the *maximum* consistent with revenue; and while any relaxation of the law, on the one hand, does not benefit the consumer, its stringent enforcement with a regulation of the business will not diminish the amount which appetite or industrial necessity demands for consumption. If it be urged that the bill as reported by the commission is too restrictive and arbitrary in its character, destructive of small private interests, and as imposing large additional restrictions and expenses upon all engaged in the business, it may be replied that the amount of good which must inevitably accrue to the whole country by the course recommended—if the same will insure an enforcement of the law and the collection of the revenue—is sufficient to justify a disregard of the interests of a comparatively small number of individuals. The commission, therefore,

*See Special Report (No. 5,) on Distilled Spirits.

express the hope that Congress will not too readily listen to the appeals of those who are more anxious to subserve their own interests than the interests of the country.

Fermented liquors.—The next source of revenue to which the commission ask attention is that derivable from *fermented liquors*, which, like distilled spirits, are capable of sustaining, without injury to the country, a heavy taxation. From this source the following revenues have accrued for the fiscal years 1863, 1864, and 1865:

1863	$1,558,083 41
1864	2,223,719 73
1865	3,657,181 06

From September 1, 1862, to March 3, 1863, the tax was one dollar per barrel of not more than thirty-one gallons; from that date to April 1, 1864, sixty cents; and since that time, *one dollar*. The number of barrels upon which the tax was received, as nearly as can be ascertaided, was 1,765,827 in 1863; 3,459,119 in 1864; and 3,657,181 in 1865.

By the census of 1860 the number of breweries then existing in the United States was returned at 1,269, affording a product of nearly four million barrels (3,812,346.) The commission, after a careful review of this branch of industry, and personal consultation with nearly every leading brewer of both ale and lager-beer in the United States, are of the opinion that the number of barrels of beer produced and consumed in the country during the fiscal year 1865 was nearly or quite 6,000,000, and that the annual increase of product at the present time is about ten per cent. per annum, mainly of lager-beer. If this opinion be correct, it is apparent that the government received for the above year but little more than sixty per cent. of its just dues from this source.

Upon the announcement of the appointment of this commission in the spring of 1865, the National Brewers' Association appointed a committee of three of their most prominent members to visit Europe, and examine, carefully and in detail, the results of the working of the systems of taxation in regard to fermented liquors adopted in those countries of Europe where the demand for such liquors is more general and extensive than in the United States.

The report of that committee, comprising a great amount of information touching this industry, now so rapidly developing itself in the United States, has, by vote of the Brewers' Association, been placed in the hands of the commission, and is now at the disposal of Congress for publication if they deem it expedient. The commission believe that its publication would be of great benefit to the brewing interest of the country, and, indirectly, to the revenue; and they therefore recommend it.

As the present rate of tax imposed upon fermented liquors, viz: one dollar per barrel of thirty-one gallons, is in excess of the rate imposed by any of the states of Europe (Austria excepted;) and as the present rate, moreover, in the opinion of the commission, after full consideration, is believed to be fully up to the revenue standard; and as such is all but unanimously acquiesced in by the brewing interest of the country, they would, therefore, recomend *that the existing rate be neither increased nor diminished.*

The determination of the proper mode of collecting the tax on fermented liquors, and preventing the large amount of fraud which has heretofore, undoubtedly, been committed in regard to the same, has been to the commission a subject of no little difficulty. By reference to their Special Report, (No. 6,) it will be seen that a tax on malt in this country is not practicable; neither is the plan, also investigated by the commission, of gauging and assessing the liquor, either in the "*coppers*" during the process of manufacture, or subsequently, while in the fermenting vats. Abandoning both of these methods, therefore, they have, with the full concurrence and assistance of the leading brewers of the country, devised a plan for collecting the tax by means of a stamp, printed on insoluble parchment paper, to be affixed to each barrel sold and removed from the place of its manufacture, with a requirement that the same be cancelled by the retailer or consumer. Specimens of the stamps designed for this purpose have been prepared for submission to Congress, while the full details of the plan for using them are given in the special report referred to. With the adoption of this system, and the retention of the present rate of excise, the commission estimate that the government may rely upon an immediate annual revenue, from fermented liquors, of at least *five millions of dollars.*

Cotton.—The attention of the commission has been especially given to the *cotton* product of the United States, as a source of revenue, and they would refer to their Special Report, (No. 3,) and also to the testimony accompanying the same, as embodying all the information requisite for the formation of a correct opinion on this subject. As the result of their investigations, the commission recommend that a tax of *five cents per pound* be levied on and after July 1, 1866, upon all cotton the product of the United States; and that the same be collected of the manufacturer at the place of consumption, and of the merchant or factor at the port of export, upon all foreign shipments. Such a plan will not interfere with the growth and cultivation of this staple, or its free movement throughout the country, and will reduce the machinery and the expenses of collection to their *minimum.*

The above proposed rate of taxation on cotton, it is believed, will not prove in any degree detrimental to any national interest, and will yield a revenue, at twenty-two dollars per bale, of *twenty-two* millions of dollars for every million of bales produced and sold for consumption. With a crop of three millions of bales, and a tax of five cents per pound, the government might derive an annual revenue of $66,000,000; or of $88,000,000 on a crop of four millions of bales, which would be less than the crop of 1859-60. Of this sum—if the consumption of the United States shall reach, in either of these years, the consumption of 1860—the inhabitants of the United States would pay about $21,000,000; and it is believed that there are few taxes which can be levied which would be so slight a burden to the consumer. The consumption of cotton per head in the United States, at the highest point ever attained to, has not exceeded twelve pounds. A tax of five cents per pound would, therefore, be an average of about sixty cents to each individual per annum.—(See Special Report, No. 3.) As the crop of the present year, in the opinion of competent persons consulted by the commission, is not likely to be less than two millions of bales—and if good seed can be obtained, may exceed this figure—the commission are of the opinion that the government may safely rely for the fiscal year ending June 30, 1867, upon a revenue from this source of *at least forty millions of dollars.*

With an increase of the crop, in subsequent years, beyond two millions of bales per annum, accompanied by a consequent reduction of the market price of the same, a corresponding reduction of the proposed rate of tax may probably be found expedient; but, in any event, the commission believe that for the future an average revenue from cotton of *at least fifty millions of dollars* may undoubtedly be relied upon.

Tobacco.—In respect to tobacco, the commission, as the result of their investigations, are unanimously of the opinion *that the tax should not be laid upon the leaf.* The commission, from lack of time, are not now able to report specially on this subject, but will do so at the earliest practicable moment.

The following tables show the amount of revenue derived from cigars and cheroots, chewing and smoking tobacco, and snuff, for the several fiscal years since the internal revenue system has been in operation:

Cigars, cheroots, &c.:	
1863	$476,589 29
1864	1,255,424 79
1865	3,087,421 51
Tobacco, chewing and smoking:	
1863	2,576,888 67
1864	7,086,684 74
1865	8,017,020 63
Snuff:	
1865	283,352 00

The total amount received in 1865 from tobacco and its manufactures was $11,387,799. The amount received from tobacco for 1865 would, undoubtedly, have been much greater, had it been possible to prescribe effective revenue regulations respecting the immense stock of tobacco held in the southern States at the close of the rebellion.

The average annual taxable production of the different kinds of manufactured tobacco from September 1, 1862, to June 30, 1865, was 42,809,168 pounds. This amount, at the present rate of excise, would return an annual revenue of $15,736,795. With some amendment of the present law, and with the exhaustion of the stock in the country made in anticipation of the tax, which is now nearly effected, the commission believe that the government may safely rely upon an annual revenue from this source for the immediate future, of *at least eighteen millions of dollars* ($18,000,000.)

Incomes.—In respect to the income tax the commission have not, from want of time, been able to give this subject the attention which its importance demands. Although in many respects an obnoxious tax, yet, falling as it does mainly on accumulation, it will probably be sustained with less detriment to the country than any other form of taxation—the excise on spirituous and fermented liquors and tobacco excepted. The discrimination at present in the rate levied on incomes under and in excess of $5,000 is, however, unjust, being in fact a tax on the results of successful industry and business enterprise; and the commission recommend that this discrimination be abrogated, and the rate be equalized at *five* per centum.

When the tax upon incomes was first imposed, an exemption of six hundred dollars upon the annual gains, profits, or earnings of every person was allowed. This was deemed sufficient at that time to enable a small family to procure the bare necessaries of life; but with the large increase in the cost of living there was not a corresponding advance in the receipts of those receiving but small incomes. As the purchasing power of six hundred dollars was fully equal at that time to one thousand dollars now, it would be, in the opinion of the commission, an act of justice, as well as of sound public policy, to extend the limit of the sum exempted. They therefore recommend that in the future assessment of incomes one thousand dollars be exempted from taxation.

The commission furthermore believe that in exempting one thousand dollars from liability to assessment under the income tax, the ends of public policy have been fully subserved; and they would therefore recommend that in assessing the income tax no allowance whatever be made for house-rent, or at least that the amount allowed to be deducted for rental should not in any case be allowed to exceed three hundred dollars.*

* The commission understand that the internal revenue bill, as it was originally draughted, and as it passed the House of Representatives, contained a clause limiting the amount to be deducted for rent in the estimation of incomes to $200, and providing that persons residing in their own houses should be assessed for income on the value of the rental of such houses exceeding $200.

As the law now stands, rentals of an excessive and unreasonable amount are often deducted; and the gain to the revenue in the city of New York alone, from the repeal of that part of the act authorizing the deduction of rentals, would, in the opinion of revenue officials, amount to over two millions of dollars per annum.

In view of the necessity for the speedy removal of other forms of taxes which tend to check the development of the industry of the country, the commission would recommend no further change for the present in respect to the income tax.

The total receipts from this source since and including 1863 are as follows:

Fiscal year 1863	$455,741 26
Fiscal year 1864	14,919,279 58
Fiscal year 1865	20,567,350 26

It should, however, be observed that the tax on the incomes of 1862, assessed in 1863, is mainly included in the receipts of the fiscal year 1864, less than half a million of dollars having been collected in 1863; and the receipts for 1865 consist almost entirely of the tax assessed in 1864 upon the income of 1863. The receipts, therefore, from the income tax assessed in 1865 do not appear in the report of the Commissioner for that year, made November 30, 1865.

By a report, however, of the Commissioner to the Revenue Commission it appears that the total receipts from the tax upon incomes from July 1 to December 1, 1865, were $54,549,128. A small part of the income tax of 1864, assessed in 1865, was collected prior to July 1, but how much cannot readily be determined; and a small part, moreover, remained uncollected on December 1, 1865. The additional collections made or to be made since that period will, in the opinion of the commissioner, further augment the receipts for the income tax of 1864 to at least fifty-eight million of dollars.

For the future, with the changes above recommended, the commission believe that the government may safely rely on an annual revenue from this source of about fifty millions of dollars.

Banks.—From the excise on banks and railroads the amount received during the fiscal year 1865 was $13,579,594, and the commission assume the collection of a similar amount for the immediate future.

Petroleum.—The receipts from refined petroleum and coal oil since 1863 have been as follows:

1863	$649,962 09
1864	2,255,328 80
1865	2,047,212 77

For the first quarter of the fiscal year ending June 30, 1865, the internal revenue receipts from the tax on refined petroleum and coal oil were $302,411 63; for the corresponding quarter of 1866 the receipts were $810,056 09, showing a gain of $507,644 46.

The tax upon petroleum was ten cents per gallon, and upon oil distilled from coal exclusively, eight cents, until June 30, 1864, after which the rates were twenty and fifteen cents respectively.

By the amended act of March 3, 1865, a duty was imposed of ONE DOLLAR on each barrel of crude petroleum of forty-five gallons. The amount received from the time the tax went into effect until the close of the fiscal year ending June 30, 1865, was $229,546 10. For reasons which will be found in detail in the Special Report (No. 7) on this subject, the commission recommend *that the tax as thus imposed on crude petroleum be repealed, and that the rates of tax on refined coal oil, petroleum, naphtha, benzole, &c., be retained as at present.*

They are also of the opinion that when the uses of all the elements of petroleum and of the distillates of oil-yielding coal and shale have been more fully developed, it will be possible for the government to derive a much larger revenue from these articles, with a much lower rate of excise than is now imposed.

For the next fiscal year the commission believe that a revenue in excess of $3,000,000 may be relied on from refined coal oil and petroleum.

Naval stores.—Under the present excise law a tax of twenty-four cents per gallon is imposed upon spirits of turpentine, and six per cent. *ad valorem* on rosin. Owing to the fact that the principal portion of these productions are manufactured in sections of the country over which the revenue laws have not until recently been enforced, the revenue derived from the same has been inconsiderable; that from spirits of turpentine for the fiscal year 1865 having been but $8,461 48.

It is represented to the commission that the tax as at present imposed upon rosin and distilled turpentine is unequal and oppressive; but as the supply of these articles from the United States to a great extent controls the prices of the world, they are of the opinion that the tax on spirits of turpentine and rosin should not be wholly remitted, and that no drawback on their export to foreign countries be allowed.

The product of turpentine distilled in 1860 was returned by the census as 12,174,851 gallons, and of rosin at 1,126,569 barrels. At the present rate of twenty-four cents per gallon the turpentine product of 1860 would yield a revenue of about three millions of dollars, ($2,921,964;) and assuming the valuation of the rosin product of 1860 to be at least two dollars per barrel, the revenue from this source, at six per cent. *ad valorem*, would yield over $135,000. It is evident, therefore, that the revenue from these products, in view of the large domestic and foreign demand, is likely to be very considerable, and will fall in part upon the foreign consumer. For the future the commission estimate the revenue from these articles at two millions of dollars.

Licenses.—The receipts from licenses for the several years during which the internal revenue system has been in operation have been as follows:

1863	$6, 824, 178 42
1864	7, 145, 388 71
1865	12, 613, 478 67

With the extension of the revenue laws over a large section of our country where they were before inoperative, and as the result of some changes which the commission will recommend hereafter in regard to the levying and collecting of the excise upon clothing and other articles of wearing apparel, the amount likely to be received from this source will undoubtedly be much augmented; and the commission assume *fifteen millions of dollars* as the receipts for the fiscal year ending June 30, 1867. The receipts of revenue in Great Britain during the year 1865 from the same source were £2,159,804, ($10,799,020.)

Stamps—No part of the revenue is probably collected so easily, with such small expense, and with comparatively so little fraud, and which in the future can be augmented so readily without detriment to the industry of the country, as that derivable from stamps. The following are the receipts which have hitherto accrued from this source:

Fiscal year 1863	$4, 140, 175 29
Fiscal year 1864	5, 894, 945 14
Fiscal year 1865	11, 162, 392 14

Our adhesive revenue stamps now embrace *eight* different classes or sizes, and thirty-two denominations, varying from *one cent* to *two hundred dollars*. They are engraved on steel, in an elaborate manner, and are believed to possess every guarantee against counterfeiting which the best skill and knowledge can afford. To this security are to be added the safeguards of gumming, and especially perforation—processes necessary to perfect every stamp, and requiring costly and peculiar machinery. Thus the revenue stamps test the counterfeiter's skill quite as effectually as the engraved currency, while little or no facilities whatever of utterance are afforded him; their use, furthermore, is specific, and their value bears no comparison with the gains which may be made by a fraudulent issue of the national currency. These statements find practical exemplification in the fact that *we have yet to hear of the first successful counterfeit of an adhesive revenue stamp.*

The rapid increase in the revenue receipts from stamps is owing in a considerable degree to the recent requirements of law, whereby receipts of money (over twenty dollars) and of property, matches, photographs, &c., are required to be stamped; but at the same time the natural advance in business throughout the country, the greater familiarity of the people with the law, and its more rigid enforcement by the government, have powerfully contributed to swell the receipts from this source.

Of the stamps thus far consumed, it appears from a report made to the commission by the government contractors for the manufacture of stamps, that *six-sevenths* of the entire consumption consist of the two-cent bank-check and receipt stamps, the various proprietory stamps, and of the one-cent stamps required to be affixed to matches.

The most important results in this department of the revenue, therefore, *flow from the smallest stamp taxes universally diffused.* Thus one-third of the revenue received from stamps in the fiscal year 1865 were derived from the three items of "bank-check," "receipt," and "match stamps;" and from the first two, (bank-check and receipt stamps,) the receipts for the fiscal year 1865 averaged about $200,000 per month.

Considering the small actual tax imposed on each bunch of matches—*one cent*—and the insignificance of the business, as contrasted with many others, this product of industry probably affords the largest *comparative* revenue accruing under the excise. The law as at present happily framed, imposes a penalty on the manufacturer of matches, as well as upon the retailer, who sells them without the requisite stamps affixed; so that the public are thus, as it were, constituted a general corps of detectives; while the amount of gain likely to accrue to the retailer from the evasion of the law is too small, in any one instance, to tempt to the commission of fraud.

As has already been stated, the quantity of matches manufactured in anticipation of the tax (which took effect August 1, 1864) was so large, that up to the present time (January, 1866,) the government has failed to derive from this article its legitimate revenue. For the fiscal year 1865, the revenue received from matches was probably about *one million of dollars;* but since then, as the stock manufactured in anticipation of the tax has diminished by consumption, the business of the match manufacturer, and consequently the revenue to the government, have correspondingly increased. This rapidity of increase is strikingly exemplified by reference to the following return,* made to the commission, of the stamps (of one cent denomination) purchased by one of the leading match manufacturers of the country. Thus, for the five months from January, 1865, to May inclusive, the number used monthly was 660,000; in June and July, 1,155,000 each; in August and September 1,760,000 each; and in each of the months of October and November 2,090,000, making an increase from May to October of 1,430,000, or over 216 per cent. in five months. Dur-

*Previous to September 1, 1864, it was the custom of match manufacturers to put about fifty matches in a bunch; but since that date, in order to reduce the tax, they have caused each package to contain one hundred. The adoption of this method, therefore, practically reduces the tax one half.

ing the last six months the manufacturer referred to purchased no less than 10,895,000 one-cent stamps, which were affixed to the same number of bunches of matches, and paid the government for the same *a tax of* $108,950 !

From the returns submitted to the commission, of the match manufacture of the United States, it appears that there are now in the country about fifty large establishments, and that from the present demand for the consumption of matches they anticipate it will require for the next fiscal year a production of 2,400,000 gross, or 345,600,000 bunches; which will yield a revenue of $3,456,000.

The revenue derived from the stamp excise in Great Britain for the year ending March 31, 1865, was £9,531,947 ($47,655,735.) This, however, includes legacy and succession duties, the taxes on insurance, gold and silver plate, and on newspapers, which, under the United States excise system, are included in other departments. Excluding the receipts from these sources, the amount returned from stamps under the British excise was £3,531,717, ($17,658,585,) showing an excess of more than six millions of dollars as compared with the receipts from the same source in the United States for the last fiscal year. The commission, however, from such examination as they have been able to give to the subject, are inclined to the opinion that the capacity of this source of revenue in the United States will prove very much greater than the results of the experience of Great Britain. In proof of this they have but to call attention to the facts before cited in reference to matches.

Another illustration to the same effect may also be found in playing cards. In Great Britain the amount received in the year ending March 31, 1865, from a stamp duty of three pence (six cents) per pack on cards was £8,801, ($44,005,) indicating a manufacture of 704,080 packs. In 1860 the average number of packs of cards manufactured in the United States was believed to be in excess of six hundred gross per week, or about four and a half millions of packs per annum. This, with a stamp duty corresponding with that levied in Great Britain, would have yielded a revenue of $269,568. The high prices of paper, colors, and other materials have considerably reduced the demand for cards within the last four years; but it is the opinion of a committee of card manufacturers, as presented to the commission, that, with a uniform stamp tax of five cents per pack, an annual revenue of at least two hundred thousand dollars may be derived from this source.*

With this and some other amendments relating to proprietary medicines, and similar stamped articles, the commission are of the opinion that a revenue of *at least twenty millions of dollars* may be hereafter collected from stamps.

Legacy and succession duties.—When it is considered that the entire property of the country probably changes hands once in thirty-two years, (the lifetime of a generation,) it is evident that a small rate of tax, in the form of legacy and succession duties, must be productive of a large revenue. As such taxes, moreover, unless excessive, have little influence in checking the development of industry, their adoption and enforcement as a part of the present revenue policy of the country is to be strongly recommended. Thus far—by reason, probably, of some imperfections—the law relative to this subject in the United States has been practically a dead letter, as is proved by the very inconsiderable amount ($546,703) which accrued from it during the last fiscal year. From the corresponding fiscal year the amount received from the same source in Great Britain was £2,337,994, ($11,689,970.)

---

* From returns made to the commission it appears that a single playing-card manufacturer in New York city paid for stamps in the year 1865 on the product of his manufacture $41,731 10. Of these stamps two-thirds were of the two-cent and four-cent denomination. The number of packs returned as manufactured by this firm in 1862 was one and a half million, (1,500,000.) During the last fiscal year, owing mainly to the high price of paper, the manufacture and sale of playing cards has probably diminished to the extent of fifty per cent.

The commission submit the form of a bill intended to render the execution of the present law more effectual, and they are of the opinion that, with its adoption, or by the enactment of some equivalent provisions, a revenue of at least *three millions of dollars* may be secured from this source.

By an estimate made for the commission by a gentleman connected with the surrogate's office of the city of New York, the amount of property annually passing in that city by will or inheritance by kin is about thirty-one millions of dollars, which, if assessed at the present lowest rate of legacy duty, one per cent., would have yielded an amount in excess of one-half the receipts from this source for the whole country during the last fiscal year.*

Tax on gross receipts.—From gross receipts the revenue for the fiscal year 1865 was $9,697,866. Under this head are included, mainly, the taxes levied on transportation and intercommunication; and as the majority of them, railroads excepted, yield but inconsiderable amounts, and are in opposition to the general system of revenue which the commission recommend, sound policy requires that they should be repealed as soon as practicable.

Thus the receipts from bridges and toll-gates for the fiscal year 1865 was $75,269; from canals, $92,421; from ferries, $126,133; from stage-coaches, wagons, &c., $469,188; and from railroads, $5,917,293.

Under this head are also included telegraph and express companies, the former of which pay five per cent., and the latter but three per cent. on the gross amount of their receipts. For this discrimination the commission can see no good reason. Express companies, as at present constituted are, for the most part, monopolies, and the average rate of profits paid by them is believed to far exceed the ratio of profits in almost any legitimate business. The commission, therefore, recommend that the tax on the gross receipts of telegraph and express companies be equalized, and are inclined to the opinion that the tax on receipts of express companies might be well advanced to a higher figure than five per cent. An increased revenue from such an advanced rate will compensate in some degree for any reductions that may be made on the taxes now levied on bridges, toll-roads, ferries, ships, &c.

The revenue receipts from telegraph companies, for the fiscal year 1865, were $215,050 62; and from express companies $529,275 89.

Under the present law (section 120) the dividends and interest upon the bonds of certain corporations therein enumerated are made liable to the income tax, which is payable by the proper officer of such corporations. The commission are unable to discover any valid reason why the moderate dividends of banks and railroad companies should be thus taxed, while the larger profits of express companies, manufacturing and other corporations, are omitted. As these returns are invariably made by an officer who has no pecuniary interest therein, it is believed that they are uniformly more nearly correct than the average returns of income made by individuals; and they, therefore, recommend an amendment of the law, which will include in the provisions of the above section all important incorporated companies for whatever purpose organized.

The commission assume that the revenue derivable from gross receipts for the fiscal year ending June 30, 1867, will continue as at present, about $9,000,000.

Tax on sales.—Under this head are included the sales by auction, by merchandise, stock and gold brokers, &c.—the whole affording a net revenue of $4,062,243 54.

The present rate of tax upon the sales of stock-brokers is one-twentieth of one per cent., or five dollars on the sale of ten thousand dollars of the par value

*The value of the whole real estate and personal property in the United States in 1860 was upwards of sixteen thousand millions of dollars, (16,159,000,000.) Allowing thirty-two years as the lifetime of a generation, and assuming the legacy and succession duty at an average of one per cent., the receipts from this source should yield annually five millions of dollars.

of the stocks sold. The testimony of the leading brokers in New York dealing in stocks, as sworn to before the commission, seems to establish the fact that the above rate is far too heavy to be raised from the whole amount of business transacted. The business is not able to pay it, and in consequence of this, there can be no doubt that the tax, as now imposed, is largely evaded. By the regular members of the stock-exchange of New York and other cities the tax is probably regularly paid, but the business done at these centres forms but an inconsiderable part of the great daily transactions in stocks, bonds, and other securities. Of the remainder of the business a very large part, undoubtedly, escapes taxation altogether. As an illustration of this, it may be stated that there are a large number of dealers who employ brokers to sell stocks, and then deliver them themselves, paying to the broker simply his commission for selling. The broker does not follow up such transaction, cannot control it, and cannot enforce the payment of the tax.

It is the opinion of experienced men in Wall street that if, during the last twenty years, the present rate of taxation had been paid on all their transactions, the revenue received by the government would far exceed what those engaged in the business during that time are now worth.

It should also be borne in mind that the stock-brokerage business is taxed otherwise most frequently; a tax being imposed on every certificate of stock taken, and on every contract for the delivery of stock. The rate of stock-brokerage is, on the average, one-eighth of one per cent.; the ordinary commission of merchants is two and half per cent.—twenty times as large as the commission of brokers. To reach the same result at the end of the year, a broker must do twenty times as much business as a merchant does; hence twenty times as many checks must be passed, which checks all bear stamps; thus showing that the stamp duty upon checks in brokerage is twenty times as much as it is on the general mercantile business of New York.

It is the opinion, further, of those most conversant with the stock-brokers' business of New York, that if it were possible to absolutely enforce the law as it at present stands, the brokerage business for the sale of stocks would be nearly or completely extinguished.

From a review of the whole subject, in which they have been aided by the judgment of the leading members of the New York stock-exchange, (one of them having formerly been a prominent member of the Committee of Ways and Means, that draughted the internal revenue law,) the commission would recommend that the present law imposing a tax of five dollars on every ten thousand dollars, or one-twentieth of one per cent. on the par value of all stocks sold, be repealed, and in lieu thereof a tax *of one dollar on ten thousand dollars, or the one-hundredth* ($\frac{1}{100}$) *of one per cent. on the par value of the stock be substituted, and collected in the following manner:*

That each sale of stock be accompanied by a bill or memorandum of sale with necessary stamp attached, and in default of affixing the necessary and required stamp on such bill of sale, the parties selling the stock and receiving the money shall be liable to a penalty, one-half to go to the informer and the remainder to the government; the same to be recoverable at any time prior to the expiration of twelve months from the date of the transaction.

Such a tax thus levied can, in the opinion of the commission, be collected almost universally, will fall equally on all, be oppressive to none, and will afford to the government an increase of revenue.

It should also be stated that the bulk of the transactions in government securities at present is done (according to the statements made to the commission) at abont *one-sixteenth* of one per cent. ($\frac{1}{16}$ of one per cent.) profit, which is $6 25 on $10,000. If the present tax of $5 on $10,000 be deducted from this, ($6 25,) it does not afford sufficient profit to continue the business. Furthermore, as the business of the great cities increase, the transactions become more concentrated, and much larger business is done at a smaller rate of profit than formerly. The large dry-goods jobbers of New York, who a few years ago sold goods to the value of one million dollars per annum at from ten to fifteen per cent. profit, now sell *from thirty to forty millions* per annum at from two to five per cent. profit; and what is thus true of the dry-goods business is more strikingly true of the transactions of the stock-brokers.

In adopting, therefore, the principle of subjecting large and frequent business transactions, turning on small profits, to the *minimum* specific tax, the government will but follow a long-recognized and sound commercial policy.

There is at present no tax imposed on government securities, but they are included in the phrase, "stocks, bonds, or other securities," of the section (99) which subjects brokers' sales to taxation. The commission believe, however, that it would be a sound and wise policy to exempt all transactions for the sale and purchase of national securities from every form of internal taxation.

The commission also recommend that the rate of tax levied on the sales of exchange and gold-brokers be made to correspond with that proposed in reference to sales of stock-brokers, and they submit a form of bill to that effect.

From the aggregate tax on sales, the commission assume, for the future, an annual revenue of at least four millions of dollars.

Miscellaneous.—For the fiscal year ending June 30, 1865, the revenue receipts of the United States from miscellaneous and incidental sources were $32,978,284 47.

For the year ending June 30, 1867, the Secretary of the Treasury estimates the receipts from lands and miscellaneous sources (premium on gold, confiscated property, penalties, &c.) at twenty-one millions of dollars.

For the future, although it is to be expected (and hoped) that a large part of the revenue now included under the head of miscellaneous (viz., all derived from the premium on gold) will be diminished; yet it is altogether probable that, under any circumstances, a considerable amount of revenue will always be derived from miscellaneous sources.

For the fiscal year 1867, the commission adopt the estimates of the Secretary of the Treasury—*viz., twenty-one millions of dollars;* and they are of the opinion that in subsequent years an equivalent amount will accrue from incidental sources—sales of land, fines, and penalties, new forms of taxation, or unexpected increments of old ones.

AGGREGATE ESTIMATES.

A recapitulation of the foregoing estimates gives us the following aggregate results for the fiscal year ending June 30, 1867:

From customs		$130, 000, 000
From excise, viz:		
Distilled spirits	$40, 000, 000	
Fermented liquors	5, 000, 000	
Tobacco and its manufactures	18, 000, 000	
Cotton, (raw)	40, 000, 000	
Coal oil, refined petroleum, &c	3, 000, 000	
Spirits of turpentine, and rosin	2, 000, 000	
		108, 000, 000
Licenses	15, 000, 000	
Incomes	40, 000, 000	
Salaries	2, 000, 000	
Banks	15, 000, 000	
Stamps	20, 000, 000	

Gross receipts	9,000,000	
Sales	4,000,000	
Legacies and successions	3,000,000	
		108,000,000
Miscellaneous receipts, 1866–'67		21,000,000
Aggregate		$367,000,000

Adding to the above sum the amount received in the fiscal year 1865, from the various direct and indirect taxes on industry, which, excepting the amounts derived from the excise on spirits, beer, tobacco, cotton, petroleum, and naval stores, the commission estimate at about *sixty-eight millions of dollars,* we have as the gross revenue possible to be derived from all sources, under the present rates, with the amendments above proposed, FOUR HUNDRED AND THIRTY-FIVE MILLIONS OF DOLLARS, ($435,000,000.)

The estimates of the Secretary of the Treasury for the expenditures of the fiscal year ending June 30, 1867, including interest on the public debt, are, as already stated, two hundred and eighty-four millions of dollars. Allowing the annual expenditures to be increased *sixteen millions of dollars* above these estimates, (making an aggregate of three hundred millions of dollars,) and setting aside *fifty millions* additional for the reduction of the principal of the public debt, A SURPLUS WILL REMAIN (assuming the correctness of the estimates of the commission) APPLICABLE FOR THE REDUCTION OF TAXATION, OF EIGHTY-FIVE MILLIONS OF DOLLARS, ($85,000,000.)

These estimates of revenue, as above submitted, are less in the aggregate than what the commission believe will actually be realized, without some unlooked-for interruption of the trade and industry of the country; and the results of their continued investigations and enlarged experience deepen their convictions *that the capacity of all the great sources of revenue have been under rather than over estimated.*

It was the opinion of the late Commissioner of Internal Revenue, founded upon his large experience, that *if the excise law, as it stands, were thoroughly and exactly enforced,* THE REVENUE FROM THE EXCISE ALONE WOULD EQUAL OR EXCEED FIVE HUNDRED MILLIONS OF DOLLARS ($500,000,000) *per annum;* and in this opinion the commission, from their own observation, fully concur. It need, therefore, be no matter of surprise, that with an increased efficiency and experience on the part of the revenue officers, the average monthly and quarterly receipts of internal revenue also continue progressively to increase.

Accepting, then, the results indicated as substantially correct, the possibility of adopting and carrying out the revenue policy advocated by the commission, viz., of concentrating the sources of revenue, and of relieving industry of all those burdens which tend to check its development, is demonstrated.

Such a system—which, in contrast with the present "*diffused*" system, may be termed the "concrete"—is, in the opinion of the commission, the only one adapted to the age and to our condition—the only one compatible with great fiscal results, and with that large freedom to industry and circulation which alone can ever adequately supply the coffers of an enterprising, competitive, and free people.

Concentrated taxes can be easily, cheaply, and surely collected, and distribute themselves with a satisfying equality; for it is to be remembered that a tax on one of the necessaries of life is, in effect, a tax upon all, without the vexations of infinitesimal application. "The oil operators find that one well, intelligently sunk in the right spot, will drain the whole basin, better than many, with less expense, and no disturbance of the surrounding country. In like manner we must draw our revenue from few sources, and avoid the error of many and useless perforations."

Again, the productiveness of a tax—like, for example, the tax on industry—is not its first consideration. The three hundred millions of revenue annually required to meet our national expenditures and interest is a very large amount to take from the resources of the nation; but it is nothing serious in comparison to the blight which may result from the manner of taking it—a blight which ruins the harvest it cannot gather. Freedom from multitudinous taxes, espionage, and vexations; freedom from needless official inquisitions and intrusions; freedom from the hourly provocation of each individual in the nation to concealments, evasions, and falsehoods; freedom for industry, circulation, competition, everywhere—give the nation these conditions, and it will give in return a flowing revenue. Deprive the people of freedom in industry, and there will be disappointing revenues, discontent, embarrassment, and demoralization everywhere—cheerfulness and prosperity nowhere.

It may, however, be urged in opposition to the plan of the commission for relieving manufacturing industry from taxation, that the enormous profits which have recently accrued to manufacturers is a good reason for continuing to impose upon them, at least, some considerable taxation. It should, however, be borne in mind, that the present and recent condition of affairs is entirely abnormal, and cannot continue for any great length of time; and that for every case cited as an illustration of excessive profits realized by persons or corporations engaged in manufacturing, there is an equal or greater number in which no profit whatever has been realized; and furthermore, that the profits in the first instance are quite as likely to have accrued from a superior ability and discretion exhibited in management, as from any actual advantages of the business.

It is an error, moreover, to assume that manufacturing establishments, large or small, are always profitable. It can, undoubtedly, be shown, that in most departments they do not yield large profits in more than three years out of ten, and they scarcely ever escape two years of heavy losses in every ten years. These losses arise from a variety of causes, such as the fall of prices, disasters to machinery, the bankruptcy of customers, commercial revulsions attended with stoppage of business and cessation of demand. Fluctuation of prices is the bane of domestic industry, for though a great rise yields at times an enormous profit, it carries fear and perilous change into every business, and causes men for years to stand on the very verge of insolvency. Not less than a third of those who engage in the production of any commodity subject to competition from abroad, and the special fluctuations of foreign trade, are utterly ruined before they can attain that capital and strength which will enable them to maintain themselves under all contingencies.

Men who are paying from $6,000 to $60,000 annual tax cannot continue it five years, and most of them not three years. A conjunction of any heavy loss, with such a burden of tax, will inevitably crush them, and at the same time produce a diminution of revenue.

It should also be remembered that, as the law imposing taxation on the products of industry now stands, the tax is liable to fall equally upon the losses of the manufacturer as upon his profits. Many instances of the former character have been cited to the commission,* in some of which the effect of the tax,

---

* The commission would call attention, in this connexion, to the following extracts from the testimony of a witness having large experience and knowledge of the manufacturing industry of New England, taken by them in their investigations relative to cotton as a source of revenue:

Question. What is the condition of the cotton-manufacturing industry in this country at the present time, (October, 1865?)

Answer. The results are, certainly, very profitable to the manufacturer, and have been for the last three months.

coming conjointly with losses, has been to compel a discontinuance of the business.

But notwithstanding the demonstration which the commission believe they have presented of the desirability, and also of the practicability, in a financial point of view, of so amending the revenue system of the United States as to relieve industry and simplify the collection of taxes, they are not prepared to recommend that an entire and radical change be immediately made.

In the present condition of the currency, and of the trade and commerce of the country, any financial estimate which can be made of the future must be somewhat problematical, and is liable to be affected by causes which the most sagacious cannot now foresee.

The commission, therefore, recommend that while the system proposed by them should be accepted substantially as the revenue policy of the country for the future, the change from the old to the new system should be made gradually, and only so fast as experience and renewed examination of the subject will demonstrate that it can be done with prudence and safety.

The present condition of the revenue, however, warrants, in their opinion, a recommendation that at least the following reductions or changes be made, to take effect at the commencement of the next fiscal year, July 1, 1866, or sooner, if, in the judgment of Congress, it is considered expedient:

1st. *A repeal of section* 100 *of the amended act of March* 3, 1865, *(generally known as schedule A,) such of its provisions as relate to and impose a tax upon "billiard tables" excepted.*

The taxes imposed under this section and schedule, viz: on wagons, carriages, watches, pianos, plate, yachts, &c., although laid mainly on articles of luxury, are inquisitorial in their character, and are productive of more annoyance to the people and of trouble and expense to the government than is commensurable with any revenue derivable from them.

Thus, for the fiscal year 1865, the revenue derived from gold plate amounted only to $126 62; from piano-fortes, $7,751 82; from watches, $9,138 61; from yachts, $2,098 33; and from billiard tables, $67,754. The amount by which they will be reduced in consequence of a repeal of section 100, the tax on billiard tables excepted—taking as a basis the returns of the fiscal year ending June 30, 1865—is $459,822 54.

2d. *A repeal of all that part of section* 94 *of the amended act of March* 3, 1865, *which provides for the assessment and collection of taxes on repairs of engines, cars, carriages, ships, &c.*

Taxes of this character are taxes upon prudence and economy, and their existence upon the statute book can only be justified by imperative necessity.

The following examples strikingly illustrate the difficulty and annoyance of

---

Question. How has the business been, as regards profit, for the last twelve months?

Answer. The results of the business for the six months previous, say from the 1st of January to the 1st of July, (1865,) were disastrous—extremely disastrous—to the cotton manufacturers; many of the large companies making up with a loss of from $50,000 to $300,000 for the six months.

Question. Can you give any specific instances of losses sustained by cotton corporations during the last twelve months?

Answer. Yes; I can give an instance of a corporation, having 18,000 spindles only, that made up with a loss of $96,000, say from the 1st of December, (1864,) to the 1st of June, (1865.)

Question. How much tax did they pay during that time?

Answer. I should say $12,000. Another mill of about the same size lost $120,000 for the six months.

Question. What tax did they pay?

Answer. They must have paid $18,000 tax.

interpreting and enforcing the tax upon repairs: thus a worker in iron or tin makes a stove one hour, upon which he pays a six per cent. manufacturing tax, and the next hour repairs a stove, on which, if the repairs exceed ten per cent. of the value, he is required to pay a tax of three and six-tenths per cent. A blacksmith in like manner makes a taxable article, and then in a like manner repairs one just like it. Neither of these persons can reasonably be expected to keep separate accounts of these transactions, upon which the rates of tax differ. Furthermore, the tax on repairs must necessarily depend entirely upon the workman's own estimate of the value of the article before the repair, as it is not taxable unless its value is increased ten per cent. by the repair; and the assessor, or assistant, cannot, and should not, be present as a spy to appraise all articles repaired.

Again: if the worker in wood repairs a wheelbarrow worth one dollar, by adding ten cents to its value, it is taxable, but if he repairs a carriage or piano worth five hundred dollars, no tax accrues unless he adds fifty dollars to its value. The tax, with this limitation, therefore, is generally favorable to articles of luxury, and bears stringently upon articles of necessity.

Again: by the present limitation of the tax on manufactures and repairs, to such manufactures and repairs, as together exceed the rate of six hundred dollars a year, (or fifty dollars a month,) and a tax on the difference when the same exceeds the rate of six hundred dollars, and does not exceed the rate of one thousand dollars, a new calculation must often be made after it is ascertained that the repairs have increased the value ten per cent. Thus, if the manufactures and repairs amount to eighty dollars, which amount is less than the rate of one thousand dollars per year, (estimated monthly,) then the tax is upon the excess of fifty dollars, namely, thirty dollars. The tax upon this excess, namely, thirty dollars, is to be apportioned at different rates of tax, in the proportion which the amount of repairs bears to the amount of manufactures.

It is, moreover, often found practically impossible to assess a tax on repairs upon the principles of the present law. Thus, for example, a wheelwright repairs a carriage to the amount of three per cent., and knows nothing more about it. The owner or his agent then passes it to another tradesman, blacksmith, trimmer, or painter, neither of whom knows what the extent of entire repairs may be, nor the value of the carriage before the repairs. The result is, that the repair, however extensive, must go untaxed, or the owner must be taxed. By the strict construction of the present law, it is doubtful whether an owner can be taxed as a manufacturer, unless he furnishes materials in whole or in part, and whether the subject of repair furnished by the owner is in itself a material for the repair. For it is the "repair" which is by the law made a manufacture. But whether this be the case or not, it is the universal testimony of all revenue assessors and collectors that all taxes which are intermittent, occasional, or exceptional, like this on repairs, should be avoided, inasmuch as the tax is not understood by the tax-payers, is difficult of collection, tends to render the law odious and inquisitorial, and requires more labor and expense on the part of the government to collect it than is compensated by any revenue accruing therefrom.

The revenue derived from this source during the fiscal year, 1865, was as follows:

From repairs of engines, cars, carriages, &c.	$294, 437 15
From repairs of ships, steamboats, and other vessels	36, 835 61
Making the whole reduction of the revenue by the repeal of this section, assuming as a basis the returns of 1865	331, 272 76

3d. *A repeal (subject to certain exceptions) of all that part of section 94 which provides for the assessment and collection of taxes on wearing apparel.*

Of all the taxes imposed under the present revenue system, none, probably, has been more effectual in "grinding the faces of the poor" than this; while there are few which have given more annoyance and trouble to the revenue officials intrusted with their assessment and collection. The main object which induces the commission to ask for a repeal of this portion of the law is a desire to free from taxation a great multitude of small operators, such as milliners, dressmakers, shoemakers, and small tailors.

The products of industry, whose exemption from excise is recommended, are, in the main, of prime necessity to the poor as well as to the rich, and do not admit, beyond a certain extent, of any economy in their use. The component parts of clothing, such as are taxed within the extent of that portion of the law referred to, are furthermore, almost without exception, heavily taxed before being fabricated, and an additional tax on them, therefore, as finished articles, necessarily involves excessive duplication of taxation.

By the operation of this law, moreover, small taxes are collected from a great number of small and poor operatives—milliners, dressmakers, shoemakers, and others—in a manner unworthy the dignity of a great nation, and obviously not contemplated by the original framers of the law.*

It is doubtless true, that many who are engaged in the manufacture of wearing apparel are in affluent circumstances, and are abundantly able to pay the tax; but the condition of the great majority is far otherwise; and the commission, after a review of the whole subject, can see no way of making a discrimination between the two classes. Besides, if it be assumed that the tax in this instance falls upon the consumer, the repeal of this section of the law will consequently be for the relief of the whole people, rather than for the benefit of the producers, or manufacturers. The commission, therefore, recommend the following enactment:

"That on and after July 1, 1866, wearing apparel of all descriptions, whether made to order or for general sale—clothing, boots, shoes, gloves, mittens, moccasins, hats, caps, and bonnets, or other articles of dress made for the wear of men, women, or children—shall be exempt from excise: *Provided*, That such exemptions shall not apply to any articles of clothing manufactured for sale by weaving, knitting, or felting, (hats excepted;) nor to any articles made separately for sale as constituent parts of clothing, or for the ornamentation of the same; or to any article made from fur, or fur-skins dressed with the fur on, or from India-rubber; or to hoop-skirts, or paper collars: *And provided further*, That every person, firm, or corporation, who shall manufacture any of the foregoing articles, exceeding annually the sum of one thousand dollars, shall pay

---

* The character of this taxation may be better illustrated by the following copies of returns from the book of the collector of the eighth district of New York, for September, 1865:

	Amount of tax.
Louisa Epstein, milliner	$1 04
Sarah Abernethy, dressmaker	1 20
E. Gallagher, milliner	1 58
Ann Furman, dressmaker	1 75
Nathan Stern, manufacturer of cloaks	42
&c., &c.	

The total collections in this month, in the above district, from twenty-four persons pursuing the above vocations, amounted to only $49 23.

From the ninth district of the same city the commission have also before them a return of assessments for the month of November, 1865, on thirteen persons, for repairs to clothing, &c.; the specific amount charged to each ranging from 51 cents to $5 83, and showing an aggregate of but $28 57. The value of the monthly industrial product on which the above taxes were assessed ranged from $15 up to $162, but the returns of only two exceeded $100; while those of the majority were under $60.

five dollars for a license; if exceeding two thousand dollars, ten dollars; and for every additional one thousand dollars, five dollars."

The amount by which the revenue will be reduced by a repeal of the excise on these articles, taking as a basis the returns for the fiscal year 1865, will be as follows:

Clothing	$6, 820, 936 65
Boots and shoes	3, 280, 627 29
Gloves, mittens, &c	30, 180 14
Making an aggregate of	10, 131, 744 08

This amount will be somewhat further augmented by the revenue from hats, caps, and other articles, the revenue from which, not being returned separately, cannot be ascertained by the commission.

4th. *A repeal of the excise duty of two dollars and forty cents per ton levied upon pig iron; the repeal of the duty of six cents per ton levied on mineral coal, and of the duty of one dollar per barrel on crude petroleum.*

These articles are all raw materials lying at the basis of great branches of industry; and it is for the interest of the country that their production and sale should be, to the greatest possible extent, increased and cheapened.

The reduction of the revenue by the repeal of the duties on these articles, adopting the returns of the fiscal year 1865 as a basis of computation, will be as follows:

From pig iron	$1, 484, 382 82
From coal	835, 993 91
From petroleum	
	2, 320, 376 73

The amount of revenue derived from the tax on crude petroleum, (one dollar per parrel,) for the fiscal year ending June 30, 1865, was $229,545 94. As the revenue from this source was not included in the aggregate estimates of future receipts heretofore given, no allowance is now made for it in the above reductions.

For similar reasons to the above, and in view of the termination of the reciprocity treaty, the commission would recommend that the duty now imposed on bituminous coal of foreign production, imported into the United States, be reduced from one dollar and twenty-five cents to fifty cents per ton.

The quantity of coal imported into and exported from the United States during the fiscal year 1865, according to the returns of the Treasury Department, is as follows:

Imported under the reciprocity treaty, *free of duty*, 13,025,432 bushels, valued at	$1, 209, 504
Paying duty, 6,131,608 bushels, valued at	568, 076
Exported, of domestic production, 3,708,264 bushels, valued at	1, 348, 371
Exported, of foreign production, 25,536 bushels, valued at	3, 437

5th. *A repeal of all excise taxes on printed books, magazines, pamphlets, reviews, and all other similar printed publications.*

The amount by which the revenue will be reduced by exempting these articles from taxation, taking as a basis for estimate the returns for the fiscal year ending June 30, 1865, will be $354,528.

Assuming that all the taxes above indicated are repealed, the aggregate reduction of the revenue likely to be experienced, therefore, taking the returns of the fiscal year 1865 as a basis for estimate and comparison, will probably amount to about fifteen millions.*

But, in addition to the reductions above specifically referred to and recommended, the commission would further recommend, *that on and after the 1st day of July*, 1866, *the taxes levied and paid upon all goods, wares, and merchandise, enumerated in section* 94 *of the amended act of March* 3, 1865, *be reduced fifty per centum; and that no allowance or deductions whatever, in the payment of the same, for freight, commissions and other expenses of sale, be authorized or permitted.*

Such a reduction would at once compensate, in great part, for the excessive duplication of taxes now complained of; and, with the continuance of the prosperity of the country, (which such a reduction must necessarily promote,) would not, in the opinion of the commission, impair the revenue to an extent sufficient to cause any anxiety.

The adoption of further reductions, the commission recommend, should be made dependent on the experience of another year.

REDUCTION OF THE PUBLIC DEBT.

In their estimates of revenue and expenditures, it will be seen that the commission have assumed fifty millions of dollars as the sum that may be set aside, annually, for the redemption of the principal of the public debt. They, however, do not wish it to be understood that they are in favor of the withdrawal of any such amount, *at present*, from the annual revenues of the nation, for such a purpose. On the contrary, they believe that it is for the interest of the government that taxation should be reduced, at the earliest possible moment, to its *minimum*, thereby making sure the future industrial development of the country; and that no considerable sum should be, for the present, raised by taxation, for the reduction of the principal of the public debt.

The burden of taxation is now, undoubtedly, at its *maximum*, and the pressure of local taxation increased to pay the interest on local war expenditures is, probably, more severely felt than even the burden of national taxation, inasmuch as the general government has taken to itself nearly every source of revenue, except the single one of real estate, which had been before burdened with large expenditures for schools, roads, and other matters with which the local governments stand charged.

Cases can be cited in which taxation upon real estate even now falls but little short of confiscation ; and in others, where property has been but partially improved, the demands for the several classes of taxes absorb nearly the whole receipts derived from it; the burden in every case becoming more and more severe with every step in the direction of appreciation in the gold value of the currency in which the taxes must be paid. Justice and wise policy, therefore, would seem to demand that the national government should not now adopt any measures calculated to maintain or increase these burdens; but, on the contrary, should do all in its power to diminish them. Such a course, so far from protracting the time at which the national debt can be discharged, would, it is believed, greatly accelerate it; inasmuch as "the power of contributing to the public revenue increases almost geometrically as the activity of the societary circulation increases arithmetically."

Looking to the past, we find that while our population has been accustomed to duplicate itself in about twenty-four years, our production has been supposed to increase twice as rapidly, or to quadruple itself in the time required for the

---

* The probable reduction, consequent upon the changes in the income tax recommended by the commission, does not need to be taken into account in this estimate, inasmuch as it was fully allowed for in the estimates heretofore given of the revenue likely to be derived from this source.

duplication of the other. While looking to the future, in view of this fact, we have reason to believe that the power of national production ten years hence will be more than twice as great as it is at present. That it will be so, provided that we soon remove all those taxes that now tend to impede national development, cannot be doubted; and if so, the revenue system, which may be now framed to yield three hundred millions of dollars per annum, cannot fail to yield, in 1875, at least double that amount.

In confirmation of these views, the commission would refer to the experience of Great Britain, whose revenues have, in the short period of twenty years, (from 1842 to 1862,) increased fifty per cent.; or, from £48,000,000 ($240,000,000) to £72,000,000, ($360,000,000) notwithstanding the exemption from taxation, during the same period, of 1,119 out of 1,163 articles that had been previously subject to impost duties.

The more completely, therefore, that we now close our eyes to the existence of the principal of our debt, and the more we give our attention to the adoption of measures tending to increase the productive power of the country, and to reduce the rate of interest payable on public and private liabilities, the more rapidly will be the increase in the money value of the landed property of the Union, the more readily will all the local taxes be paid, and the sooner shall we arrive at that condition of affairs in which it will be possible to boast that the war debt, local and general, whether held at home or abroad, has been once again extinguished.

THE RECIPROCITY TREATY.

In accordance with the resolutions of Congress and the notification of the Executive, the commercial arrangement known as the "reciprocity treaty," under which the trade and commerce between the United States and the British provinces of North America have been carried on since 1854, expires on the 17th day of March, 1866. The consideration of the effect which the termination of this important commercial arrangement is likely to have upon the revenue, as well as upon the trade and commerce of the United States, has legitimately formed a part of the duties devolving upon the commission, and has also been especially commended to their attention by the Secretary of the Treasury. The commission do not, however, propose to present in this connexion any review of the history of the treaty, or of the circumstances which, in the opinion of Congress, have rendered its termination expedient. This work has already been performed under the auspices of the Treasury Department, by E. H. Derby, esq., of Boston, to whose able and exhaustive report the commission would refer, without, however, indorsing its conclusions. There are, however, certain points connected with this subject to which the commission would ask special attention.

The first of these is, that during the continuance of the reciprocity treaty the trade and commerce between the United States and the British North American provinces *has increased* in ten years *more than three fold*, or from seventeen millions in 1852, to sixty-eight millions in 1864; so that at present, with the exception of Great Britain, the commercial relations between the United States and the British North American provinces outrank in importance and aggregate annual value those existing between this country and any other foreign state.*

* The value of the import and export trade of the United States with the following countries for the year ending June 30, 1864, was, according to the treasury report, as follows, (in round numbers:)

Great Britain	$317,000,000
British North America	68,000,000
Spanish West Indies	57,000,000

It may also, they think, be fairly assumed, that taking into consideration the growth of the two countries in population and wealth, (that of Canada for the last ten years having preserved a nearly equal ratio in this respect with that of the United States,) the trade as at present existing is really but in its infancy, and that the future may be expected to develop an increase equally as great as that of the past.

A change in the conditions under which a reciprocal commerce of such magnitude is carried on, and is now developing, ought not, therefore, to be made without the most serious consideration.

As regards the present treaty, the commission, as the result of their investigations, have been led to the conclusion that its continuance, under existing circumstances, unless accompanied with certain important modifications, is not desirable on the part of the United States.

They, however, are also unanimous in the opinion, that in view of the close geographical connexion of the United States with the British provinces, (rendering them in many respects but one country,) and of the magnitude of the commercial relations existing between them, it would be impolitic and to the detriment of the interests of the United States to decline the consideration of all propositions looking to the re-establishment of some future and satisfactory international commercial arrangement. Such a course would be in entire opposition to the spirit of the age, the liberality of our people, and the policy of rapidly developing our resources as a means of diminishing the burden of our public debt.

In view of such an arrangement, the question of whether either of the parties to the treaty has, or has not, conformed to the spirit of its stipulations, is of little importance. It is the future, not the past, that we are to consider; and if advantageous terms for the future are offered—terms which are calculated to promote the development of the trade and commerce of the United States, encourage good feeling and prevent difficulties with our neighbors, and at the same time protect the revenues of the country from serious and increasing frauds—it would be, in the opinion of the commission, most impolitic to disregard them.

The offer on the part of the provincial authorities to re-negotiate in respect to the commercial relations of the two countries, is in itself an expression of desire to make an arrangement that must be in every respect reciprocal, inasmuch as it is evident that no treaty can, for any length of time, continue that does not conduce to the benefit of both parties.

It is evident that the necessities of the United States will for many years require the imposition of high rates of taxation on many articles, and that with the production of such articles, free or assessed at low rates of duty in the British provinces, the enforcement of the excise laws on the borders will be a matter of no little difficulty, annoyance, and expense; and under all ordinary conditions a large annual loss of the revenue must inevitably occur. The experience of all the nations of Europe has shown that to attempt to wholly prevent smuggling, under the encouragement of high rates of duty, is an utter impossibility. If, however, such an arrangement can be made with the British provinces as will insure a nearly or quite complete equalization of duties, excise and customs, it must be apparent that all evasions of the revenue laws by smugglers would instantly come to an end, and that the attainment of the above result would be of immense advantage to the United States in a revenue point of view.

France	29,000,000
Hamburg and Bremen	29,000,000
Mexico	20,000,000
Brazil	19,000,000
China	19,000,000
British West Indies	12,000,000

Again, it is also urged that under the existing system the products of American industry subject to high rates of excise are injuriously brought into competition with similar products of provincial industry which are subjected to little or no excise, and then admitted into the United States free of duty. That such is the fact cannot be denied, and is itself a reason why the abrogation or modification of the present reciprocity treaty has become imperative. But if it were possible to effect such an arrangement with the British provinces as would allow the imposition of duties equivalent to the American excise on all articles of provincial production passing into the United States, it seems clear that the aforementioned objection would be entirely removed.

As the whole subject, however, is now before Congress for consideration, the commission do not consider it as within their province to submit any specific recommendations, but would content themselves with merely pointing out that under certain circumstances, conditions of great advantage to the United States, in a revenue point of view, might be secured.

ORGANIZATION AND ADMINISTRATION OF THE REVENUE SYSTEM.

Under the terms of the act authorizing the commission, they were required to consider the best and most efficient mode of raising the revenue, and were intrusted with power to "inquire into the manner and efficiency of the present and past methods of collecting the internal revenue."

In accordance with this provision the commission have devoted as much time as was at their command to the consideration of the above subject.

It must be obvious, in the outset, that however perfect may be the system of revenue law devised, unless an efficient and judicious administration of the same is also provided for, the results will be anything but satisfactory.

As the case now stands, there can hardly be said to be any general and efficient organization of that department of the revenue which relates to the customs. The system devised in the infancy of the nation has been gradually enlarged and modified to meet the requirements of an increasing and now enormous commerce; but so imperfectly and irregularly has this been done, that the whole system at present seems wanting in method and centralization; and the government, in this department of its business, is obliged, as it were, to do the work of a giant with the toy instruments of a child. The commission believe, furthermore, that there is not, at this time, any individual connected with this branch of the revenue who possesses such an acquaintance with the relations of our customs system to the trade and commerce of the country as is possessed by the supervising official of the customs departments of either Great Britain or France; and what is more, there probably never will be any such, so long as appointment and continuance in office are made dependent on political considerations.

As regards the New York custom-house, the channel through which about two-thirds of the custom receipts of the whole country pass, want of time has prevented the commission from making extensive personal inquiry; but judging from the numerous statements presented to them, and from the evidence elicited by the Committee on Public Expenditures (H. of Rep., 38th Cong., 2d sess., Report No. 25—1865,) they feel satisfied that the necessity of reform in the manner of doing business in this institution was never more urgent than at present.

Of the officers employed in the New York custom-house, it is believed that a majority of them have no special qualifications for their places, and little knowledge of the law under which they discharge their duties; while the estimates presented to the commission of the annual losses experienced by the government, through the frauds perpetrated in connexion with this institution, range from twelve to twenty-five millions of dollars.

A very large part of these frauds arises from the undervaluation of invoices, coupled with neglect and incompetence in the department of the appraisers. To enter into any detailed account of the manner in which these frauds are perpetrated would, however, require more space than is at the command of the commission in the present report; but as an illustration of the common, systematic, and shameless manner in which it is conducted, they would state that they have had exhibited to them two invoices received during the past few months from one of the leading and most respectable houses of one of the chief cities of Europe, one of which invoices, sworn to falsely for the payment of duties, was nearly forty per cent. less in amount than the other which was transmitted for the private account of the importer.*

The attention of the commission has, furthermore, been called to a case which has occurred very recently, concerning a foreign publication, imported in sheets into New York, for which an American house offered to double the price at which the sheets were invoiced, and use them as a raw material for the manufacture of printing paper, although rags and like materials are admitted free of duty. The sheets of the publication in question were invoiced with their covers at three farthings, could be bound for a fraction of a cent each, and are sold in the American market at from eighteen to twenty-five cents.

The effect of such frauds is not to be measured merely by the actual loss of revenue sustained by the government, but also includes the injury inflicted upon the honest importer or the American manufacturer, who is forced to submit to a competition against which no skill or industry will enable him to protect himself. And it is undoubtedly true that, in this way, no tariff enacted of late years has fully accomplished the end it was intended to subserve.

Another prolific source of fraud in the customs is connected with the present system of refunding duties paid or alleged to be paid in excess. "The number of such cases pending in the New York courts averages five hundred and over a year, sometimes running up to one, two, or even three thousand, and involving millions of dollars," to which must be added an aggregate of costs of no small dimensions. In some of these cases, it is the conviction of old and experienced custom-house officials that the government has been made to refund duties three or four times in succession, and that a large part of the business can be characterized as nothing less than shameless and systematic robbery, involving, it would seem, not unfrequently, collusion on the part of government officials.

---

* The following is a list of prices, per thousand litres, at which Rhine wines have been recently passed through the custom-house, and a list of the real prices discovered by reference to the books of the importers:

Custom-house invoice.	Real invoice.
220 florins	530 florins
150 "	330 "
250 "	580 "
180 "	450 "
110 "	240 "
320 "	700 "
350 "	700 "
194 "	460 "
153 "	320 "

All these goods were passed by the New York appraisers at the lowest prices. (Report of the Committee on Public Expenditures, page 93.)

"There are probably no more honorable merchants in the Union, or in the world, than are to be found in New York, but we have also always a large number who look upon our revenue laws as simply an instrument to be set aside, if possible, in order to defraud the revenue. There is no moral restriction whatever imposed on them. They look upon our revenue laws, as they do in Europe, as barriers which they are justified in getting over, if they can. Catch them once, and they will laugh at you, and say you are not smart enough to catch them again. One of them, who paid $10,000 the other day, said to me, 'I do not believe you will be smart enough to catch me again.' They do not consider it any disgrace to violate the revenue laws." (Testimony of C. S. Franklin, deputy naval officer, Congressional Report, page 101.)

It ought to be clearly understood by the people of the country that a continuance of this laxity in the management of the customs revenue is equivalent to increased taxation; and that every dollar taken from the revenue under various pretences in this department must, necessarily, be made up by an equivalent assessment.

In regard to the Internal Revenue department, the commission have no allegation of fraud to present; but at the same time are constrained to say that, in point of organization and administration, it is very far from what it should be. In proof of this, they have but to cite the opinion of the late Commissioner, before referred to as concurred in by the commission, that if the law, as it now stands, could be fully and effectually executed, the receipts from it would not fall short of $500,000,000 per annum; or, in other words, that a complete administration of the law would justify wiping out more than one-half of the excise tax from the statute book.* If we admit the truth of this statement, even in an approximate degree, the commission might here rest their argument in favor of the necessity of reorganization. They will, however, briefly call attention to some of the leading imperfections of the present system.

One of the most prominent of these is a lack of power and authority in this department to control itself, especially in the matter of expenditures. In regard to this latter, the law itself allows but little discretion, and what little there is, is vested in officers of the Treasury Department, who, although they may be the most faithful and vigilant guardians of the public moneys, have little or no experience in connexion with the collection of the internal revenue, or practical knowledge of its workings. It therefore, undoubtedly, often happens that in an honest desire to prevent the waste of public money, a small sum may be saved at an expense of one of much greater magnitude.

Thus, as illustrations of this character brought to the notice of the commission, they might cite cases where vigilant officers, who have devised plans at slight expense for simplifying returns, or detecting fraud, have been obliged, after the government has adopted their recommendations, and been benefited by their services, to have the small expenditures thus incurred deducted from their salaries—a course equivalent, in fact, to offering a premium for continued inefficiency and want of method. Again: officers who have been detailed on special service, and have performed such service, bringing back thousands of dollars to the treasury, have had their accounts for small expenditures, even when approved by the Commissioner, disallowed or reduced by the auditing officers. The commission would not be understood as intending to censure the auditing officers for the course pursued by them, as it was undoubtedly in strict accordance with the law; but they would say that they do not think it is for the interest of the government or the country to allow the revenue system to be curtailed of its usefulness, either by reason of such laws, or by any special interpretation placed upon them.

Another cause of imperfection in the internal revenue system is undoubtedly due to a limitation in the number of highly competent and responsible officers, and to the inadequacy of the salaries paid to them. Starting less than four years since with one Commissioner and one clerk, the business of the internal revenue has increased to such an extent that probably it now exceeds in magnitude the entire Treasury Department previous to the war, and is at present receiving more money every quarter than the whole annual revenue of the gov-

* Thus a committee of the Association of Journeymen Boot and Shoemakers of the city of New York, in a return to the commission, estimate the value of the boot and shoe industry in that city as being $16,867,200 per annum. Deducting fifty per cent. from this to represent the exemptions of $1,000 to each manufacturer, allowed by law, and for overestimates, the amount of revenue which ought to have accrued to the government from this source, under the six per cent. manufacturing tax, would be $506,016, while the amount actually collected was less than $100,000.

ernment prior to 1860. The amount of mailable matter which leaves the office is reported to average one and a half ton daily.

With all this labor and responsibility, the internal revenue is but a bureau of the Treasury Department, and, with the exception of the Commissioner, deputy commissioner, and cashier, no provision has been made for clerical assistance independent of the department.

With the present organization of the office, the commission believe that no one man can be found mentally or physically competent to faithfully discharge all the duties devolving upon and expected from the Commissioner; while the clerk in charge of the division of accounts is required to possess as high an order of qualifications, and to perform more intricate, responsible, and laborious duties than any employé of any private firm or corporation in the country. The salary of the former of these officials is now fixed by law at four thousand dollars per annum, and that of the latter at eighteen hundred dollars.

The operations of the internal revenue, and also of the customs, affect the character of nearly every industrial and moneyed interest in the country ; and all experience has shown that great numbers of designing persons are ever on the alert to take advantage of imperfections in the law, and of the inexperience of officials, to evade the law and defraud the government.

The only counter-check, therefore, for government to rely upon is the integrity, faithfulness, capacity, and experience of its agents; and for the government to endeavor to procure and retain the services of men competent to discharge responsible trusts at less salaries than is paid by leading banks, or private mercantile firms or corporations, will not only, probably, be impossible, but will result in very poor economy.

The system under which drawbacks are allowed on products of American industry exported from the country which have previously been subjected to excise, is also represented as being very imperfect and complicated, and as presenting an obstacle to the resuscitation and development of our trade with foreign nations, impaired by the events of the last four years.

With the adoption, however, of the policy recommended by the commission, viz: of removing the excise from nearly all products of industry, many of these difficulties will undoubtedly be obviated.

The present system of the allowance of moieties of forfeitures and penalties to informers is also undoubtedly exercising a very demoralizing influence. In a mere pecuniary point of view, however, no expenditures of the government probably produce so large a return, both direct aud indirect, as flow from the distribution of these moieties, and so long as the present organization of the revenue is retained the commission find it difficult to devise a better arrangement.

Attention should also be called to the fact that the chief business of the office of the internal revenue at Washington, and the chief depository of its records and papers, are located in a building which is not fire-proof, and that at any moment the whole machinery of the department is liable to be thrown into great confusion, with the infliction of irreparable losses, by reason of circumstances against which there is now no adequate provision.

But an imperfection in our whole revenue policy more serious and radical than any yet adverted to, and which affects alike both the customs and the excise, is that of making the appointment, retention, and promotion of officers of the revenue dependent on other circumstances than qualifications of good behavior. So long as this policy prevails—a policy never adopted by any private firm or corporation having a due regard to their own interests, and one entirely ignored by all the leading states of Europe—a thoroughly efficient and economical administration of the revenue. coupled with the education of a competent corps of officials, cannot reasonably be expected. Under the present system, inspectors of spirits have been appointed who were entirely ignorant of the hydrometer and disregarded its use; and inspectors of tobacco, who required to be instructed as to the nature of the different varieties of this article when manufactured, previous to entering upon the discharge of their duties.

The commission are also informed that efforts for the removal of competent officers have, in some instances, undoubtedly been made for the sole reason that in the faithful discharge of their duties they have interfered with the private interests of wealthy and influential individuals.

The commission consider it imperative that some action should be speedily taken by Congress on this subject; and that the necessities of the country should override any advantages that now may accrue in the distribution of patronage in the revenue department of the government. Good men, honest, competent, and efficient, should be sought out and placed in all the positions requiring tact, skill, and judgment, and on such salaries as will enable them to live and continue honest; they should, moreover, hold their situations by such assured tenure as to induce application and faithfulness. Thus would the government have the benefit of experience, every year growing more and more valuable.

To remedy the imperfections of the existing revenue system, which the commission have thus briefly alluded to, an entire reorganization of the whole machinery and policy of its administration seems necessary; but, before offering any suggestions on the subject, they would call attention to some of the peculiarities of the administration of the British revenue.

The leading features of the British administrative system consist in placing the customs and excise under the charge of separate and distinct boards of commissioners, each consisting of five members and a secretary. To each is also attached a law officer of great ability and large salary,* which are respectively known as the solicitor of the customs and solicitor of the excise. To these separate boards of commissioners (which the commission understand it is now contemplated to unite) very large powers are intrusted to make and amend the regulations under which the revenues are to be assessed and collected; and in respect to the appointment of all subordinate officials, who, before receivnig such appointments, are required to undergo strict examinations as to education, business qualifications, health, and moral character. No distribution of moieties of fines and forfeitures to informers is allowed, but the boards of commissioners are empowered, at discretion, to pay for information, to distribute rewards, and to promote in office for good service.

Superannuated and faithful officers are also allowed pensions on retirement from office. To such an extent, moreover, is the British revenue, in all its departments, divorced from party and politics, that all officers and employés of the revenue are even deprived of the right of suffrage while in service, though otherwise qualified; while it is understood that no influence on the part of any member of Parliament, or even of the chancellor of the exchequer, will avail for the securement of an appointment under the revenue, unless the candidate receive, at the same time, the approval of a majority of the board of commissioners, under whose supervision his duties are to be discharged. The consequence of this is, that the administration of the British revenue law is constantly improving, while frauds and defalcations on the part of the officials are rarely, if ever, heard of.

The responsibility of the collection, preparation, and publication of statistics of British revenue, trade, and commerce—to the accuracy and clearness of which we would bear testimony—is divided between the respective boards of commissioners and the board of trade. The decision of all law points connected with the revenue, and the publication and legal enforcement of the same, appear to devolve upon the respective revenue solicitors.

* The salary of the solicitor of customs is £2,000, ($10,000 in gold,) and the appointment is for life.

Whether a plan analogous to the British system, as thus presented, could be advantageously carried out in detail in the United States, and whether the same would be in all respects in accordance with the spirit of our institutions, is a question upon which the commission are not prepared to express an opinion, but they have no doubt that some of its leading features must form the basis of any sound national revenue policy.

In proposing a plan of change, however, they would suggest that the work of a reorganization should commence in the office of the Secretary of the Treasury itself. This office, with the exception of that of the Executive, is now undoubtedly the most responsible and important of any under the government; and the position of its occupant, as respects the future condition of the country, is not unlike that sustained by the commander-in-chief of the army during the most critical period of the war—a position in which the nation cannot afford to allow any risks of mistakes in judgment. With far more power than is intrusted to the British chancellor of the exchequer, or the French minister of finance, the office of the Secretary of the Treasury is at the same time, by long usage and custom, in many respects merely clerical. He is called upon, at one hour, as a member of the cabinet, to participate in the decisions of grave political questions, and in the next to decide upon the transactions of his lowest subordinate. Intrusted with the supervision of the expenditures of hundreds of millions annually, he is also the final arbiter for the settlement of the most insignificant disbursements. It is also the assumed privilege of nearly every individual in the country to address him on all subjects connected with either public or private interests; and courtesy and usage demand that, in all instances, a reply of some nature should be given. The demands thus made at present upon the time and attention of the Secretary of the Treasury are wholly inconsistent with a proper consideration of those great questions of finance submitted to his decision, upon the wise determination of which the future welfare of the nation is inevitably dependent. To impose, therefore, any subordinate and trivial duties on this great officer of state is both to degrade his office and to imperil the financial interests of the country.

The business of the Treasury Department, as at present constituted, may be classified under three heads: First, the collection of the revenue; second, the supervision of its expenditures; and, third, the management of the public debt and the national currency.

The commission would suggest that the first of these—the collection of the revenue—be transferred from the immediate responsibility of the Secretary of the Treasury, and, subject only to his general supervision, be placed under the charge of a new officer, subordinate only in rank and in amount of salary to the Secretary, who shall be styled the Under-Secretary of the Treasury in Charge of the Revenue; and that to this officer should be assigned the general oversight and direction of the collection of the revenues, and the preparation of an annual exhibit of the condition of the revenue, trade, commerce, and industry of the country.

If it were also allowed to the Secretary and the Under-Secretary of the Treasury to participate, on the floor of the House of Representatives, in all debates on revenue questions, the business of legislation might, probably, be greatly facilitated.

The commission would also propose that, in connexion with this new department of the Treasury, there should be appointed a commissioner of the customs, and a commissioner of the excise; with a solicitor of the customs and a solicitor of the excise; and that these five officers should constitute a board, to be known as the board of commissioners of the revenue, of which the Under-Secretary of the Treasury should be the chairman.

To this board should be referred the determination of all rules and regulations relating to the collection of the revenue; the expenditures to be incurred in respect to the same; the management of all revenue processes at law; and the distribution of all moieties, received from forfeitures and penalties, in reward for good service and for valuable information. They would also propose that no subordinate officer of the revenue should receive a commission until his qualifications for the proper discharge of his duties had been examined into and approved of by the board of commissioners.

In the departments of the commissioners of customs and excise, they would further propose, that each of the leading sources of revenue be recognized as a division of the revenue, and that the same be placed in charge of an officer, to whom the incentive of a permanent position and a good salary should be offered as an inducement for the attainment of a thorough acquaintance with, and efficient management of, his special trust.

This plan, which the commission have merely presented in outline, seems to them susceptible of being carried out in a manner which would remedy nearly all the imperfections of the present system, and greatly conduce to the best interests of the country; and if, in the judgment of Congress, it may seem expedient, and sufficient time be allowed for a careful study and examination of the whole subject, the commission will be prepared to submit a bill in accordance with the above suggestions.

If Congress should concur in the opinion that a reorganization of the revenue system, either according to the plan proposed, or some other, be expedient, the commission recommend that the change should be made as soon as practicable, especially before, in the Internal Revenue department, custom has developed into routine, and usage has acquired, through time, the binding effect of law. It required the best efforts of the most enlightened ministers of finance in France (Count Mollier, the Marquis d'Audiffret, and others) for thirty or forty years to replace the cumbrous and awkward system of finance which prevailed in that country at the commencement of the present century with the existing system, which is now acknowledged to be one of the best, if not the very best in Europe. It ought also to be borne in mind that no revenue system, in its details, can or ought to be considered permanent. As resources develop, as forms of industry and commerce modify or change, and as revenue receipts, from particular sources, increase or diminish, the rate of taxes and the method of assessing them will need to be correspondingly modified. To prepare the basis for such changes by legislation would seem to require that the industry, the commerce, and the revenue of the country should be made the subject of special and continued study and investigation by some competent persons.

The commission feel certain that such labor, properly executed, would be of immense service, if not indispensable, to Congress.

The discharge of such service, however, does not seem to properly devolve upon congressional committees, to whom should be assigned the duty of examining and passing judgment, rather than of preparing material and digesting statistics.

The commission, therefore, would commend this subject to the special attention of Congress, and recommend that some arrangements for continued inquiry and investigation, of the nature indicated, should be provided for, either in connexion with or independent of the regular administration of the revenue.

In the mean time, in order to provide for a more perfect administration of the law in certain respects, the commission present the following forms of bills, which they would recommend to the attention of Congress:

First. A form of bill authorizing the Secretary of the Treasury to appoint, in such one or more collection districts as he may deem advisable, "*solicitors of the revenue*," who shall discharge the duties, now devolving on United States district attorneys, in all cases relating to frauds or violations of the revenue laws.

The commission believe that the experience of the last three years, in the administration of the internal revenue, warrants the adoption of such a measure. In the British system this plan has been found to work very advantageously.

Secondly. A form of bill, authorizing the Secretary of the Treasury to appoint officers, to be known as supervisors of the revenue, who shall discharge such general and specific duties as are therein enumerated.

Thirdly. A form of bill, authorizing commissioners of the courts of the United States, under certain circumstances, to take cognizance of cases of forfeiture and frauds committed under the revenue laws of the United States, and to give judgment in respect to the same, in accordance with the laws, subject to appeal to the district courts of the United States.

CONCLUSION.

In submitting this general report, the commission would again state that they have been unable, from lack of time, to consider many of the topics of importance which have been referred to them. A number of special reports on various sources of revenue, with forms of bills, as by law directed, are herewith submitted, and others will be presented at the earliest practicable moment.

Among the separate reports which will be submitted is one by an individual member of the commission in relation to national securities—a topic which has already excited some discussion, and is likely to produce more. It is thought by a majority of the commission that this report, and the bill accompanying it, should be referred, with your consent, to Congress, not only on account of the importance of its suggestions, and the arguments by which they are sustained, but as a preventive of crude projects and plans which may be presented to Congress by those who have not devoted so much time to the consideration of the subject. If the policy of a sinking fund shall be adopted by Congress, that suggested in the report alluded to is worthy of consideration.

The commission also desire to say that, in respect to some of the points discussed in their reports, there is a difference of opinion existing among its members, but that each recommendation of the commission offered is sustained by a majority of the commission, and that, as regards the report as a whole, it has their unanimous concurrence.

The commission would also again allude to the very great difficulty which they have experienced in their investigations in obtaining exact statistical information. The returns furnished by the Treasury Department do not, in any degree, correspond with those furnished to the commission by the trade, or published in the various commercial circulars; and these latter, furthermore, do not always agree with each other. They cannot, therefore, claim that the statistics of production and consumption, given by them in their general and special reports, are absolutely correct. They are, however, believed to be approximately so, and are the best results derivable from the data placed at their disposal.

The commission, furthermore, in closing their report, would take occasion to express their sense of obligation to the Secretary of the Treasury and to all officers connected with his department—especially to the late and present Commissioners of Internal Revenue—for the prompt and effective assistance which has at all times been rendered to them in furtherance of the objects of their investigations.

As another gratifying feature of their labor, the commission are also enabled to report a most cheerful and prompt co-operation on the part of the representatives of nearly all the industrial interests of the country, for all which services they herewith tender their unqualified acknowledgments.

Respectfully submitted:

DAVID A. WELLS.
STEPHEN COLWELL.
S. S. HAYES.

Hon. HUGH McCULLOCH, *Secretary of the Treasury.*

SPECIAL REPORT No. 1.

Report of the United States revenue commission on tea as a source of national revenue.

TREASURY DEPARTMENT,
Office of the United States Revenue Commission, January, 1866.

SIR: The following are the estimates of the consumption of *tea* in the United States since 1813:*

	Pounds.
1813 to 1820, mean annual consumption....................	3,300,000
1821, mean annual consumption..............................	4,473,000
1830, mean annual consumption..............................	6,873,000
1831 to 1841, mean annual consumption....................	12,448,000
1841 to 1850, mean annual consumption....................	16,246,000
1850 to 1861, mean annual consumption....................	27,363,965

For the ten years from 1831 to 1841 the mean annual consumption of *tea* in the United States is believed to have been 12,448,000 pounds. Assuming the average number of the free population in this period to have been 13,137,000, we have $\frac{95}{100}$ of a pound as the consumption *per capita.*

For the nine years from 1841 to 1850 the mean annual consumption of tea in the United States is estimated at 16,246,000 pounds, which, for an average free population of 17,819,000, would be equal to $\frac{91}{100}$ of a pound *per capita.*

It would thus appear that from 1831 to 1850 (a period of nineteen years) the increase in the consumption of tea in the United States only kept pace with the increase of population.

During the eleven years from 1850 to 1861 the whole amount of tea imported into the United States was 351,314,031 pounds. During the same time there were exported from the country 50,310,420 pounds, leaving for home consumption 301,003,611 pounds, or an average of 27,363,965 pounds per annum.

Assuming the average number of the free population for this period to have been 24,640,000, we have, therefore, $1\frac{11}{100}$ of a pound as the average annual consumption of *tea per capita* for that period; showing a gain of one-fifth ($\frac{20}{100}$) of a pound on the average of the years included between 1831 and 1850, or an increase in consumption of between six and seven per cent. per annum, while the increase in population was only three and a half per cent. per annum.

This great increase in the consumption of *tea* may be referred, in part, to the great prosperity of the country and the opening of the California trade; partially to the increased facilities and cheapness in transportation, by railroad, to all parts of the country, and partially to the cheapness of *tea* itself. From 1850 to 1856 the import of *tea* into the United States was largely in excess of consumption; so that in January, 1856, there was an estimated stock of *tea* on hand of at least 30,000,000 pounds. During the next five years, however, or from 1857 to 1861, inclusive, the excess of the imports over the exports fell short of consumption, so that on the 1st of January, 1862, the country was almost bare of tea.

The annual consumption of *tea* for the whole country for the year previous to the breaking out of the rebellion was estimated at about 30,000,000 pounds. Of this amount, the States which seceded and the State of Kentucky—in all comprising a free population of 8,000,000—are estimated to have consumed 3,000,000 pounds, or $\frac{37}{10}$ of a pound *per capita;* while the remaining States, with a free population of 20,000,000 consumed 27,000,000 pounds, or $1\frac{35}{100}$ of a pound *per capita.*

* There are records showing the quantity of tea shipped from Canton to the United States s far back as the year 1784–'8.

Of this consumption by the free States, about 17,000,000 pounds may be set down to the credit of the "black" teas, and 10,000,000 pounds to "green" teas.

The following, according to the returns made to the commission by the Treasury Department, were the gross importations of *tea* into the United States for the fiscal years 1861–62, 1862–'63, 1863–'64 :

1861–'62	24, 739, 983 pounds.
1862–'63	29, 761, 006 "
1863–'64	37, 229, 176 "

As no allowance is here made for re-exports, the above figures do not in any way represent the consumption of the country. This, the commission, from data obtained from the trade in New York, believe to have been approximately as follows for the years ending December 31, 1861, 1862, 1863, 1864, and 1865 :*

	Green Japan.	Black.	Total.
	Pounds.	*Pounds.*	*Pounds.*
1861	7, 485, 000	18, 035, 000	25, 520, 000
1862	13, 871, 600	13, 597, 000	27, 468, 600
1863	14, 490, 680	12, 415, 685	26, 906, 365
1864	13, 564, 295	9, 573, 251	23, 137, 546
1865 †	18, 874, 199	10, 979, 234	29, 853, 433

It would thus appear that the effect of the war was to reduce the average consumption of *tea* in the loyal States during the war, as compared with the year 1860–'61, *less than five per cent.* There is no allowance made in this calculation for smuggling. Whatever quantity may have been smuggled has increased the consumption to that extent.

The influence of the imposition of a duty on *tea* in restricting consumption has, in the opinion of the commission, been very slight as compared with other causes. For some time past, the first cost of the article itsef in China has been unusually high. High rates of freight have also been paid in gold for its transport in neutral vessels, (from five to seven cents per pound,) while the high premium upon gold operating on prime cost, freight and charges, has forced the price to the consumer to more than twice what it would have been with a hundred per cent. increase of duty, and gold at or near par.

By referring back to the record of the imports heretofore imposed on *tea* imported into the United States, we find that, by the act of April 11, 1816, the following comparatively heavy schedule of duties was adopted :

On Bohea	by American vessels,	12 c. per lb. ;	by foreign vessels,	14 c. per lb.
Souchong and other black	do.	25 "		do.	34 "
Imperial and gunpowder	do.	50 "		do.	68 "
Hyson and young hyson	do.	40 "		do.	56 "
Hyson skin and other green	do.	28 "		do.	38 "

These duties amounted to from seventy-five to a hundred per cent. on Bohea, and sixty to a hundred per cent. on Souchong and green, according to the then existing prices.

This act remained unaltered until March, 1833, when, by an act previously

* This estimate of consumption is based upon imports, direct and indirect, and upon the quantity of *tea* re-exported. The movement of *tea* between the United States and the Canadas is also included, but it does not, however, include the consumption of the Pacific States.

† During this year we had *four* months of actual war, and less than six months of peaceful internal commerce with the lines of communication open with all parts of the country. The trade statistics for the six months ending June 30, 1865, indicate that the consumption of tea, for that period, was in excess of fifteen millions pounds for all kinds.

passed, (July, 1832,) all duties on *tea* imported in American vessels were remitted; the former rates being, however, retained as respects teas imported in foreign vessels. The importation in the latter class of vessels was, however, very small. The following table shows the quantities of *tea* imported and re-exported for the several fiscal years, ending September 30, from 1828 to 1840, inclusive.

Year ending—		Imports.	Exports.
		Pounds.	*Pounds.*
September 30, 1828		7, 707, 437	1, 417, 846
1829		6, 636, 790	1, 033, 995
1830		5, 182, 867	526, 186
1831		8, 609, 415	1, 736, 324
1832		9, 906, 606	1, 279, 462
1833	dutiable	2, 051, 182	748, 297
	free	12, 588, 640	964, 482
1834		16, 274, 769	3, 081, 126
1835		14, 412, 380	2, 080, 742
1836		16, 381, 126	1, 896, 342
1837		16, 973, 742	2, 508, 020
1838	dutiable	4, 066	2, 435, 302
		14, 414, 046	
1839	dutiable	9, 756	1, 592, 033
		9, 340, 061	
1840	dutiable	25, 119	3, 120, 692
		19, 981, 476	

After the repeal of the duties in 1833, the importations (as will be seen by reference to the table) increased very considerably, but being almost wholly in American vessels, very little revenue accrued from them. For the year ending June 30, 1850, the imports were in American vessels, free, 28,244,462 pounds, and in foreign vessels, dutiable, 508,355 pounds.

Up to 1846, *tea* imported in foreign vessels continued to pay the rates of duty imposed on the same in 1816, but in the act of 1846 they were left to pay *twenty* per cent. as unenumerated articles.

By the tariff of March 3, 1857, *tea* imported indirectly paid *fifteen* per cent., also as unenumerated.

By the act of August 5, 1861, which took effect on its passage, *teas* imported in American vessels were again charged with duty for the first time since 1833; the duties being *specific*, and upon all *teas* at the rate of *fifteen* cents per pound.

By the act of December 24, 1861, this rate was increased to *twenty* cents per pound; and by the act of June 3, 1864, the rate was further advanced on all *teas* to *twenty-five* cents per pound, and has since then remained unchanged.

In answer to a call made on the Treasury Department for information respecting the customs revenue derived from the importations of specific articles, the commission were informed at the outset of their labors, that "it is impossible to define the precise amount of the revenue received from the duties levied at various times upon tea. No distinct return of the actual receipts of revenue from particular articles was received until the commencement of the current fiscal year" (1865.) And again, "it cannot definitely be said what amount of revenue has been received from teas since the duties of 1861 were laid. The import statement embraces all going into warehouse, and the exports are not only from warehouse, without payment of duty originally, but also from stocks which have paid duty, and on which drawbacks are not admitted."

In November, 1865, however, in answer to a second call of the commission for information, the department furnished the following statement of the imports of *teas* and the duties accruing on the same, for the fiscal years ending June 30, 1862 and 1865, inclusive, from the *five* ports of Boston, New York, Philadelphia, Baltimore, and San Francisco.* As to the reliability of these statements the commission express no opinion. It will be observed, however, that there is a wide discrepancy between the returns of the department and the tables indicating consumption furnished to the commission by the trade in New York.

Year ending—	Amount.	Rate.	Duty accrued.
	Pounds.	*Cents.*	
June 30, 1862	315, 283	15	$47, 292 45
1862	11, 773, 307	20	2, 354, 661 40
Total	12, 088, 590	......	2, 401, 953 85
1863	18, 711, 646	20	3, 742, 329 20
1864	33, 195, 957	20	6, 639, 191 40
1865	18, 595, 314	25	3, 999, 524 50

Present consumption of tea—Estimating the total population of the whole country in 1866 at 36,000,000 of all classes, the commission believe it will be perfectly safe, and probably within the mark, to base a calculation for present revenue upon an annual consumption of 30,000,000 pounds of all kinds of tea; which consumption, the duties remaining the same as at present (i. e. twenty-five cents per pound,) *will yield a revenue of seven millions five hundred thousand dollars* ($7,500,000,) *showing a gain of revenue as compared with the estimated consumption based on trade returns of* 1864, *and at the then rate of duty (twenty cents per pound,) of two million eight hundred and seventy-two thousand four hundred and ninety-one dollars* ($2,872,491.) With a fall in the price of gold and a continuance of the general prosperity of the country, the commission, in common with some of the leading trade authorities on this subject, are further of the opinion that the consumption of *teas* in the United States will continue to increase hereafter at the rate of at least three and a half (3½) per centum, or about one million of pounds per annum, giving thereby a proportionate increase of revenue.

The consumption of *tea* in different countries of Europe during the year 1860 was estimated as follows:

Great Britain	2.659	pounds	*per capita.*
Russia	.20	"	"
German States	.011	"	"
Belgium	.02	"	"
France	.089	"	"
Austria	.0013	"	"

In the United States, during the same year, the consumption of *tea, per capita*, for the whole population, was probably about *one* pound.

In Great Britain, during the year 1860, two and a half pounds of tea were consumed for every one and a quarter pound of coffee. In the United States, for the same year, about six and a half pounds of coffee were consumed for

* From San Francisco, only until April 30, 1864.

every pound of *tea*. It may here be remarked that one pound of *tea* is generally considered as equal to three pounds of coffee.

At present the consumption of *tea* in Great Britain is largely in excess of that of any of the other countries of Europe, as well as that of America. "The recent rise and present magnitude of the British *tea* trade," says McCulloch, "are among the most extraordinary phenomena in the history of commerce."

The quantity of *tea* consumed in Great Britain in 1830 is estimated at 31,676,000 pounds; in 1840, it was estimated at 37,588,000 pounds; and in 1848, at 48,734,000 pounds. Since 1852 the increase in the quantity of *tea* retained for consumption in Great Britain, according to the official returns, and the distribution of consumption *per capita*, has been as follows:

Year.	Population.	Pounds consumed.	Consumption per capita.
1853	27, 806, 145	58, 834, 087	2.115
1854	27, 961, 569	61, 953, 041	2.215
1855	28, 116, 993	63, 429, 286	2.255
1856	28, 272, 417	63, 278, 212	2.238
1857	28, 427, 841	69, 159, 843	2.433
1858	28, 583, 265	73, 217, 484	2.561
1859	28, 738, 689	76, 362, 008	2.657
1860	28, 894, 113	76, 842, 016	2.659
1861	29, 049, 540	77, 949, 464	2.683
1862	29, 204, 964	78, 817, 060	2 698
1863	29, 360, 388	85, 206, 779	3.902
1864	29, 515, 812	88, 637, 099	3.003

This extraordinary consumption of *tea* in Great Britain cannot, in the opinion of the commission, be regarded as any indication of prosperity on the part of the consumers. The view taken by the most recent chemical authorities in relation to the physiological action of *tea* is, that it tends to diminish the waste of the system, and therefore supplies to a certain extent the lack of other nutritious food. That the same conclusion has been practically arrived at, through experience, by the working and poorer classes of Great Britain seems evident from the statement made by Professor Leone Levi, in 1860, in his work on British Taxation—that *tea*, next to bread, is regarded by the above-mentioned classes as a pure necessity of life. "In various parts of England," he continues, "those whose wages range from eight shillings (two dollars) to twelve shillings (three dollars) per week almost live upon bread and *tea*, and the women especially take it at all meals. Many of the working classes use *tea* three times a day; and among the working females tea and sugar constitute the chief articles of their diet. In Ireland *tea* and sugar are consumed even by the poorest, although they thereby deprive themselves of more nourishing food; and in the south of Ireland, among the agricultural population, those who cannot afford to use these articles for general diet, purchase small quantities, about sixpence worth, at Christmas and other holiday times."

If the above supposition that the extraordinary increase in the consumption of *tea* in Great Britain during the last thirty years is due in great part to the circumstances of its being used as a substitute for other and more concrete food, it is evidently useless to expect that any increase in the consumption of *tea* in the United States will take place from similar causes.

It might possibly be further inferred that a part or all of the enormous increase in the consumption of *tea* in Great Britain was due to a progressive decrease in the rates of duty. An examination of the subject will not, however, in the opinion of the commission, warrant any such inference.

Tea is probably less affected in price to the consumer, by any increase or decrease of duty, than any other article that enters into consumption among a civilized people. There is practically but one producing country, and the trade, therefore, partakes of the features of a monopoly; a decrease of duty inuring to the advantage of the producer, and conversely an increase of duty inuring to the disadvantage of the producer. This statement is abundantly proved by the following table, taken from the report of the British commissioners of customs for 1865:

Year.	Average rate of duty.		Average price of tea per lb. in bond.		Year.	Average rate of duty.		Average price of tea per lb. in bond.	
	s.	*d.*	*s.*	*d.*		*s.*	*d.*	*s*	*d.*
1848............	2	2¼	1	0¼	1857...........	1	5½	1	5 4-10
1849............	2	2¼	1	1	1858...........	1	5	1	4⅝
1850............	2	2¼	1	3¼	1859...........	1	5	1	6⅝
1851............	2	2¼	1	2½	1860...........	1	5	1	6¾
1852............	2	2¼	1	0¼	1861...........	1	5	1	5
1853............	1	11¼	1	3¼	1862...........	1	5	1	7 3-16
1854............	1	6½	1	3½	1863...........	1	1$\frac{1}{10}$	1	6 11-16
1855............	1	8	1	3	1864...........	1	0	1	6¼
1856............	1	9	1	2¾					

We see, therefore, that while the duty on tea was reduced in Great Britain, between the years 1848 and 1864, to the extent of fifty-five per cent, the average price of *tea* in bond during the same period exhibited a corresponding increase of about fifty per cent.; and this, too, notwithstanding that (as the report of the commissioners of customs states) heavy importations of tea into Great Britain in 1862 and 1863 overstocked the market, leaving on hand in 1864 a much larger stock than was held in any previous year; showing that the advance in the price of tea in Great Britain was not owing to any diminution of supply, but rather resulted from a decrease of duty, in spite of a heavy supply.

When the intelligence reached China, by telegram, of the last reduction of sixpence per pound in the British duty, the price immediately responded in an equivalent advance, owing partly to the more extreme views of the Chinese sellers—who are shrewd merchants and sensible of their monopoly—and partly to the increased competition among the English merchants as buyers.

There being no material competition among buyers of tea of the green descriptions in the Chinese market, except for the American market, an inference that a further increase of duty in the United States (if Congress should deem the same expedient) would fall on the producing country to a considerable extent, is, therefore, fully justified. Owing to the large profits of the trade, it is reasonable also to infer that not an inconsiderable portion of any increase of duty would be borne by the middle-men, who stand between the importer and consumer, rather than by the consumer.

The staple tea of Great Britain is Congou, of which there is little or no consumption in the United States; and this, together with "Souchong," (both coming under the general denomination of "black") forms, almost exclusively, the consumption of the British people. On the other hand, no "Congou," and probably not more than 2,000,000 pounds of "Souchong," are used in the United States, whose consumption is mainly of "Oolong," (which is properly a "green" tea, though classed as black,) "green," and "Japan" (also a green tea, and, until recently, unknown to commerce.) The "Bohea," which was so extensively used in the United States thirty or forty years since, is not now imported.

Attention should also be called, in this connexion, to the fact that the increase of the *per capita* consumption of *tea* in the United States has kept pace with the *per capita* increase in Great Britain since 1834.

Since 1840 the average rates of duty imposed on *tea* in Great Britain have been as follows:

	s.	*d.*		
From 1840 to 1845	2	2½	sterling	per pound.
From 1845 to 1852	2	2¼	"	"
In 1853	1	11¼	"	"
In 1854	1	6½	"	"
In 1855	1	8	"	"
In 1856	1	9	"	"
In 1857	1	5½	"	"
From 1858 to 1862	1	5	"	"
In 1863	1	$1\frac{1}{10}$	"	"
In 1864	1	0	"	"

During the year 1865 the duty was further reduced to sixpence per pound, at which rate it now remains.

Tea, with the exception of sugar and tobacco, constitutes the most productive article on the list of British customs. The largest gross receipts from tea in any one year, were in 1852 and amounted to £5,985,484; equal to about $29,927,420, in a consumption of 54,724,425 pounds, under the duty of 2*s.* 2¼*d.* In this year the receipts from tea exceeded the receipts from sugar, wines and spirits, or tobacco, and constituted more than one quarter of the entire custom receipts. The gross revenue derived from the duties imposed on tea, imported into Great Britain during the five years from 1860 to 1864 *inclusive*, has been as follows:

1860	£5,442,923	or about	$27,214,615
1861	5,522,320	"	27,611,600
1862	5,582,793	"	27,913,965
1863	4,652,822	"	23,264,110
1864	4,431,868	"	22,159,340

The quantity of *tea* imported and consumed in France, Austria and Belgium is small, and the revenues derived therefrom very inconsiderable.

Cost of tea.—By far the largest proportion of the cost of tea to the American consumer is made up of the profits of the jobbers and retailers.

When it is considered that the "ship-off" price of good *tea* is about eighteen taels per pecul, or eighteen cents per pound, and that to be deducted from this is the export duty, two and a half cents, the toll levied at the various mandarin stations on its transit to the shipping port, the expense of packing, as well as two or three profits before it reaches the hands of the exporting merchant, it will readily be seen that the portion of the price going into the hands of the original pickers and producers must be very small. The average day's wages of those people do not probably exceed ten cents. The cost of staple grades of black (Oolong) *tea*, which is the staple *tea* of American commerce, is about *thirty cents gold*, laid down in New York, free of duty—that is to say, "in bond;" this includes all charges, selling commission, freight, insurance, &c.; all over this price being profit. The profits of the *tea* trade, after leaving the importer's hands and before reaching the consumer, have been enormous. This statement accounts for the very numerous shops where nothing but tea (and perhaps coffee) is dealt in as a specialty; and it is probably within the truth to say, that of the profit paid by the consumer, probably not more than one-fourth reaches the original importer. In proof of this statement the following test was made:

A pound of Oolong tea was purchased of each of two different and respectable grocers in New York, on the same day, at one dollar and a half ($1 50) per pound. This tea was immediately taken to one of the leading "tea brokers," and valued by him at a market price of ninety (90) cents for one of the samples, and ninety-three (93) cents for the other. The market for tea at this time was very steady, and had been so for some months; gold was also steady, at 146 *a* 147, and had not been below 144 for months, nor had it touched 150 for a like period. The broker's valuation, returned to the commission on the samples submitted to him, was the price at which the tea would have been sold by the importer. The tea in question cost probably about eighty (80) cents (currency) in New York, laid down, including duty and all charges; the profits of the importer ranged from ten to thirteen (say 12) cents per pound, while the balance of the cost to the consumer—about fifty-eight cents (or seventy-two per cent. on the cost to the importer)—was taken by whoever stood between the importer and consumer. A condition of trade that permits such an iniquitous profit to be made out of the consumer, certainly needs reformation. It is impossible to say what profits have been paid by the consumers of tea in remote sections of the Union; but it is probable that the average of two or three cents per pound will cover the cost of transportation to the remotest sections of the Atlantic and western States. Fifteen cents in gold (five for the importer and ten for the trade) is a liberal profit to be divided between the importer and whoever may stand between him and the consumer, making forty-five cents for a good tea, suitable for the middling classes, and as good probably as they are in the habit of using, allowing for duty.

"Green" *teas* cost more than "black," but the consumption of the former is giving way to that of Oolong and Japan *teas.*

Rates of duty.—As regards the rate of duty, the commission are inclined to the opinion that the present rate (i. e., twenty-five cents per pound) is the proper revenue standard, and they would recommend that the same *be neither increased nor diminished.* But whatever may be the duties laid upon tea, they should, as now, *be made specific and without distinction of quality.*

The almost infinite varieties of grades and values of tea, and the impossibility of precisely indicating any distinctive and certain lines of demarcation between the several qualities, render the assessment of discriminating or *ad valorem* duties extremely difficult, and the attempt to institute such a system, after having been tried in Great Britain, has been abandoned as impracticable. Specific duties, moreover, discourage the adulteration of teas, and encourage the importation of good qualities, thus indirectly benefiting the consumer.

Differential duties.—By the present law a differential duty of *ten per cent. ad valorem* upon indirect importations of *tea* (i. e., *tea* imported from the place of production through other countries,) is imposed in addition to the regular duty. The bulk of the indirect importations of *tea* at present are made *via* England. All such *teas* come to the American consumer laden, probably, with the cost of two freights paid to the British carrying trade, one of which, probably, would be an expensive steamer freight.*

Such indirect importations also come laden with the expense of landing, stowing, taring, fire insurance, &c., &c., with, perhaps, one or more selling commissions of two and a half per cent. each, altogether amounting to, perhaps, *thirty*

---

* Freight by the Liverpool steamers is 60s. per ton. Freight to England from China is about $12, equal in all to more than *four cents gold* on a pound of tea.

per cent. on the market value in England.* Every package of *tea* landed in England is opened, and being thus exposed to the air, absorbs moisture which increases its weight and deteriorates its quality. The increase in weight on English *teas* landed in New York is about three per cent.; the cost of which increase falls, of course, upon the consumer, and augments the profit to the English merchant in proportion.

The New York charges on a sale of *tea by wholesale* (exclusive of the duties) are about *fifteen per cent*, but they are all paid to our own people, and are, therefore, no loss to the country. It may doubtless be objected, that it is the interest of the consumer that there should be no obstacles in the way of indirect importations, if thereby he can get his *tea* cheaper. It is not probable that he would get his *tea* any cheaper; probably the difference between the American market price and the cost of indirect importation laid down in New York would disappear before it (the English tea) reached him, and therefore the indirect importation would not benefit the consumer, whose interest, next to that of the government and the country, is to be consulted. It is of the first importance to the American consumer that he should not unnecessarily pay thirty per cent. of the cost of the *tea* away out of the country; but it is his interest and the real interest of the country, that all of the cost of the *tea* which is not paid to the producing country should be paid within the United States, thereby hastening the time when the government can abolish the duty altogether, or reduce it to a very low point. If the present differential duty of ten per cent. *ad valorem* were abolished, it is probable that in a very few years direct importations of *tea* would cease entirely, and London would become the commercial emporium of this country, so far as regards *tea*, as it now is of Continental Europe. Even with the present duty, large quantities are now indirectly imported, and the trade is passing out of the hands of the American importers.

The following table shows the great increase of the export trade of Great Britain in tea, and the decreased *direct* import trade of tea to the United States:

Total exports of tea from China and Japan to the United Kingdom and United States.

	Season			
To Great Britain, season	1861-2	107,351,649 lbs.	To the United States	29,068,746 lbs.
" " "	1862-3	118,692,138 "	" " "	21,941,427 "
" " "	1863-4	119,689,238 "	" " "	24,204,193 "
" " "	1864-5	121,236,870 "	" " "	18,093,462 "

The superior advantages of the liberal bonded-warehouse system of Great Britain, her large market, her great and commanding resources of capital, necessarily place the United States on the defensive, if we desire eminence either as a commercial or manufacturing nation.

Advices from New York *via* London, thence by telegram to Point de Galle, thence by steamer to China, reach China in thirty days, so that the American market could not be short supplied with *teas* for any length of time, and therefore circumstances favoring indirect importation could only be of temporary duration.

The commission, therefore, recommend that the present differential duty of ten per cent. ad valorem be repealed, and in lieu thereof a specific duty of ten cents per pound on all indirect importations of tea be substituted.

With this differential duty the American merchants will be enabled to go into the importing business with some degree of security against loss, if they manage their business properly; and, by an active, healthy competition with

* Indirect importations of tea *via* England, are paid for originally by *opium* from British India, or cotton and woollen manufactured goods, or metals, or other merchandise the produce of Great Britain. Teas imported direct are paid for to a great extent by the products of American industry.

each other, to keep prices at a low point. American importers are now thrown into competition with English merchants under the most unfavorable circumstances. The interest of money in England is only half what it is in the United States, and this is the great item of cost to the merchant in importing and carrying a stock of *tea*, so that he can be ready at all times to supply the market. The *tea* business requires a large capital, and a comparatively high rate of interest is the greatest obstacle with which our merchants have to contend. The heavy stocks of *tea* constantly on hand in Great Britain are against them. During the year 1864, the surplus stock thus held was estimated at upward of 100,000,000 pounds. Any portion or all of these heavy accumulations, may be at any time precipitated upon the American market, to the derangement of all the business of the American importer, whose transactions, involving a period of at least eight months, are subjected to all this risk, and against which he cannot possibly protect himself.

No abatement of duty in consequence of damage.—It is a provision of the British tariff that "No abatement of duty shall be made on account of damage received by any *tea* during the voyage; but it shall be lawful for the importer to separate the damaged parts, and to abandon the same to the commissioners of the customs for the duty." The commission deem it of importance that an analogous provision should be incorporated into the American revenue system, and they would further enlarge the scope of the act for the following reasons: It frequently happens that *teas* damaged by fire in bonded warehouses, as well as by salt water on the voyage of importation, are sold at auction, and the duties on the same are remitted *pro rata*, according to the *pro rata* deterioration of value; such teas, however, the commission are informed, are generally made over and pass into consumption, thus taking the place of sound *teas*, and defrauding alike both the government and the consumers. This business of renewing, by various methods, and revending damaged *teas*, is believed to constitute a considerable part of the business of the so-called popular "*tea companies*" which of late years have been established in most of our large cities.

The commission, therefore, recommend that an amendment of the revenue law be enacted to this effect: "That all *teas* or *coffee*, damaged by water or otherwise on the voyage, or by fire, water, smoke, or otherwise, while in bonded warehouses, on which duties accruing, or any portion thereof, are remitted, shall be abandoned to the government and forthwith entirely destroyed, under the direction and supervision of the collector of the port."

The commission, in conformity with the act authorizing their appointment, submit herewith a form of bill, in accordance with the recommendations made by them in the foregoing report.

Respectfully submitted for the commission:

DAVID A. WELLS, *Chairman.*

Hon. HUGH McCULLOCH,
Secretary of the Treasury.

A BILL for an act relative to duties on tea.

Be it enacted by the Senate and House of Representatives of the United States of America in Congress assembled, That from and after the passage of this act the differential duty of *ten per cent. ad valorem* now imposed on all teas imported indirectly and other than from the place of production, be repealed, and in lieu thereof a duty of *ten cents* per pound be levied and collected on all teas thus imported, in addition to the duty imposed thereon when imported directly from the country of its production.

And be it further enacted, That from and after the passage of this act no abatement of duty shall be made on account of damage received by any *tea* or *coffee* during the voyage, or while in bonded warehouse, but it shall be lawful for the importer or owner to separate the damaged parts, and to abandon the same to the government; and the same shall be forthwith entirely destroyed, under the direction and supervision of the collector of the port.

SPECIAL REPORT NO. 2.

Report of the United States revenue commission on coffee, &c., as sources of national revenue.

TREASURY DEPARTMENT,
Office of the United States Revenue Commission, January, 1866.

SIR: The following table exhibits the quantities and value of coffee imported into the United States, with the rates of duty and the revenue accruing therefrom, for the nine fiscal years from June 30, 1856, to June 30, 1864, inclusive:

Year ending June 30.	Gross importation.	Value.	Rates of duty from places other than where produced.	Rates of duty from places where produced.	Duties accruing.
	Pounds.				
1856	235,241,362	$21,573,558	20 per c't.	Free.	$11,872 40
1857	240,676,227	22,426,758	20	Free.	7,975 80
1858	189,211,300	18,369,840	15	Free.	4,313 85
1859	264,436,534	25,086,029	15	Free.	3,404 40
1860	202,144,733	21,888,797	15	Free.	17,228 70
1861	142,624,717	15,727,791	15	Free.	947 40
1861, (act of March 2, 1861)	41,874,938	4,840,506	Free.	Free.	
Total, 1861	184,499,655	20,568,297	....	....	947 40

	Gross importations.	Imports entered for consumption and paying duty.	Rates of duty.	Duties accruing.
	Pounds.	Pounds.		
1862.—Act of March 2, 1861	28,784,312	None.	Free.	None.
Act of August 5, 1861,	58,868,644	16,574,297	4 cents.	$662,971 88
Act of Dec'r 24, 1861,		39,804,720	5 cents.	1,990,236 00
Total 1862	87,652,956	56,379,017*	....	2,653,207 88
1863	80,461,614	63,022,803*	....	3,151,140 18
1864	131,622,784	98,700,782*	....	4,935,039 10
1865	104,316,581	82,353,638*	....	4,117,681 00

* Five ports—Boston, New York, Philadelphia, Baltimore, and San Francisco. From San Francisco only to April 30, 1864.

The above tables are based on returns furnished to the commission by the Treasury Department.

For the fiscal years ending June 30, 1866 and 1867, the commission estimate the imports for consumption and the duties accruing as follows:

Year ending—	Imports for consumption, (estimated.)	Rates of duty.	Duties accruing (estimated.
June 30, 1866..........................pounds..	135,000,000	5 cents.	$6,750 000
June 30, 1867..........................pounds..	160,000,000	5 cents.	8,000 000

As a matter of interest, we also present, in this conn xion, a series of tables based on the Monthly Commercial Tables, published for the trade in the city of New York, showing the estimated annual consumption of coffee in the United States for the several calendar years from 1852 to 1865, inclusive. The discrepancies which exist between these latter and the treasury returns may be accounted for, in part, by the fact that the treasury returns from 1856 to 1861, inclusive, only indicate gross importations, and from 1862 to 1865, inclusive, are incomplete.

Estimates from New York Commercial Tables and Reports.

			Estimated consumption.	
Atlantic States:				
Year ending December 31, 1852......	91,514	tons, or	204,992,000	pounds.
1853......	78,432	"	175,688,000	"
1854......	80,126	"	179,481,000	"
1855......	93,920	"	210,378,000	"
1856......	97,423	"	218,228,000	"
1857......	77,039	"	172,566,000	"
1858......	112,167	"	251,255,000	"
1859......	99,380	"	222,610,000	"
1860......	79.068	"	177,112,000	"
1861......	83,500	"	187,046,000	"
1862......	39,728	"	88,990,000	"
1863......	35,589	"	79,720,000	"
1864......	48,700	"	109,087,000	"
1865......	57,208	"	128,146,000	"
Average, five years, 1852 to 1856, inclusive,	88,283	tons, or	197,753,000	pounds.
Average, five years, 1857 to 1861, inclusive,	90,231	"	202,118,000	"
Average, ten years, 1852 to 1861, inclusive,	89,257	"	199,936,000	"
Average, four years, 1862 to 1865, inclusive,	45,306	"	101,486,000	"

Previous to the war, the United States ranked first among coffee-consuming countries—the average consumption from 1857 to 1861, inclusive, having been upwards of two hundred millions of pounds per annum, or ninety thousand tons, an amount equal to nearly twenty-nine per cent. of the average annual export of all the coffee-producing countries from 1856 to 1864. The rapidity with which the consumption of coffee in the United States has increased during the last forty-four years is also noteworthy in this connexion, the annual consumption in 1821 having been estimated at that date at only 5,306 tons.

It would also appear from a discussion of the above tables that, while the annual average consumption of the country for the six years immediately preceding the war was about two hundred millions of pounds, the war at once reduced the importations (as compared with this average) seventy-two per cent. in 1862 and sixty eight per cent. in 1863. From this point, however, consumption has increased rapidly, rising from sixty-three millions of pounds in 1863 to ninety-nine millions in 1864, (treasury estimates,) and one hundred and twenty-eight millions (commission estimates) in 1865. It is also interesting to notice, in this connexion, some of the disturbances and fluctuations of the trade in coffee occasioned by the war. Thus we find that during the first ten months of 1861, out of 781,830 bags of Brazilian coffee imported into the five principal Atlantic ports of the United States, 626 bags only were re-exported during the same period; while, during the first ten months of 1864, out of 485,292 bags of Brazilian coffee imported, 61,910 were re-exported, mostly to Europe. Again, during the first ten months of 1865, out of 551,591 bags Brazilian coffee imported, only 8,035 were re-exported during the same period, and these were sent mainly to Mexico.

Attention should be called, in this connexion, to the circumstance that of the importations of 1863 and 1864, and the first half of 1865, a very large proportion was purchased by the government for the use of the army and navy, the average monthly consumption of these two branches of the service ranging, according to estimate,* from fifteen thousand to twenty thousand bags per month, averaging one hundred and forty pounds each, or from thirty to forty per cent of the entire imports entered for consumption during the same periods. During the first five months, however, immediately succeeding the termination of hostilities, the increased demand for coffee for consumption in the United States not only made good the cessation of the large government demand, but also entirely cleared the market of a stock which had been considered by the New York trade as sufficient to meet the wants of the country for several months to come.

With the continuance of peace, and the general progress of the country uninterrupted, coupled with a reduction in the price of gold, the commission unhesitatingly express the opinion that the consumption of coffee in the United States will rapidly approximate to the annual average of the ten years prior to the year 1860—say to about two hundred millions of pounds—and in this opinion they are happy to state that they have the concurrence of the best commercial authorities on this subject in the country.

Previous to the year 1861, coffee, when imported in American vessels from the place of its production, and coffee, the growth of the possessions of the Netherlands, imported from the Netherlands, was admitted into the ports of the United States free of duty. By the act of August 5, 1861, however, a uniform duty of four cents per pound was imposed upon all coffee, which rate, by the act of December 24, of the same year, was further advanced to five cents per pound, and has since remained unchanged.

It is instructive, in this connexion, to compare the present rate of duty, as fixed by law, upon coffee imported into the United States, with the rates imposed upon the same imported article by some of the leading countries of Europe. They are as follows:

Great Britain	(3*d*.) 6 cents.
France	8 cents.
Russia	8 cents.
Zoll-Verein	3 cents.
Austria	4½ cents.
Sweden	2 cents.
Norway	3 cents.
Spain	4 cents.

* The commission applied to the Quartermaster General for information in respect to this matter, but no notice was taken of their application.

The average rate of duty on coffee in the above specified eight countries is therefore about the same (five cents per pound) as that imposed by the present tariff of the United States.

The amount of revenue received under the five-cent rate of duty, since and inclusive of 1863, in the United States, has been as follows:

Year ending June 30, 1863	$3,151,140
Year ending June 30, 1864	4,935,039
Year ending June 30, 1865, (treasury estimate)	4,117,681

For the current fiscal year 1865–66, the commission, in view of the present amount of imports, as ascertained both from official and private sources, estimate the amount of revenue as likely to accrue from the duty on coffee, at $6,750,000; and for the next fiscal year, 1866–67, they are of opinion that the revenue from the same source, with the same rate of duty (five cents,) will not be less than $8,000,000; or nearly $4,000,000 in excess of the estimated duties from this source during the fiscal year ending June 30, 1865. Furthermore, with the return of the country to the average annual rate of consumption of coffee for the five years immediately preceding the war—a return which high prices can only check and delay, but not prevent—a duty of five cents per pound may undoubtedly be relied on to furnish a certain and constant revenue of at least ten millions of dollars per annum. Under these circumstances, therefore, the commission can but regard the existing rate as the proper revenue standard, and recommend that it be retained unchanged.

The following table shows the average monthly range of prices of Rio coffee per pound in New York for the three years, 1860, 1863, and 1864:

	1860. Gold.	1863. Currency.	1864. Currency.
January	11½ to 12½ cts.	28 to 30½ cts.	33½ to 34 cts.
February	11½ to 12½ cts.	31 to 33 cts.	33½ to 34 cts.
March	12½ to 13¼ cts.	34½ to 35½ cts.	36 to 37 cts.
April	13½ to 14 cts.	31½ to 33½ cts.	39 to 40 cts.
May	13½ to 14¼ cts.	31½ to 33½ cts.	45½ to 47 cts.
June	13 to 14 cts.	30 to 32 cts.	43 to 44 cts.
July	13½ to 14½ cts.	30 to 31 cts.	44 to 46 cts.
August	15 to 15½ cts.	26½ to 28 cts.	47½ to 52 cts.
September	13¾ to 15¼ cts.	27½ to 28 cts.	48½ to 50 cts.
October	14 to 15¼ cts.	31 to 32½ cts.	36½ to 37¼ cts.
November	14 to 15¼ cts.	32 to 33½ cts.	41½ to 43 cts.
December	13¼ to 14½ cts.	32½ to 34 cts.	43 to 44½ cts.
Average	13$\frac{16}{100}$ to 14$\frac{21}{100}$ cts.	30$\frac{50}{100}$ to 34$\frac{08}{100}$ cts.	40$\frac{96}{100}$ to 42$\frac{42}{100}$ cts.

The following table shows the average prices of coffee in New York at the close of the calendar years 1862, 1863, 1864, and 1865:

	Java, per pound.	Rio, per pound.
1862	33 to 34 cents currency.	27 to 30½ cents currency.
1863	40 to 41 cents currency.	33 to 34¾ cents currency.
1864	to 50 cents currency.	41½ to 45¼ cents currency.
1865	28 to 29 cents gold.	17½ to 20 cents gold.

The bulk of the coffee consumed in the United States prior to the war appears to have been in the western and southwestern States. The annual requirements of the southern States for consumption were formerly estimated at from *thirty* to *thirty-five* thousand tons; while the imports of coffee into the port of New Orleans prior to 1860 were from three hundred thousand to four hundred and twenty thousand bags per annum. In 1860, the requirements of the various ports of the United States were as follows:

	Pounds.
New York	63,523,547
New Orleans	47,380,326
Baltimore	28,257,480
Philadelphia	15,431,985
Boston	9,409,849
Other ports	13,108,736
Total	177,111,923

It should also be remarked, that the consumption of tho western and south-western States is confined almost exclusively to Brazilian coffee. In New England the consumption of coffee appears to be diminishing, and the consumption of tea increasing. It is also the opinion of the dealers that a larger proportion of adulterated coffees is used in New England than in any other section of the country. In the western States and middle States substitutes for, rather than adulterations of, coffee are used.

But notwithstanding the enormous consumption of coffee in the United States, an examination of the whole subject has led the commission to the conclusion, that even before the war its use was restricted to less than *one-half* of the population. Thus, assuming the average annual consumption of the country to be two hundred millions of pounds, and the average consumption of each person using coffee to be one-fourth of a pound a week, (a low estimate,) or thirteen (13) pounds per annum, we have, as the number of consumers of coffee, *fifteen and one-half millions,* or somewhat less than *one-half* of the entire population. Estimates, furthermore, made by authorities in New York, restrict the consumption of imported coffee to a much less proportion than the one above indicated.

A part of the large decrease in the importation of coffee during the last five years is undoubtedly due to the very general introduction and use of adulterated coffee or substitutes for coffee. The business of preparing such adulterations or substitutes, which for many years has been somewhat extensive, received a great encouragement from the extraordinary advance in the prices of coffee in the years 1863 and 1864. The principal substances made use of are the root of the chiccory, peas, and rye, burnt and ground. Of these, the two former are undoubtedly wholly innoxious, and by many the addition of chiccory to coffee is considered as effecting a marked improvement in the resulting beverage. Rye-coffee, on the other hand, is reported in some instances to have produced decidedly deleterious effects; but the truth of such reports may be doubted. It has also come to the knowledge of the commission that a favorite material for adulterating both coffee and pepper in New York and Philadelphia has been stale black bread, the surplus stock of emigrants arriving from Europe, and also condemned ship bread. This refuse material, collected on the arrival of vessels in port, or purchased with eager competition at the auction sales of condemned naval stores, and burned and crushed, is said to yield a product so closely resembling ground coffee, in color and weight, as to be exceedingly difficult of detection. Molasses boiled down, and reduced by heat to the state of *caramel,* is also largely used as a material for coloring and adulterating coffee and coffee substitutes; the headquarters of this department of the business being apparently in Philadelphia.

With the close of the war, and the decline in the price of coffee, the demand for adulterated or cheap coffee substitutes is reported to the commission to have largely decreased; but that the consumption of these spurious articles will always be considerable, and will, to a certain extent, diminish the revenue derived from imported coffee, cannot be doubted.

The bulk of the chiccory used in the United States at present is of foreign growth, and is subjected to a duty of four cents upon the root and five cents upon the ground.

The following table shows the quantity, rates of duty, and duties received on the chiccory imported into the ports of the United States for the fiscal years ending June 20, 1862, 1863, 1864, and 1865, as returned to the commission by the Treasury Department:

Year ending—	Imports entered for consumption.	Rates of duties.	Duties received.
June 30, 1862, root, pounds	3, 878, 341	1 cent	$38, 783 41
June 30, 1862, ground, pounds	3, 190, 845	2 cents	63, 816 90
Total, 1862, pounds	7, 069, 186		102, 600 31
June 30, 1863, root, pounds	1, 785, 017	2 cents	$37, 500 34
June 30, 1863, ground, pounds	3, 430, 088	3 cents	102, 902 64
Total, 1863, pounds	5, 215, 105		140, 402 98
June 30, 1864, root, pounds	1, 380, 955	2 cents	$27è619 10
June 30, 1864, ground, pounds	4, 444, 391	3 cents	133, 331 73
Total, 1864, pounds	5, 825, 346		160, 950 83
June 30, 1865, root,* pounds	11, 904	4 cents	$356 80
June 30, 1865, ground, pounds	1, 675, 113	5 cents	83, 755 65
Total, 1865, pounds	1, 687, 017		84, 112 45

The price of chiccory root (foreign growth) before the war was two and three-eighths cents per pound. The present price, duty paid, (December, 1865,) is nine cents (currency.)

The increase of the rate of duty on foreign-grown chiccory since 1861, from *one* and *two* cents to *four* and *five* cents per pound, has naturally had its effect to stimulate and encourage the growth of this article in the United States, especially in some of the western States, and the quantity annually produced is reported as already very considerable. As the only use which can be made of chiccory is the adulteration of coffee, and as every pound so used diminishes to the same extent the consumption of coffee, and, consequently, the revenue (American chiccory being at present untaxed,) it would seem necessary, in order to make the duty on coffee wholly effectual, that some excise should be imposed, not only upon the production and use of this home-grown material for adulterating coffee, but also upon the preparation and sale of *all* spurious and adulterated coffee.

In Great Britain the preparation and sale of coffee, adulterated other than with chiccory, is forbidden by statute, and the enforcement of the law is made

*Re-exported 2,984 pounds.

a part of the duty of the officers of the inland revenue. In the United States a measure of so restrictive a character would not probably be deemed advisable; but, in legislating on the subject, it should be borne in mind that if there is any class of individuals whose interests the government can afford to disregard, it is certainly those whose profits in business are based upon the sale to the public of spurious and adulterated articles in the place of those which are pure and genuine.

The commission, therefore, recommend, as an experimental measure, that a license fee of fifty dollars ($50) be required of each and every person cultivating chiccory for sale; and that a license fee of one hundred dollars ($100) be also levied and collected from all persons, firms, or corporations engaged in the preparation or manufacture of adulterated coffee, or in the preparation or manufacture of substances other than coffee, to be sold under the name of or as substitutes for coffee.

They would also recommend that the existing excise of one cent per pound on ground coffee be repealed, and that an excise of two cents per pound be imposed upon all ground coffee manufactured for sale, and upon all substances other than coffee, manufactured for sale under the name of or as substitutes for coffee; and that such excise be collected by means of stamps affixed to the packages in which such preparations are sold. Were excise duties on adulterated coffee, or substitutes for coffee, advanced to a still higher figure, the sale of such spurious articles would not probably be appreciably restricted, owing to the much greater value and cost of the coffee which they imitate or represent, and to the price of which such adulterations are made to approximate. The imposition of some excise would, however, to some extent, diminish the premium or fraud afforded by the greatly increased cost of coffee.

The following table shows the revenue which has been derived from the excise on ground coffee and coffee substitutes for the fiscal years ending June 30, 1863, 1864, and 1865:

	Rev. received. (Currency.)
Fiscal year ending June 30, 1863, (rate of excise 3 mills)	$58, 846 01
" " 30, 1864, " "	80, 198 81
From June 30, 1864, to March 31, 1865, (rate of excise 3 mills).. From March 31, 1865, to June 30, 1865, " 1 cent)..	284, 069 96

The experience of Great Britain, in respect to the use of chiccory for the adulteration of coffee, has been as follows:

In the original act imposing a duty on foreign-grown chiccory, no reference whatever was made to the home-grown product, it being regarded as too inconsiderable in amount to merit attention. The duty on foreign chiccory, however, so rapidly promoted the cultivation of the plant in Great Britain, and to such an extent affected the revenue derived from imported coffee, that, in 1861, an excise, by act of Parliament, was imposed of 8*s.* 6*d.* per cwt. on all British chiccory. This rate was further increased, in 1862, to 11*s.*; in 1863, to £1 1*s.* 9*d.*; and in 1864, to £1 4*s.* 3*d.*, or equal to about five (5) cents per pound (our present duty); thereby making nearly a complete equalization as respects the duties on coffee and foreign and home-grown chiccory. This large and rapid increase in the rates imposed on chiccory appears to have little or no effect in restricting its production or consumption.

The quantity of domestic chiccory assessed for duty in Great Britain, in 1864, was 1,233,972 pounds, yielding a revenue of about $52,000; while the quantity of foreign chiccory imported was returned for 1864 at 11,151,168 pounds, yielding customs revenue of £129,104 ($645,520,) as compared with a revenue of £64,220 ($321,100) in 1863.

One effect, however, of the additional duties imposed on domestic chiccory in Great Britain, as reported by the commissioners of inland revenue, has been to cause the adulteration of chiccory itself with cheaper materials—as roasted peas, mustard seed, husks, &c.—and for this fraud the arrest and punishment of persons is noticed in the report of the commissioners for 1864.

The experience of Great Britain in respect to the duties on the importation of coffee is also pertinent to this subject. In 1807 the duty on coffee imported into Great Britain was one shilling and eight pence per pound; and the quantity entered for home consumption amounted to 1,170,000 pounds, yielding a revenue of $806,000 (£161,245.) In 1808 the duty was reduced from one shilling and eight pence to seven pence; and in 1809 the annual importation for home consumption had increased to upwards of nine millions of pounds, yielding, notwithstanding the reduction of duty, a revenue of $1,229,000 (£245,800.) Ten years later, in 1819, the duty having been raised from seven pence to one shilling a pound, the quantity entered for home consumption, in 1820, fell to six million eight hundred and sixty-nine thousand (6,869,000) pounds, yielding a revenue of $1,701,000 (£340,223.) In 1824, the duty on West Indian coffee being again reduced, the quantity entered for consumption largely increased; and in 1830, the annual import was returned at twenty-one million eight hundred and forty thousand (21,840,000) pounds, producing a net revenue of $2,790,000 (£558,000.) In 1839, the duty on British coffee was still further reduced to four and one-fifth pence (or eight and two-fifth cents) per pound; and in 1847, the consumption was returned at 37,441,000 pounds per annum. At this time the introduction and use of chiccory as a substitute for coffee began to seriously affect the annual importations; so much so that, in 1850, the annual amount returned for consumption was only 31,166,000 pounds. In 1851, the duties on coffee were still further reduced in Great Britain to threepence (six cents) a pound, which rate is still in force. The consumption of coffee, however, in Great Britain, owing probably to the increased use of chiccory, does not increase even with an increase of population; the total importations entered for home consumption in 1864 being only 31,591,122 pounds, as compared with 36,983,000 pounds in 1853; while the duty collected from imposts on coffee was £17,433 less in 1864 than in the preceding year 1863. The importation of cocoa into Great Britain also exhibits a similar reduction.

It is also interesting to note, in this connexion, the great disparity in the amount of coffee consumed per annum in Great Britain and the United States, the population of the two countries being nearly the same. Thus the present demand for consumption in the former country is about sixteen thousand tons; and in the latter sixty thousand tons, or an average of ninety thousand tons for the ten years preceding 1861, equal to about 200,000,000 pounds.

In order to further aid in estimating the future relation of the article of coffee to the commerce and revenue of the United States, the following data are submitted.

The total amount of coffee annually supplied to the world by various coffee-producing countries, from 1856 to 1864 inclusive, is estimated as follows:

	Tons.
Calendar year 1856	301, 680
" 1857	316, 940
" 1858	314, 880
" 1859	326, 300
" 1860	351, 570
" 1861	339, 100
" 1862	283, 810
" 1863	310, 070
" 1864	272, 390

Annual average product 313,000 tons, or 701,120,000 pounds (2,240 pounds to the ton, the custom-house standard.)

The average annual production of the various coffee-producing countries, during the period above mentioned, was as follows:

	Tons.
Brazil	151,730
Java and Sumatra	61,370
Ceylon	29,860
St. Domingo	23,210
Venezuela:	
Maracaibo, Laguayra, Porto Cabello	15,870
Cuba	5,670
Porto Rico	5,780
Jamaica	2,010
Dutch and French West India islands	1,000
New Grenada and Guatemala	900
Costa Rica	4,900
Africa and Arabia	2,360
Bombay, Madras, and the Malabar coast	5,000
Singapore and Macassar	1,970
Manilla	1,370

giving, as above stated, an average yield of the principal producing countries of 313,000 tons for the years 1856–'64 inclusive.

The amount of coffee available for export from all coffee-producing countries for the crop-year ending June 30, 1866, is estimated by Mr. H. E. Moring, of New York, the best recognized authority on this subject in the United States, at 294,000 tons, distributed as follows:

Producing countries.		Tons.	Per cent.	Average last 3 yrs.
Brazil	1,900,000 bags at 160 lbs.	135,700	46	124,360
Java and Sumatra	800,000 piculs at 130 lbs.	46,500	16	56,127
Ceylon	750,000 cwts. at 112 lbs.	37,500	13	33,687
St. Domingo	400,000 bags at 130 lbs.	23,300	8	23,210
Venezuela, New Grenada, and Costa Rica	450,000 bags at 110 lbs.	22,000	7½	22,943
Cuba, Porto Rico, Jamaica, and West India islands		16,000	5	15,553
Manilla, Singapore, Malabar coast, Bombay, Madras, Africa, and Arabia		13,000	4½	12,880
Total		294,000	100	288,760

The demand for consumption of coffee in all non-producing countries for the year ending June 30, 1866, is also estimated by the same authority at three hundred thousand tons, distributed as follows:

	Tons.	Per cent.
German Zoll Verein	66,000	22
United States* (including the Pacific coast)	60,000	20

* The estimated sources of supply to the United States for the fiscal year ending June 30, 1866, are as follows:

From Brazil 716,800 bags, *a* 160 lbs., or	51,200 tons.
From Java, Venezuela, St. Domingo, &c., 160,000 bags, *a* 125 lbs	8,900 "
Total	60,100 "

Holland and Belgium	43,000	14⅓
France	32,000	10⅔
Austria	24,000	8
Switzerland, Italy, Turkey and Southern Europe	22,000	7⅓
Prussia, Sweden, and Denmark	22,000	7⅓
Great Britain	16,000	5⅓
Australia, Cape of Good Hope, South America, Canada, &c.	15,000	5
Totals	300,000	100

Assuming the above estimates to be correct, it follows that the total demand for coffee for the present year is likely to exceed the total supply by about six thousand tons. "Few articles," says McCulloch, "exhibit such variations, not only of consumption, but also of growth and price, as coffee. These are occasioned partially by changes of commercial regulations and duties, and partially also by the circumstance that the coffee-plant requires four or five years before it comes into bearing; so that the supply is neither suddenly increased when the demand increases, nor diminished when the demand falls off."

The cultivation of the coffee-plant is necessarily confined to a narrow tropical belt, beyond which its culture cannot be profitably pursued. Its production in the climates suitable for its growth seems to have been already stimulated to nearly if not its utmost extent. In Java and the East Indies generally the quantity gathered increases very slowly, if at all; indeed, in some parts of the east, we understand that the cultivation of the plant has in many instances been abandoned for that of the sugar-cane; the latter being considered as much the surest and most profitable crop. At present the only countries which are increasing their annual exports of coffee to any considerable extent are Venezuela and the island of Ceylon; the exports from the latter showing an annual increase of about three thousand tons. In Brazil, the largest by far of all the coffee-producing countries, the amount exported has largely decreased since 1861, and the present prospect of an increase of the crop is not flattering. We submit, in this connexion, the following extract of a recent letter on this subject, submitted to the commission, from one of the leading factors in Rio de Janeiro:

"The manner in which the economy of the coffee plantations of Brazil is conducted is as follows: the virgin forest, of which a good deal still belongs to each plantation, is burned down, and the young plantations made upon the rich soil thus gained begin to give a fair yield in the fourth year, and last about twenty years. At the expiration of that period the coffee-trees are too old to yield a crop, and are abandoned. Thus the heaviest work of a Brazilian coffee plantation consists in clearing the forest and in making new plantations to take the place of the old ones which have become exhausted.

"In 1848, there were plenty of laborers in Brazil for all purposes, and the coffee plantations were in the most prosperous and productive condition. Since then the importation of negroes (slaves) into Brazil has entirely ceased, and the cost of slaves is three or four times as great as it formerly was. The consequence is that the price of labor has also greatly increased, while the mortality of the slaves—who were mostly newly imported and not accustomed to the climate and hard labor—is always excessive.

"As, furthermore, it had always been found more advantageous to import male rather than female slaves, the deaths among the black population since 1848 have uniformly been largely in excess of the births. The laboring classes of Brazil, which are mainly slaves, are, therefore, rapidly diminishing in number; and the lack of a supply of labor began to be sensibly felt by the planters as far back as 1854 and 1855.

"The labor at present available is probably sufficient to keep the existing plantations in order, and to gather the crops, but it is beyond a doubt insufficient to perform the work necessary to the formation of the new plantations which are requisite to maintain the present average annual production of coffee. In 1848, a very large number of new plantations were formed, which since then have gradually yielded an abundant crop, while the old ones, also, only gradually ceased to be productive, so that the crop really continued to augment until about 1860. Since that period, the amount of coffee produced has gradually diminished. This decrease was at first attributed to temporary causes, but is now acknowledged to be due to a lack of a supply of labor. We are, therefore, convinced that the Brazilian crop will not reach for many years so high a figure as formerly, and that two millions of bags, equal to 143,000 tons, would be the outside which could be produced in this province (Rio de Janeiro) in a very abundant crop. The crop of the present year, 1865, will probably not reach this figure, and we are of the opinion that not more than sixteen or seventeen hundred thousand bags will be exported from this port during the next crop-year, 1st July, 1865, to 30th June, 1866."

From the above statements and the accompanying letter, it seems evident that, irrespective of any contingencies pertaining to the present year, the coffee trade has reached a point where the demand for consumption is largely (and for a considerable time is likely to be) in excess of the supply; and if it be also considered, in this connexion, that the consumption of coffee in Europe has been increasing for the last fifteen years at an average annual rate of over three per cent., and that the average annual rate of increase of consumption in the United States for the ten years prior to 1859 was about two per cent., the conclusion is irresistible that the price of coffee will continue to advance until it has reached a point sufficient to check consumption, and thus equalize the supply and demand for this commodity. By some authorities the opinion is entertained that this check to consumption will not be given until the price of coffee assimilates closely to that of tea. How far such an anticipated increase in the price of coffee may affect its consumption in the United States, and consequently the revenue to be derived from its importation, time and experience alone can determine.

Respectfully submitted for the commission.

DAVID A. WELLS, *Chairman.*

Hon. HUGH McCULLOCH,
Secretary of the Treasury.

A BILL for an act relative to the excise on ground coffee, spices, &c.

Be it enacted by the Senate and House of Representatives of the United States of America in Congress assembled, That any person, firm, company, or corporation, who shall hereafter cultivate or produce, or in any manner be engaged in the cultivation or production of, chiccory as a commodity for sale, or for use in the manufacture of any article or compound intended to be sold as coffee, or as a substitute for coffee, shall first obtain a yearly license for that purpose in the manner provided by law in other cases, except that no bond shall be required, and shall pay therefor the sum of fifty dollars; and any person who shall in any manner engage in the production of chiccory for the purposes aforesaid without the license herein required having been obtained, or who shall sell, or offer for sale, or manufacture for sale, or dispose of to other persons, any chiccory so produced without license as aforesaid, shall forfeit the same, and shall also forfeit and pay a fine not exceeding five hundred dollars, to be recovered with costs of suit.

SECTION 2. *And be it further enacted,* That every person, firm, company, or corporation, who shall hereafter be engaged in the manufacture or preparation of adulterated coffee, tea, or spices, or of any material for use in the adulteration of the same, or of any article, material, or compound intended for use as a substitute for coffee, tea, or spices, shall obtain from the proper officer a yearly license for that purpose in the manner prescribed by law, and shall pay therefor the sum of one hundred dollars, and shall give a bond in such amount as the collector of the district may deem proper, conditioned that he or they will not sell or dispose of any article so manufactured by him or them without having affixed thereto the proper stamp as hereinafter required, and will also comply with all provisions of law relating thereto; and it shall not be lawful to engage in or carry on such business without such license having first been procured; and every person who shall engage in or carry on such business without having obtained a license as herein required shall forfeit all implements used therein, and all articles so manufactured and materials for manufacture, and shall forfeit and pay in addition thereto a fine of five hundred dollars, to be recovered with costs of suit.

SECTION 3. *And be it further enacted,* That on all ground coffee prepared or manufactured for sale there shall be paid, as hereinafter mentioned, when sold, an excise tax of two cents per pound; and on all compounds and mixtures of coffee ground and adulterated, or mixed with other materials, and sold, and on all articles or substances other than coffee, prepared or manufactured and sold as coffee, or intended to be used as a substitute therefor, there shall be paid a duty of two cents per pound; and on all adulterated teas prepared and sold there shall be paid an excise tax of twenty-five cents per pound; and on all preparations and manufactures of spices—to wit, pepper, mustard, pimento, cloves, clove-stems, cassia, and ginger—ground and sold, and on all articles and substances prepared and sold as spices, or as a substitute therefor, there shall be paid an excise tax of two cents per pound: *Provided,* That no exemption from payment of duty or tax shall apply to the manufacture of any of the articles mentioned or referred to in this section, but the tax thereon, as herein required, shall be paid without reference to the amount of product of such manufacture: *Provided further,* That all ground coffee, whether pure or adulterated, and all articles, compounds, and preparations, manufactured and sold as coffee, or as a substitute for coffee, and all adulterated teas, and all ground spices, whether pure or adulterated, and all substitutes therefor, manufactured for sale, as aforesaid, shall be sold only in packages; and every package thereof shall have affixed thereto when sold, or offered for sale by the manufacturer, an excise stamp corresponding in value to the rate of duty required, as before mentioned, and also the name of the manufacturer and place of manufacture, and the quantity contained in such package; and such stamps shall be purchased of the collector of the district, and shall be furnished by the Commissioner of Internal Revenue. In determining the value of the stamps required, each package containing less than one pound shall be accounted as one pound, and any fractional part of a pound in any package containing more than one pound in excess of one-sixteenth of a pound, shall be accounted as equivalent to another pound.

SECTION 4. *And be it further enacted,* That any manufacturer of any of the articles herein mentioned as subject to an excise duty, to be paid by affixing stamps as aforesaid, who shall sell, or offer for sale, or in any way dispose of, and suffer to go out of his possession, any of said articles without having the proper stamps affixed thereto, or without his name stamped on the package, shall forfeit the same, together with all the implements of manufacture, and all the stock and material found in his possession, and shall for each offence pay a fine of five hundred dollars, to be recovered with costs of suit.

And any dealer, other than the manufacturer thereof, who shall sell, or offer for sale, or have in his possession, any of the articles before mentioned, without the proper excise stamps affixed thereto as herein required, shall forfeit the same, and shall pay for each offence a fine of one hundred dollars, to be recovered with costs of suit.

SECTION 5. *And be it further enacted,* That all acts and parts of acts inconsistent with the provisions of this act are hereby repealed.

SPECIAL REPORT No. 3.

Report of the United States revenue commission on cotton as a source of national revenue.

TREASURY DEPARTMENT,
Office of the United States Revenue Commission, January, 1866.

SIR: The consideration of cotton as a source of national revenue, merely, involves a discussion on the part of the commission of the following points:

1st. Can a tax be imposed upon the cotton product of the United States, thereby enhancing its cost to the consumer, without detriment to the national interests, present and prospective; and if so, what rates of taxation are expedient?

2d. Admitting the expediency of imposing a tax on American cotton, in what manner can such tax be best levied and collected?

3d. Assuming the imposition of the tax, shall a drawback on the export of American manufactured cotton be allowed; and if so, to what extent, and under what conditions?

1st. Can a tax be imposed upon the cotton product of the United States, thereby enhancing its cost to the consumer, without detriment to the national interests, present and prospective; and if so, what rates of taxation are expedient?

A discussion of the foregoing proposition would seem to require, on the part of the commission, a statement and review of the cotton production of the United States, and its relation to the manufacturing industry of this country and Europe *prior* to the commencement of the rebellion, in 1861; a review of the cotton product of the world, and the state of the cotton manufacturing industry *since* that period; and, finally, an estimate from the above and other data respecting the future. This we propose to give in the order as above stated.

Notwithstanding the increase in the successive crops of cotton from 1845 to 1859 and 1860, there was, with some fluctuations, a gradual increase in the price until, and including, the sales of the year 1861; and although the crop of 1860 probably amounted to a surplus for the time being, the short crop of 1861 would have again, in the ordinary course of trade, restored the price to the average level of the preceding five or six years.

1st. *The following table exhibits the comparative crop of cotton produced in the United States for various years, from* 1825 *to* 1861:*

Years.	Bales.	Years.	Bales.
1825–'26	720, 027	1851–'52	3, 015, 029
1826–'27	957, 281	1852–'53	3, 262, 882
1830–'31	1, 038, 848	1853–'54	2, 930, 027
1835–'36	1, 360, 725	1854–'55	2, 847, 339
1839–'40	2, 177, 835	1855–'56	3, 527, 845
1840–'41	1, 634, 945	1856–'57	2, 939, 519
1842–'43	2, 378, 875	1857–'58	3, 113, 962
1844–'45	2, 394, 503	1858–'59	3, 851, 481
1846–'47	1, 778, 651	1859–'60	4, 675, 770
1850–'51	2, 355, 257	1860–'61	3, 656, 086†

* These crops are given at the actual number of bales, and their commercial weight; not at the estimated census weight of exactly four hundred pounds each.

† Average yearly production in the five years from 1825–'26 to 1829–'30, 850,432 bales; in the ten years from 1830–'31 to 1839–'40, 1,368,000 bales; in the ten years from 1840–'41 to 1849–'50, 2,117,443 bales; in the ten years from 1850–'51, 3,251,312 bales; and in the year 1860–'61 the crop was 3,656,086 bales.

The total production for thirty-six years amounted to 71,619,716, and the average yearly crop during that period 1,989,436 bales.

The demand for cotton for manufacturing purposes in the United States in 1860 was estimated at about 400,000,000 of pounds.

The demand for the manufacturing industry of England for the same year was 2,523,200 bales, of an average weight of about four hundred and thirty pounds each, or 1,083,600,000 pounds. For the continent of Europe the same year the demand for consumption was 713,813,000 pounds, making the total consumption of the United States and Europe, for the year 1860, 2,197,400,000 pounds, or about 5,110,000 American bales, of four hundred and thirty pounds each. The product of American cotton for that same year was 4,675,770 bales.

The proportion of American cotton consumed by the manufacturing industry of the world during 1860 was as follows: In England *eighty-seven and a half per cent.;* upon the continent of Europe about *seventy-five per cent.;* and in the United States *one hundred per cent.* In the same year American cotton comprised a little less than *seven-eighths* of the consumption of Europe and the United States. Of the remaining *eighth,* about *three-fifths* were supplied from the East Indies, and the balance from South America (Brazil) and Egypt.

The following table exhibits the amount of cotton consumed in the United States from 1847 *to* 1861, *inclusive:*

Years.	Consumed in the United States.	Foreign export and stock on hand.	Total crop.
	Bales.	*Bales.*	*Bales.*
1847–'48	616, 044	1, 731, 590	2, 347, 634
1848–'49	642, 485	2, 086, 111	2, 728, 596
1849–'50	613, 498	1, 483, 208	2, 096, 706
1850–'51	485, 614	1, 869, 643	2, 355, 257
1851–'52	699, 603	2, 315, 426	3, 015, 029
1852–'53	803, 725	2, 459, 157	3, 262, 882
1853–'54	737, 236	2, 192, 791	2, 930, 027
1854–'55	706, 412	2, 140, 927	2, 847, 339
1855–'56	770, 739	2, 757, 106	3, 527, 845
1856–'57	819, 936	2, 119, 583	2, 939, 519
1857–'58	595, 562	2, 518, 400	3, 113, 962
1858–'59	927, 651	2, 923, 830	3, 851, 481
1859–'60	972, 043	3, 697, 727	4, 669, 770
1860–'61	843, 740	2, 812, 346	3, 656, 086

The following table exhibits the average price in England of United States upland, Brazil and Pernambuco, and East India Surat cotton, from 1800 *to* 1865:

Years.	United States Uplands.	Brazil and Pernambuco.	East India Surat.	Years.	United States Uplands.	Brazil and Pernambuco.	East India Surat.
	per lb.	per lb.	per lb.		per lb.	per lb.	per lb.
1800	26*d.*	32½*d.*	14*d.*	1848	4¼*d.*	6*d.*	3¼*d.*
1810	18½	26	15½	1849	5⅛	5½	3⅞
1811	14	20½	11½	1850	7¼	7⅞	5⅛
1812	18	23	14	1851	5¾	7½	4
1813	25½	29	17½	1855	5¾	7	3⅞
1814	30	31½	21½	1856	6	7⅛	4⅜
1815	21½	31	17½	1857	7¼	8¾	5⅜
1820	11½	15½	8½	1858	6¼	8¼	4¾
1824	8½	11⅜	6⅝	1859	6¼	8⅜	4¾
1825	11⅝	15⅛	6⅞	1860	5½	8¼	4⅛
1826	6¾	10½	5½	1861	7¾	9½	5⅞
1830	6⅛	8¼	5	1862	18	17⅞	12
1835	10¼	14⅛	7½	1863	24	24¼	19
1840	6⅜	9¼	4⅝	1864	27	28	19¼
1845	4⅜	6⅜	3	1865	19½	19½	15
1847	6⅜	7⅜	4½				

The following are the prices of "middling" cotton in New York, in cents: At the close of 1861, 37 to 38½; 1862, 67 to 67½; 1863, 81 to 82; 1864, 117 to 120; 1865, 51 to 53.

The average crop of American cotton for twenty years, to 1860 inclusive, was as follows: From 1841 to 1850, 2,117,443 bales per annum; from 1851 to 1860, 3,251,312 bales per annum. This large increase, however, was not sufficient to meet the demand, as will be proved by the following comparison of prices in Liverpool. Thus, the average price in Liverpool, from 1841 to 1845, inclusive, was $5\frac{10}{100}$ pence; from 1846 to 1855, $5\frac{54}{100}$ pence; from 1856 to 1860, $6\frac{25}{100}$ pence; or, in other words, the excess of the price of cotton in Liverpool, in 1860, over that of 1845, was $9 67½ per bale, equal to over $45,000,000 per annum. This same result also appears from the following tabular statement:

The average price of American cotton in Liverpool, in 1843, '44, and '45, was $9\frac{25}{100}$ cents. The amount of cotton imported from the United States into England from 1846 to 1860, inclusive, was as follows:

Years.	Pounds.	Price.	Excess of price.	Excess of cost.
1846 to 1849....	2,001,301,222	10 31 cts.	1 06	$21,213,792
1850 to 1855....	3,889,546,040	11 62 "	2 37	92,182,241
1856 to 1860....	4,336,100,534	12 60 "	3 35	145,259,367
Total........	10,226,947,796	....	....	258,655,400

In 1850, according to parliamentary returns, there were in Great Britain 20,858,062 spindles employed upon cotton. In 1860, early in the year there were 32,460,026 spindles, (increased to over 33,000,000 before the end of the year,) showing an increase, in ten years, of 11,601,964 spindles, or an average rate of increase of 20,718 spindles per week.

In 1850 the average weekly consumption of cotton in Great Britain was as follows:

	Bales.
American..	20,767
Brazilian..	3,310
Egyptian..	1,542
East Indian..	3,385
All others..	121
Total..	29,125

In 1860 the average weekly consumption of cotton in Great Britain was as follows:

	Bales.
American..	41,094
Brazilian..	2,164
Egyptian..	1,804
East Indian..	3,340
All others..	121
Total..	48,523

On the other hand, in the absence of a supply of American cotton in 1864, Great Britain has been able to obtain from other countries, for her own use, a quantity but little more than the annual increase in her consumption of American cotton between 1857 and 1860, when there was a full supply of American cotton.

	Pounds.
In 1860 Great Britian consumed of other sorts than American..	126, 706, 000
In 1864, under the stimulus of four prices, she only consumed of other sorts than American............................	491, 147, 470
Difference..	364, 441, 470

From 1857 to 1860, her annual increase in the consumption of American cotton was as follows:

	Pounds.
In 1858 over 1857, about..................................	97, 000, 000
In 1859 over 1858, "	115, 000, 000
In 1860 over 1859, "	100, 000, 000
In 1860 over 1857, "	312, 000, 000

It is thus clear that the entire increase in the consumption of cotton by the new spindles added in England in the ten years from 1850 to 1860, was of American production.

The consumption of the United States increased, from 1850 to 1860, about sixty per cent.

There was an accumulation of cotton fabrics—due to the excessive supply of cotton—in 1860, in the markets of the world, the effect of which would have appeared in 1861 and 1862, rather than in 1860; which might have entailed large losses upon manufacturers but for the war. Since this period the stock of goods in the hands of manufacturers and traders throughout the world has been entirely exhausted.

There are no data available to the commission for estimating the supply of American cotton for 1861 and 1862. The mills north of the Potomac were mainly operated, during those two years, upon cotton laid in from the crop of 1860 and 1861. Manufacturers were induced to take this course by the knowledge—obtained early in September, 1860—that the crop known as the crop of 1861 would be a short one; and many manufacturers purchased enough to last their mills, at full speed, for one year. When the war broke out, by decreasing their consumption, and making lighter fabrics, this heavy supply was made to last for nearly two years. In 1863, the supply of cotton for the mills of the United States north of the Potomac was about 4,000 bales per week—3,500 American, and 500 Surats; and in 1864, probably about the same, being only 25 per cent. of the full capacity of the mills. It was then demonstrated that a supply of 4,000 bales per week was the absolute and imperative need of the loyal States; and when that amount of cotton could not otherwise be obtained, it was imported from Liverpool, and taken from the supply furnished to England by blockade-runners, and East India and other imports.

The consumption of cotton in Europe in 1860, was 1,797,400,000 pounds, at an average price of a little over eleven cents a pound, amounting to $205,167,744; and of this supply, as has been stated, nearly 87½ per cent. was American. The consumption of cotton in Europe in 1864 was 928,896,810 pounds, at an average price of about 44 cents per pound, equal to $412,304,688; and of this less than 8 per cent. was American. These statistics show that the supply of 1864 was about one-half in weight that of 1860, and at about twice the cost.

The sources from which the deficiency of American cotton was supplied can be best shown by a comparison of the consumption of England for 1860 and 1864:

	1860.	1864.
	Pounds.	*Pounds.*
American	956, 894, 000	70, 049, 340
Brazilian	20, 380, 500	28, 044, 000
Egyptian	38, 885, 500	115, 705, 000
West Indian, &c	1, 260, 000	9, 276, 000
East Indian	66, 180, 000	269, 018, 820
China and Japan	....	49, 284, 000
Turkey and Asia Minor	....	19, 819, 650
	1, 083, 600, 000	561, 196, 810

It would thus appear to be demonstrated by the above statistics—and the demonstration is confirmed by all the collateral evidence that can be obtained—that while cotton may be grown in various parts of the world, the United States enjoy a practical monopoly of the best cotton lands, coupled with a sufficient supply of labor to make a full crop, and while, to produce the large crop of 1860, the United States had under cultivation less than *two per cent.* of the area of the cotton States, yet, under the stimulus of *four prices*, the other parts of the world have, during the war, been unable to fill the gap caused by the cessation of the cultivation of that small part of our territory.

The American crop of 1860 was sufficient for the 50,000,000 spindles existing in Europe and America. All other cotton made that year could have been dispensed with. These spindles, with their looms, bleacheries, and print-works, represent, at ten dollars per spindle, a fixed investment of $500,000,000. Upon these spindles the crop of 1860, which, at ten cents a pound, represented a value of about $200,000,000, was raised by the labor of a little less than a million of operatives, to a value of not less than $500,000,000.

The crop of 1860, estimated at six bales to the hand, was raised by the labor of about 800,000 laborers, each of whom represented, in that year, a cash value of $1,200; or, in the aggregate, $960,000,000; about double the capital represented by the mills and machinery employed to spin the product of their labor. With the labor of such of these former chattels, now freemen, as shall remain upon the cotton-fields, supplemented by emigration from the north and from Europe, it is evident that it is within the limits of possibility for the United States soon to regain the control of the cotton market of the world which it enjoyed prior to 1860; provided we do not, by excessive taxation, discourage the revival of this industry at the south, and render permanent the rival production which has been partially developed in other countries by the events of the last four years.

We come next to the consideration of the question, what tax can be imposed upon American cotton without detriment to the national interests, present and prospective?

In view of the statements above made, and the evidence taken, (a copy of which is herewith appended to this report, and to which special attention is requested, particularly to the answers to the questions relative to the expediency and the rate of taxation,) the commission would recommend, *that from and after July* 1, 1866, *a tax of five cents per pound be levied and collected upon all cotton raised in the United States.*

If this rate of excise is less than what it has been expected the commission would agree upon, and less than what the present circumstances might seem to some persons to warrant, it must be remembered that the cultivation of the crop for the next one or two years will be undertaken at great disadvantages. The fields, overgrown with weeds, have to be cleared; fences rebuilt; the entire equipment of cotton gins and farm implements renewed; and a revolution accomplished in the system of labor by which cotton is to be raised hereafter. Very large numbers of inexperienced men will undertake its cultivation during the coming season; many of them must fail to succeed in any event; and the cost to the cultivators must be far above the natural cost of cotton; and if, in addition to all the obstacles which are to be overcome, a tax of more than five cents per pound were levied, (which is probably not less than sixty-five per cent. of what will prove to be the natural cost of cotton in future years; or, in other words, the cost at which cotton can be raised with results to the cultivator equal to those secured on almost any other product of agriculture,) a rapid increase in the crop, such as is desired and such as is essential to the prosperity of the country, might be impeded, and a stimulus given to the product of other countries which, in the end, would be prejudicial to American interests. On the other hand, it is believed that a tax of five cents a pound may be levied, for the present, without seriously impeding cultivation in this country, and without giving any appreciable stimulus to cultivation elsewhere. On a crop of three or four million bales of cotton, which we may hope to realize within a few years, provided we leave to the cultivators, in the years 1866 and 1867, all the profit we can afford to spare them as a stimulus for their future exertions, the government would derive a revenue (at $22 per bale) of about $22,000,000 on every million of bales sold, or of $66,000 000 on a crop of three millions of bales, and $88,000,000 on a crop of four millions of bales, which would be less than the crop of 1859–60. Of this sum, if the consumption of the United States shall reach, in either of these years, the consumption of 1860, the inhabitants of the United States would pay about $21,000,000; and it is believed that there are few taxes which can be levied which would be so slight a burden to the consumer. The consumption of cotton per head in the United States at the highest point ever attained to, has not exceeded twelve pounds. A tax of five cents per pound would therefore be an average of but sixty cents to each individual per annum.

With a crop exceeding three millions of bales per annum, it will probably be found expedient, in view of a possible excess of production throughout the world over the demand for consumption, (which high prices must limit,) to reduce a five cent *per pound* excise to a lower rate. But in any event, the commission believe they have demonstrated the practicability of drawing from cotton, without detriment to any American interest, a sufficient annual revenue to allow of the removal of taxation from many other forms and products of industry less able to bear it, and the burden of which falls wholly upon our own people, and at the same time permit of a great reduction in the expense and machinery of our revenue collection.

3d. Admitting now the expediency of imposing a tax on cotton produced within the territory of the United States, the next point for consideration which presents itself is, In what manner can the tax, as above recommended, be best levied and collected? The commission are of the opinion that it would be inexpedient and difficult to attempt to collect this tax from the producers on the plantations or farms. The majority of the producers would rarely, if ever, have funds on hand at the time of gathering the crop from which to pay the tax; and, moreover, a tax upon the raw material, collected directly of the producer, is more of a burden in its effect upon production than one collected at some more remote point nearer to the consumer. Furthermore, a tax upon cotton at the point of its production would, in the opinion of the commission, necessitate a large increase of the revenue force in the States where cotton is grown—a measure to be avoided, if possible. It would also, as it seems to the commission, be impossible to protect the government against very considerable evasions of the tax if the attempt were made to collect it of the producers. Again: it is manifestly desirable that the transit or movement of cotton throughout the territory of the United States should be left as free and unimpeded as possible; and the levying of a tax at the point of production, or at the time of its first sale, and making the excise from that time forward a lien upon the cotton, would have a tendency to check this freedom of transit and impede both trade and production. The commission have, therefore, after considerable deliberation, concluded to recommend *that the tax upon the cotton consumed in the United States be levied and collected from the manufacturers, and upon the amount exported to foreign countries from the merchants at the port of export, and that no collector of customs be allowed to grant a clearance to any vessel with cotton on board, bound to a foreign port, until the owner or agent thereof has produced a certificate from the collector of internal revenue of the district in which the port is situated, that such cotton has been inspected and weighed, and that the excise tax on the same has been duly paid.* As there are but few ports in the country from which cotton would be exported, and as the entire number of establishments working cotton in 1860 was but 915,* of which one-third, probably, consume seven-eighths of the amount used in the country, the commission believe that by this method the collection of the tax upon cotton will be simplified to the greatest possible extent, the cost of its collection reduced to the minimum, and the movement of cotton left entirely free and untrammelled. They therefore, in accordance with the law providing for their organization as a commission, report herewith the form of a bill in conformity with the above recommendations.

If the levying and the collecting of an export duty on cotton are within the jurisdiction and control of Congress, the commission would not hesitate to recommend the enactment of this measure; and in any event it seems to them desirable that Congress should not be deprived of so important a privilege in relation to the regulation of our commerce. The precedents in favor of the levying and collecting of export duties, as afforded by the example of other nations, are numerous and worthy of attention. Thus from British India the following duties on exports are levied: On saltpetre, one rupee (worth 44½ cents in gold) per *bazar mound,* (which the commission understand to be about *eighty-two and one-eighth* pounds, which is equivalent to a duty of from fifteen to twenty-five per cent.) On rice, two annas per *bazar mound;* on linseed, three per cent. on the market value; on gunny cloth, (used largely for the baling of American cotton,) three per cent.; on gunny bags, three per cent.; on jute, three per cent.; *on cotton, three per cent.;* on shellac, four per cent.; on castor oil, three per cent.; and the same rate of duty on cutch, dry ginger, turmeric, twine, stick-lac, and India-rubber. Opium is a complete monopoly of the government of British India, and a heavy duty is indirectly exacted on it from all consumers. Holland has also adopted the principle of levying export duties on many of the productions of her colonies. Thus in Java the export duty on coffee shipped to the Netherlands is six per cent., but on coffee shipped to other countries the export duty is nine per cent. Sugar, the production of the Dutch colonies, pays no export duty when shipped to the Netherlands, but pays three per cent. when sent to other countries. From the production of coffee and sugar in Java, the commission understand that the Dutch government at present realizes a profit almost sufficient to pay the interest on their national debt—a debt of between four and five hundred million dollars. This large sum is not, how-

* 472 in New England; 281 in the middle States; 19 in the western States, and 143 in the southern States.

ever, wholly derived from export duties, but arises, in part, from the system of cultivation of coffee and sugar followed in Java, by which a considerable part of the profits of these crops inures to the benefit of the government. France, at the present time, levies an export duty upon rags so large as practically to prohibit their shipment from that country. China also levies an export duty upon her teas; Portugal upon her wines; while Peru pays no small part of her expenses from the export of her *guano.*

If a constitutional amendment is necessary in order to allow Congress to exercise the privilege of laying export duties whenever it may deem the same expedient, the commission, in view of the practice of foreign nations, and the profitable results flowing therefrom, have no hesitation in recommending that such an amendment be passed as soon as practicable.

3d. In regard to the third point of the discussion, namely, the allowance of drawbacks on the export of American manufactured cottons, assuming that an excise duty be levied upon the raw material, the commission would report: *that a drawback on cotton fabrics is absolutely essential, and to the full amount of the tax upon cotton, if we would maintain any export of co'ton fabrics.* Our export of cotton cloth formerly amounted to from $7,000,000 to $10,000,000 in value per annum. It consisted mainly of heavy goods, made from No. 14 yarns. These goods can now be made in England, in mills which have been built or altered since the war began, for the purpose of spinning India cotton; and in such mills heavy goods can be made, with scarcely any disadvantage in production or cost of labor, from short-staple cottons. Now, if England can make these goods from untaxed cotton, and send them to India and China, they will, of course, drive out American fabrics made from cotton on which either a tax or a duty has been paid.

It is the opinion of gentlemen most conversant with this business, who have been consulted by the commission, that the drawback allowance on exported American cotton fabrics should be as many cents per pound on the pound of cloth exported as are assessed in the form of a tax upon the raw cotton entering into the manufacture of such cloth. The loss in manufacturing will be nearly or wholly made up by the sizing of the goods; and as the practice has extensively prevailed of late in Great Britain, and might be rapidly introduced into this country, of "stuffing" cotton cloth, as it is termed, with various materials, such as starch, silicate of soda, clay, &c., to make it weigh more than the cotton entering into its composition, (a practice which has been carried to such an extent in England as to cause buyers of cotton goods in Manchester, in some cases, to claim a chemical analysis before they accept a given lot of goods,) it is evident that some special provision of the customs must be determined upon, in order to guard against fraud, previous to an allowance of the drawback. It would seem that an oath should be required of the exporter, in all cases, that the cloth upon which a full drawback is claimed does not weigh more than the cotton from which it is made; and it would also seem advisable that an examination should be made of each parcel of goods exported, with provisions for forfeiture and fine in case of attempted fraud or evasion of the law. As, however, it is necessary, in order to compete with goods of foreign production, that a practice of "stuffing," similar to that adopted abroad, should also be possible here, with regard to certain descriptions of goods, a further provision should be made, allowing goods so manufactured to be exported, with a proportional drawback. The commission have not, however, had time to fully mature a system of regulations adapted to meet these various contingencies; but in case of the adoption of their suggestions, such regulations can be promptly framed by experienced custom-house officials.

In addition to this drawback, which is provided as an offset for the tax upon raw cotton, all cotton goods *exported from this country* should be exempted from the payment of all other excise taxes; otherwise, no exports claiming the drawback can be made.

While some objections may possibly be raised against the allowance of these heavy drawbacks upon the ground that they will make the cost of cotton cloth considerably more to the consumer in this country than to the consumer abroad, it should be borne in mind, first, as we have demonstrated, that the tax upon the consumer here is a very light one; secondly, that by facilitating the export of cotton fabrics rather than of raw cotton, we enhance the aggregate value of our exports and thereby cheapen the cost of our imports.

The commission, furthermore, can conceive of no measure better calculated to resuscitate and build up the interests of the southern sections of our country and to diversify industry there, than one which would give to that portion of our population there located the opportunity, with little labor, of spinning coarse yarns sufficient to supply the markets of the world. It should be here stated that a very large portion of the cotton exported from Great Britain is in the form of yarns, and not of woven fabrics, and that the manufacture of yarns requires less than one-half the number of operatives that are required for the manufacture of woven fabrics.

The commission having recommended a large increase of the excise tax upon raw cotton, it becomes evident that there must be a corresponding change in the tariff upon imported cotton fabrics; the great demand of the United States being for goods within the limit, in point of number of yarns, which can be manufactured in England from untaxed "Surat" or India cotton, at very little disadvantage as compared with American cotton in point of production or cost of labor. *The commission, therefore, recommend that so long as there shall be a tax upon American raw cotton, there shall be in the tariff bill a specific duty on all imported cotton fabrics of as many cents per pound as are levied in the form of an excise tax upon the raw cotton.* The effect of this would be to check importation from England of goods "stuffed" with foreign substances, and secure us, so far as we do import cotton cloths honestly-made goods. This duty should be understood to be simply the offset or equivalent of the tax upon American cotton, and should only be charged when such excise tax is charged. When once imposed with this understanding, other legislation in the tariff upon cotton goods may be made entirely independent of the excise tax upon raw cotton. Provision should also be made for the importation of mixed fabrics in which cotton is a component element, and it would be safe to impose a duty upon such mixed fabrics, where the proportion of cotton is one-half or less, such as cotton-warp, "*delaines*," and worsted goods, of one-half the number of cents that are imposed upon raw cotton as an excise tax, leaving all mixed fabrics which are more than one-half cotton to pay the full duty, the same as if all cotton.

The commission would ask attention, in this connexion, to evidence taken by them, (see the testimony of Mr. John A. Lowell,) which seems to establish the fact that within a comparatively recent period the Indian department of the British government, in direct opposition to what is claimed as the established policy of that nation, with a view to discourage the importation into India of American manufactured cottons, levied and collected upon them heavy discriminating duties, which duties were sufficient, prior to 1860, to almost entirely destroy that portion of the American trade with India which before that time was large and increasing.

As regards the future supply of cotton, the commission, in view of the evidence they have been able to obtain up to the date of making their report, (January 1, 1866,) are unable to present any reliable estimate of the crop for the next one or two years. It is evident that under the fortunate stimulus of very high prices, all the cotton will be planted in the year 1866 for which good seed can be found, and a crop may be made of from two millions to two million and a half of bales. It is, however, impossible to predict with any accuracy what the exact amount of that crop will be. There can be no doubt that the high price of cotton will prove one of the best, if not the best, regulator of southern society, and that from self-interest alone, good order ought to prevail in the year 1867; and it is to be hoped and expected that in that year a crop more nearly approaching former figures will be realized.

During the war, as has already been shown, Europe drew her supplies, to make good the deficiency of American cotton, mainly from India, Egypt, Brazil, China, and Japan.

The export from China and Japan was abnormal. Neither of these countries produce more than is sufficient for the supply of their own necessities; and their export of cotton has now not only wholly ceased, but they are, as they have been before, importers of cotton from the East Indies.

The crop of India appears to have reached its maximum for the present, as famine prevailed in some parts of that country in 1865 from the over-planting of cotton. It must be remembered, in considering this statement, that famine may prevail in some portions of India with plenty in no very remote districts, for the reason that, as but a small part of the proceeds of the cotton reach the producers, they cannot afford to pay the excessive cost of transportation on food that the merchant can pay on cotton. It should also be remembered that India is not a true cotton country. Her crop is from 30 to 100 pounds an acre, against 200 to 600 in the United States; it is, moreover, of an inferior variety, and it is believed that no improvement in cultivation can make it equal to the cotton of the United States.*

Egypt is one of the most formidable rivals to the United States in the cultivation of cotton, which the events of the last four years have developed. Her crop has increased from 90,000 bales in 1859–'60, to 440,000 bales, of 500 pounds each, in 1864. But in that year so large an area of land was planted in cotton that the crop of cereals became deficient, and the planting was limited in 1865 by an edict of the Pacha to a more restricted area of country. In addition to this limit, an unfavorable season has probably reduced her crop of 1865 to 300,000 bales. But as the quality of Egyptian cotton is superior to that of the United States, except the sea island, and as emigration is being invited into her territory, it is probable that she will continue to produce a large crop of cotton, and will hold at least her present position in the markets of the world.

Turkey, Asia Minor, and other countries bordering upon the Mediterranean, have produced a considerable supply of cotton of good quality during the last four years, but it is not believed that they can maintain their position when cotton shall decline to twenty-five cents per pound in the United States. In Brazil it is not believed that cotton can maintain its position in competition with sugar and coffee, especially in view of the scarcity of labor consequent upon the cessation of the slave trade.† The supplies of cotton from other sources have been too inconsiderable to need notice.

The commission have been unable, in this report, through want of time, to enter into as full a discussion of the question of the expediency of a tax upon cotton, and its probable future effect upon production at home and abroad, as they have desired, and as the information collected by them would warrant. The testimony, however, taken by them, and herewith submitted, has been carefully prepared and edited, and is believed to embody nearly every point of interest in connexion with the subject. They would especially commend its careful examination to Congress and the country.

Respectfully submitted.

For the commission:

DAVID A. WELLS, *Chairman.*

Hon. HUGH MCCULLOCH, *Secretary of the Treasury.*

---

* See appendix A.

† See report on coffee, submitted by the commission.

APPENDIX A.

From one of the most recent contributions to our knowledge of the "Cotton Trade of India,"* we derive the following extracts :

"On no point has the public opinion of England been so egregiously misled by false reports, as on the supplies of cotton to be expected from that country" (India.)

"Cotton in most parts of India is cultivated in rotation with other crops, and is seldom looked upon as the mainstay of the ryot, but only as a subordinate product. The great staple of cultivation everywhere is breadstuffs in some shape or other; and the ryot will not neglect the raising of food for the sake of cotton, however high its price may be, for in so doing he runs the risk of starvation. No surplus stocks of grain are available to meet an emergency of this kind ; the internal commerce of India is still in the crudest possible shape ; no such thing exists as large districts devoted to special branches of agriculture, and drawing their supplies of food from others ; the rule, speaking generally, all over India, is for each locality to raise its own supplies of food, and for each separate cultivator to do the same for himself So true is this, that if the grain crops fail in any one region, a famine ensues ; and people perish by thousands even though the rest of India is unaffected. During the famine in the northwestern provinces two years ago, half a million of people are said to have died from starvation, while in most of India the crops were not deficient; but so wretched were the means of internal communication, and so little was the trade in breadstuffs organized, that supplies could not be thrown into the famished districts in time to avert this awful calamity. It is not then to be wondered at that the natives are reluctant to diminish their food-crops in order to turn their land into cotton.

"Moreover, in all parts of the Bombay Presidency, food is already very scarce and dear; the moderate increase in cotton cultivation has told largely on its price, and grain is already about twice as dear as it was a few years ago."

The conclusions to which the writer, in his essay of sixty-seven pages, is led, are stated as follows :

"*India is not able as a cotton-growing country to supply the place of America.*"

"*Large supplies of cotton can be drawn from India only by excessive prices, and whenever prices return to a normal level, the production will recede correspondingly.*"

"*No hope whatever exists of India being able to fill the void made by the stoppage of the southern trade at anything like remunerative prices to the spinner, and very little hope of her being able to provide a quality which would suitably fill the place of American cotton.*"

"If American cotton falls to tenpence (twenty cents) per pound, the cultivation of cotton in India will come to a standstill. If American cotton should ever again be grown for sevenpence (fourteen cents) per pound the swollen and artificially sustained production of cotton in India would certainly collapse, for at such prices it would not pay as a great staple crop."

A BILL for an act to provide for the levying and collection of an excise tax upon cotton.

Be it enacted by the Sentae and House of Representatives of the United States of America in Congress assembled, That on and after the first day of July, A. D. 1866, in lieu of the duties on unmanufactured cotton, as provided in "An act to provide internal revenue to support the government, to pay interest on the public debt and for other purposes," approved June 30, 1864, as amended by the act of March 3, 1865, there shall be paid upon all cotton produced within the United States, or any territory thereof, and upon which no excise duty has been levied, paid, or collected, an excise tax of —— cents per pound, as hereinafter provided; and the weight of such cotton shall be ascertained by deducting from the gross weight of each bale or package four per cent. tare for the weight of the ropes and bags on said bales; and such excise tax shall be and remain a lien thereon, in the possession of any person whomsoever, from the time such cotton is produced as aforesaid until the same shall have been paid; and no drawback shall in any case be allowed of any excise tax paid on raw or unmanufactured cotton.

SECTION 2. *And be it further enacted,* That it shall be the duty of every person, firm, or corporation, manufacturing cotton for any purpose whatever, to

---

* " ton Trade of India," being a series of letters written from Bombay in 1863, by Samu , London.

return to the assessor or assistant assessor of the district in which such manufacture is carried on, a true statement in writing, signed by him, and verified by his oath or affirmation, and a duplicate thereof to the collector of said district, on the first day of each month, or within ten days thereafter; and the first statement so rendered shall be on or before the tenth day of July, A. D. 1866, and shall state the amount of cotton which such manufacturer had on hand and unmanufactured, or in process of manufacture, on the first day of said month; and each subsequent statement shall show the whole amount in pounds gross weight, of cotton purchased or obtained, and the whole amount consumed by him in any business or process of manufacture during the last preceding calendar month, and the quantity and character of the goods manufactured therefrom; and every such manufacturer or consumer shall keep a book, in which he shall enter the quantity, in pounds of cotton, which he has on hand on the first day of July, A. D. 1866, and each quantity or lot purchased or obtained by him thereafter, and the time when, and the party or parties from whom the same was obtained, and also the quantities used or disposed of by him from time to time in any process of manufacture or otherwise, and the quantity and character of the product thereof, which book shall at all times during business hours, be open to the inspection of the assessor, assistant assessors, collector or deputy collectors of the district, or of revenue agents; and such manufacturer shall pay monthly to the collector, within five days after rendering the statement aforesaid to the assessor, the tax herein specified, subject to no deductions, on all cotton so consumed by him in any manufacture, and on which no excise tax has previously been paid; and every such manufacturer or person whose duty it is so to do, who shall neglect or refuse to make such returns to the assessor, or to keep such book; or who shall make false or fraudulent returns, or make false entries in such book, or procure the same to be so done, in addition to the payment of the tax to be assessed thereon, shall forfeit to the United States such cotton, and all products manufactured therefrom, and shall be liable to a penalty of not less than one thousand nor more than five thousand dollars, to be recovered with costs of suit, or to imprisonment not exceeding two years, in the discretion of the court; and any person or persons who shall make any false oath or affidavit in relation to any matter or thing herein required shall be guilty of perjury, and be liable to imprisonment not less than two years, nor more than five years. *Provided,* That nothing herein contained shall be construed in any manner to apply to or affect the liability of any person to any tax imposed by law on the goods manufactured from such cotton, or any law relating thereto.

SECTION 3. *And be it further enacted,* That every person, firm, company, or corporation, manufacturing or consuming cotton as aforesaid, shall immediately give notice thereof in writing to the assessor of the district where such business is carried on, and shall execute a bond to the United States, with two sufficient sureties to be approved by the collector of the district, in such form as the Commissioner of Internal Revenue may prescribe, conditioned to render the monthly statements herein required, and to pay the tax on all such cotton manufactured or consumed by him or them, and shall be sufficient in amount to secure the tax which will accrue monthly, and shall be renewed on the first day of May, annually, and oftener if the collector of the district shall require, or shall give such other and further bond as he may require; and such tax shall also be a lien, until paid, upon all the real and personal property of the person or persons to whom it belongs to pay the same, and payment of such tax may be enforced in the manner provided by law for duties upon manufactured articles; and any person or persons liable to pay such tax, who shall fraudulently evade or attempt to evade the same, shall forfeit such cotton and the product of any manufacture thereof; and shall, in addition to the tax, be liable to one hundred per cent. assessed penalty thereon, to be collected in the same manner as the original tax, and also to a fine of not less than one thousand nor more than five thousand dollars, to be recovered with costs of suit, or to imprisonment not exceeding two years, in the discretion of the court: *Provided*, That nothing herein contained shall be construed to impose such tax on cotton waste produced from the manufacture of cotton on which an excise tax or import duty has been paid.

SECTION 4. *And be it further enacted*, That it shall be the duty of all persons making shipments or removals of cotton, on which the proper excise duty or tax has not been paid, from any part of the United States or its territories to any foreign country, to cause the same to be properly inspected and weighed by a United States inspector, under the supervision of the collector of internal revenue of the district whence such shipment or removal is to be made, and thereupon, before making such shipment or removal, pay to said collector the amount of tax to which such cotton is liable, as before provided; and the said inspector shall affix proper marks upon said cotton, showing that the same has been inspected and the weight thereof, and shall certify and report the weight to the assessor of the district, and shall give to the owner thereof a certificate of inspection and weight. And the collector aforesaid, after the receipt by him of the tax on any cotton, shall, at the request of the party desiring to make such shipment or removal thereof, give a permit in duplicate, in such form as the Commissioner of Internal Revenue may prescribe, allowing such shipment or removal to be made, and stating therein the weight of each bale or package, and that the tax thereon has been paid. Such shipment or removal from the United States shall not be made, except from or through a port of entry whence merchandise is allowed by law and regulations to be exported for benefit of drawback; and the duplicate permits aforesaid shall be delivered to the superintendent of exports at the port, (or the collector having charge of matters relating to exportations where there shall be no superintendent,) who shall cause the weight of such cotton to be ascertained, and the amount thereof, not exceeding the number of pounds named in the permit, to be placed on board the vessel or other conveyance, under his surveillance, and shall at the same time deliver one of said permits to the master of the vessel or person having charge or control of the vehicle of conveyance, and shall immediately file the other permit with his certificate indorsed thereon that the quantity is correct, and that he is satisfied the tax has been paid, with the collector of customs, who may thereupon grant a clearance for the same.

SECTION 5. *And be it further enacted*, That it shall be unlawful (from and after the passage of this act) for the owner, master, supercargo, agent, or other person having charge of any vessel, to allow any cotton to be placed on board thereof for shipment to a foreign port, except under such supervision, and upon receipt of the permit before mentioned. And any master, owner, supercargo, or other person, who shall wilfully violate this provision of law, shall be liable to a fine of one hundred dollars for each bale of cotton so shipped, and to imprisonment for not more than one year. And no railroad company, or other transportation company, common carrier, or other person, shall convey or transport, or attempt to convey or transport, any cotton from the United States, or from any territory thereof, to any foreign country, without having previously obtained such permit. And any person who shall violate the provisions of this act in this respect shall be liable to a forfeiture of the vessels and vehicles employed in such conveyance or transportation, and shall be further liable to a penalty of one hundred dollars for each bale of cotton so conveyed or transported, or attempted to be conveyed or transported, and to imprisonment for not more than one year. And all cotton so shipped or attempted to be shipped or transported beyond the limits of the United States, without payment of the tax, shall be forfeited—one-half of the proceeds of the sale of the same to go to the informer; and the owner or agent of said cotton shall be liable to the tax on the same, and to one hundred per cent. thereon in addition, as penalty, and further to a fine of not less than one thousand nor more than five thousand dollars, or to imprisonment not more than two years, in the discretion of the court.

SECTION 6. *And be it further enacted,* That no collector or other officer of the customs shall grant a clearance to any vessel bound to a foreign port whose cargo consists, wholly or in part, of cotton, until the permit aforesaid, certified as to the quantity shipped in the manner before provided, shall be filed with him. And any vessel, whose owner, master, supercargo, or shipper, or the agents thereof, shall convey, or attempt to convey therein, cotton from any port or place in the United States, to a foreign country, without such permit and clearance, shall be liable to seizure and forfeiture in any court of the United States. And in case of such forfeiture, one moiety thereof shall belong to the person or persons who, in the judgment of the court, shall have first furnished the information which shall have been the cause of such forfeiture.

SECTION 7. *And be it further enacted,* That the Commissioner of Internal Revenue shall make all necessary rules and regulations for carrying into effect the provisions of this act, subject to the approval of the Secretary of the Treasury.

SECTION 8. *And be it further enacted,* That all acts or parts of acts inconsistent with the provisions hereof are hereby repealed : *Provided,* That nothing herein contained shall be construed to change or release any duties accrued, or liability or obligation created by law, prior to the time when this act takes effect, or in any manner to affect the same.

SECTION 9. *And be it further enacted,* That this act shall take effect on the first day of July, A. D. 1866.

SPECIAL REPORT No. 4.

Report of the United States revenue commission on sugar and molasses as sources of national revenue.

TREASURY DEPARTMENT,
Office of the United States Revenue Commission, January, 1866.

SIR: The following table shows the estimated consumption of foreign and domestic cane-sugar in the United States (excluding the States on the Pacific) for the years ending December 31, from 1852 to 1865, inclusive:

Years.	Foreign.	Domestic.	Tons.	Total.
	Tons.	*Tons.*		*Pounds.*
1852	196, 558	118, 659	315, 217	706, 086, 000
1853	200, 610	172, 379	372, 989	835, 495, 360
1854	150, 854	234, 444	385, 298	863, 067, 520
1855	192, 604	185, 148	377, 752	846, 164, 480
1856	255, 292	123, 468	378, 760	848, 422, 400
1857	241, 765	39, 000	280, 765	628, 913, 600
1858	244, 758	143, 634	388, 392	869, 998, 080
1859	239, 034	192, 150	431, 184	965, 852, 160
1860	296, 950	118, 331	415, 281	930, 229, 440
1861	241, 420	122, 399	363, 819	814, 954, 560
1862	241, 411	191, 000	432, 411	968, 600, 640
1863	231, 308	53, 000*	284, 308	636, 849, 920
1864	192, 660	28, 000	220, 660	494, 278, 400
1865	345, 809†	3, 500	349, 309	782, 452, 160

ANNUAL AVERAGES, IN TONS.

	Foreign.	Domestic.	Total.
Five years—1852–'56	199, 183	166, 820	366, 003
Five years—1857–'61	252, 786	123, 103	375, 889
Four years—1862–'65	252, 797	69, 250	322, 047
Ten years—1852–'61	225, 985	144, 961	370, 946

*The bulk of the crop of Louisiana and Texas in 1862, and a part of 1861, was distributed in 1863.

†The great increase in the demand for foreign cane-sugars, experienced during the year 1865, cannot be considered as normal and legitimate. The west, and especially the south, were in a great measure destitute of sugars at the close of the war, and the great demand, which sprung up since that period has been rather to supply a vacuum than a legitimate increase in consumption.

ANNUAL AVERAGES, IN POUNDS.

	Foreign.	Domestics.	Total.
Five years—1852–'56	446, 169, 920	373, 676, 800	819, 846, 720
Five years—1857–'61	566, 240, 640	275, 750, 720	841, 991, 360
Four years—1862–'65	566, 265, 280	155, 120, 000	721, 385, 280
Ten years—1852–'61	506, 206, 400	324, 712, 640	830, 919, 040

From the above table it appears that the average annual consumption of *foreign* cane-sugars in the Atlantic States, from 1852 to 1856, inclusive, was 446,169,920 pounds, and of *domestic* cane 373,676,800 pounds, making an *aggregate* of 819,846,720 pounds. During the next series of five years, or from 1857 to 1861, inclusive, the average annual consumption of *foreign* cane-sugars was 566,240,640 pounds, showing an increase of twenty-seven per cent.; while the average annual consumption of *domestic* cane-sugars was 275,750,720 pounds, showing a decrease of twenty-six and a quarter per cent.; making in all, for these five years, an average annual *aggregate* consumption of 841,991,360 pounds.

The effect of the war on the consumption of sugars in the United States first manifested itself in a striking degree in 1863. The crop of *domestic* cane sugar in 1862 was unprecedentedly large, and for the State of Louisiana alone yielded 459,410 hogsheads; or for the three States of Texas, Louisiana, and Florida, was estimated at upward of 241,000 tons. The bulk of this crop was mainly distributed for consumption in 1862; the receipts at the port of New York from New Orleans alone, in 1862, after the latter port came into the possession of the government, having been, with the exception of 1854, the largest ever known in the trade in any single year. The total consumption of cane-sugar (foreign and domestic) for the year 1862, for the Atlantic States, was estimated at 432,411 tons (or 968,600,640 pounds,) making a larger aggregate consumption than of any previous year in our history.

During the year 1863 the consumption of *foreign* cane-sugars *decreased*, as compared with 1862, 10,103 tons, or somewhat more than four per cent. (4.2;) while the *decrease* in the consumption of *domestic* cane-sugars was 138,000 tons, or seventy-two per cent.*

During the year 1864 this reduction also continued—the decrease in the consumption of *foreign* cane-sugars, as compared with 1862, having been 48,751 tons, or exceeding twenty per cent.; and of *domestic* cane-sugar 163,000 tons, or eighty-five per cent. less than in 1862.

In the year 1865, especially in the months following the close of the war, the consumption of *foreign* cane-sugar has very rapidly *increased;* the aggregate increase being upward of 153,149 tons, as compared with the consumption of 1864, or seventy-nine and a half per cent. The production and consumption of *domestic* cane-sugars, on the contrary, was almost too inconsiderable to be taken into account.

No reliable data are available to the commission for accurately estimating the consumption of raw cane-sugar in the Pacific States; but an annual average of about 10,000 tons is probably approximately correct. A considerable portion of the sugars consumed in the Pacific States are of the refined descriptions received from New York and Boston, though the recent establishment of refineries in San Francisco has begun to interfere with such shipments from the Atlantic ports.

*The bulk of the crop of Louisiana and Texas in 1862, and a part of 1861, was distributed in 1863.

In addition to the above estimates of the consumption of cane-sugars, allowance should be made for a considerable amount of clarified sugar annually entering into consumption, which is produced from molasses. This product (which is represented in the aggregate table of consumption of sugars of all kinds given hereafter) was estimated for the year 1863 at 21,250 tons, and for the year 1864 at 22,321 tons.

The manufacture of maple sugar during the past few years, owing to the great increase in the price of cane-sugar, has been prosecuted with unexampled energy; and although it is extremely difficult to arrive at any satisfactory conclusions respecting the present extent of this important crop, owing to the numerous locations, scattered throughout the northern, middle, and western States, where it is gathered in a small way, yet there can be little doubt that the estimates that are generally made, of about 28,000 tons (or 62,720,000 pounds) per annum, are rather within than in excess of the actual quantity.

The cultivation of the sorghum, under the like influence of high prices for cane-sugar, is rapidly extending throughout the western States, and is also becoming, to the same extent, a farm product of southern New England and the middle States. As yet, the expectations that have been indulged in, respecting the value of this plant as a source of sugar, have not been realized; but that sirup of a valuable quality can be easily and economically made from it has been well established. The high price of the sirups derived from the sorghum, averaging $1 20 per gallon, effectually precludes all idea of an immediate production of sugar from this source, even were an economical process for its extraction devised.

Continued experiment, however, has satisfied intelligent minds that this plant may become a future source of merchantable sugar. The quantity of sirup thus produced for the years 1862, 1863, 1864, and 1865, is estimated by the commission as follows:

	Gallons.
1862	5,000,000
1863	9,000,000
1864	16,000,000
1865	25,000,000

For the future a steady annual increase in this product may be also considered certain.

That such a rapid and large addition to the supply of the saccharine material of the country will, to some extent, affect the demand for foreign and domestic cane-sugar, and more especially of cane molasses (and consequently the revenue to be derived from the same,) cannot be doubted; and in the opinion of those most conversant with the trade, such indeed has been the effect already. It should, however, be called to mind in this connexion, that the western States have never been consumers of foreign molasses to any great extent, and that it is the new and cheap supply of saccharine material afforded by the sorghum, which has itself, in a measure, created its demand for consumption.

The following table shows the estlmated consumption of *sugars of all kinds* in the United States, from 1857 to 1865, inclusive (nine years :)

Years.	Tons.	Pounds.	Remarks.
1857	332, 065	743, 825, 600	
1858	431, 152	965, 780, 480	30 per cent. increase.
1859	478, 737	1, 072, 370, 880	1 " "
1860	464, 673	1, 040, 867, 520	$2\frac{15}{16}$ " decrease.
1861	411, 650	922, 096, 000	$11\frac{3}{8}$ " "
1862	483, 205	1, 082, 379, 200	$17\frac{3}{8}$ " increase.
1863	440, 500	762, 720, 000	$29\frac{1}{2}$ " decrease.
1864	280, 500	628, 320, 000	$17\frac{5}{8}$ " "
1865	412, 000	922, 880, 000	47 " increase.

In 1860, the consumption of sugar in Great Britain was estimated at an average of about thirty-four pounds *per capita*, or an aggregate of upwards of one thousand millions of pounds. This consumption, however, is not equally distributed in different parts of the kingdom. Thus, in 1856, the consumption in England was thirty-four pounds *per capita ;* in Scotland, thirty-one pounds ; and in Ireland, only eight and a half pounds.

In France the consumption of sugar *per capita* was estimated, in 1860, at eleven and one-third pounds ; in Belgium, at twenty-one pounds ; in the German states, at seven and three-fourths pounds ; and in Russia, at two pounds.

In Great Britain it is estimated that there are consumed nine pounds of sugar for one pound of tea and coffee. In France the proportion is nine and two-thirds pounds for one pound of coffee. In Belgium, where the coffee is usually taken without sugar, the consumption of sugar is estimated at but little more than two pounds for one of coffee.

In all the United States, if we adopt the estimates above given, the average annual consumption of sugar of *all kinds per capita*, with an assumed population of 30,000,000, for the years 1858, 1859, and 1860, was thirty and a half pounds. For the year 1864, when the consumption of sugar, by reason of the war and high prices, was reduced to its minimum, the consumption *per capita* was only twenty-one pounds. For the year ending December 31, 1865, the consumption may be estimated at thirty-one pounds *per capita.*

The average annual consumption *per capita* of *foreign cane-sugar*, for the years 1858, 1859, and 1860, in the Atlantic States, was nineteen and one-third pounds; and of *domestic* cane-sugar for the same years, eleven and two-thirds pounds.

Assuming the present average annual production of *maple-sugar* to be 28,000 tons, we have as the average annual consumption of this article, with a population of 30,000,000 as above, about *two* pounds (2.1) *per capita.*

The commission estimate the average rate of increase in the consumption of cane-sugars, foreign and domestic, in all the United States, for the ten years prior to and including 1861, to have been about three per cent. (more nearly 2.8) per annum.

With the revival of the peculiar industries of the south, the States of Louisiana, Texas, and Florida will, undoubtedly, during the *present* year (1866,)* begin to contribute again to a considerable extent to the supply of the cane-sugars

* The sugar product of Louisiana for 1865 was estimated to be insufficient for even the local consumption.

required for the consumption of the United States. As will be seen by reference to the tables above given, the amount of cane-sugar of *domestic* production annually supplied for consumption in the United States averaged 166,830 tons (or 373,676,800 pounds) for the five years next preceding 1857; and 123,000 tons (or 275,751,000 pounds) for the five years next preceding 1862. For the next few years, or so long as the labor question at the south remains at all unsettled, and probably so long as cotton continues to command twenty-five cents or more per pound, the manufacture of cane-sugars in the States above mentioned must revive but slowly; and in the opinion of the commissions the aggregate and maximum product of domestic cane-sugars, for the year, 1866 and 1867, will not exceed 50,000 tons*

For the fiscal years ending June 30, 1867 and 1868, the commission estimate that the consumption of the country will probably require an annual importation of at least 285,625 tons (or 620,000,000 pounds) of foreign cane-sugars; which estimate presupposes, for these years, an annual consumption of all kinds of sugars considerably less than for the average of the five years immediately preceding the war.

---

* It is extremely difficult to form any reliable estimates respecting the immediate future production of sugar in the southern States. History records few examples of so stupendous and rapid a destruction of a great branch of national industry as befel the sugar interest of the United States, by reason of the rebellion. The crop of 1861–62 was one of the largest ever made. The number of sugar estates returned as in operation for that year was 1,292, and the product 459,410 hogsheads of sugar, and 36,752,800 gallons of molasses. For 1864–5, on the contrary, the number of sugar estates returned as in operation was only 180, which afforded the scanty product of 6,750 hogsheads of sugar (or about thirty-seven hogsheads per *estate*) and 405,000 gallons of molasses.

Large as was the crop of 1861–'62, the crop of 1862–'63, would probably have been much larger under all ordinary circumstances. The crop in question had nearly reached maturity; the expenses incidental to grinding had already been incurred; when military necessity suddenly and violently wrested from the planter his working power—representing a capital of over one hundred and seventeen millions of dollars—leaving the canes for the mills and the corn for the use of the respective estates to rot in the fields, or to become spoil of the contending armies.

In view of these facts, it is not improbable that the estimates given in this report of the immediate future product of domestic cane-sugar is much larger than the facts will warrant. If this should prove to be the case, a larger import of foreign sugars will be required than has been estimated, to make good in all, or part, of the deficiency of the domestic crop.

An opinion is communicated to the commission, by one of the most intelligent sugar producers and factors of Louisiana, founded on a careful examination and review of the present industrial and financial condition of the sugar-producing States, that if an active capital of $25,000,000 could be obtained, coupled with a "virtual organization of labor, irrespective of color, and equally protective of the employer and employé," the sugar industry of the State of Louisiana alone might in less than four years be made to yield an annual aggregate of at least 500,000,000 pounds. All such supply of capital must, however, be furnished from abroad, as the local banks, and the sugar factors, who formerly co-operated with and made advances to the planter, have, in common with him, been greatly crippled, or entirely ruined.

Molasses.—The following table shows the estimated consumption in the Atlantic States of cane molasses, domestic and foreign, for the years ending December 31, from 1851 to 1864, inclusive:

Calendar years.	Amount consumed.	Amount imported.
	Gallons.	*Gallons.*
1851	43, 948, 018	33, 238, 278
1852	48, 257, 511	29, 417, 511
1853	55, 536, 821	28, 576, 821
1854	56 493, 019	24, 437, 019
1855	47, 266, 085	23, 533, 423
1856	39, 608, 878	23, 014, 878
1857	28, 508, 784	23, 266, 404
1858	45, 169, 164	24, 795, 374
1859	54, 260, 970	28, 293, 210
1860	47, 318, 877	28, 724, 205
1861	40, 191, 556	20, 383, 556
1862	62, 668, 400	25, 650, 400
1863	37, 569, 088	26, 569, 088
1864	32, 581, 668	28, 753, 668

The total consumption of molasses of all kinds, for the year 1862, was estimated as follows:

	Gallons.
Cane, foreign and domestic	62, 668, 000
Sugar-house sirups	21, 000, 000
Sirups from maple and sorghum	14, 000, 000
	97, 668, 000

For the year 1863:

Cane, foreign and domestic	37, 569, 000
Sugar-house sirups	25, 000, 000
Maple sirup	9, 000, 000
Sorghum	9, 000, 000
	80, 569, 000

For the year 1864:

Cane, foreign and domestic	32, 582, 000
Sugar-house sirups	20, 000, 000
Maple sirup	9, 000, 000
Sorghum	16, 000, 000
	77, 582, 000

The quantity of cane molasses taken for distilling before the excise law went into effect was very large, but since then the demand for this purpose has fallen off materially.

In the opinion of the commission an annual importation of at least twenty-five millions of gallons of cane molasses may be relied on for the fiscal years

1866–7 and 1867–8; and during the same years an annual domestic product of cane molasses, available for assessment and revenue, of about ten millions of gallons, may be also anticipated.

The following are the rates of duty at present imposed on imported sugars:

Sugars not above No. 12, Dutch standard, in color, 3 cents per pound; sugars above No. 12, and not above No. 15, Dutch standard, in color, 3½ cents per pound; sugars above No. 15, not stove-dried, and not above No. 20, Dutch standard, 4 cents per pound; sugars, refined, 5 cents per pound; sugars, stove-dried, or other sugars above No. 20, Dutch standard, in color, 5 cents per pound; sugars, refined, when tinctured or adulterated, 15 cents per pound; candy, valued at 30 cents or less per pound, 15 cents per pound.

The rates of duty imposed by several of the leading countries of Europe on the importation of unrefined raw sugars, previous to 1864, were as follows:

Great Britain, 2¾ to 3½ cents per pound—average, 3⅛; France, 2⅞ to 4 cents per pound—average, 3½; Russia, 8 cents per pound; Zoll Verein, 5 cents per pound; Austria, 5 cents per pound; Sweden and Norway, 2 cents per pound; Spain, 3½ cents per pound. Average rates of imposts in the above eight countries, 4 cents per pound.

In 1864, the imposts on foreign sugars in Great Britain were reduced, making the present rates on low grades of sugar 2 cents to 2⅓ per pound.

In Great Britain, sugar is the most productive article in the customs revenue, the importation of unrefined sugars for the years ending December 31, 1862, 1863, and 1864, having yielded, respectively, the following gross amount of duties:

1862	£6,201,250	$31,006,250
1863	6,329,850	31,649,250
1864	4,773,210	23,866,050

The aggregate of duties paid in Great Britain, for the same years, on sugars of all descriptions, and molasses, is also returned as follows:

1862	£6,641,236	$33,206,180
1863	6,717,186	33,585,930
1864	5,394,701	26,973,505

The following table, prepared from returns furnished to the commission by the Treasury Department, shows the estimated quantities of sugars imported, and the duties received on the same, for the five ports of Boston, New York, Philadelphia, Baltimore, and San Francisco,* during the fiscal years ending June 30, 1862, 1863, 1864, and 1865:

Year ending—	Quantity.	Rates of duty.	Duties received.
	Pounds.		
June 30, 1862†	652,498,301	....	$11,541,733 03
June 30, 1863	315,038,166	2½ cents.	7,875,954 15
June 30, 1863	18,611,342	3 cents.	558,340 26
June 30, 1863	2,454,460	3½ cents.	85,906 10
June 30, 1863	47,121	4 cents.	1,884 84
June 30, 1863, sugar candy	2,687	6 to 10 cents.	252 70
Total, 1863	336,153,776	....	18,522,338 05
June 30, 1864	494,812,465	2½ cents.	12,370,311 62
June 30, 1864	31,699,069	3 cents.	950,972 07
June 30, 1864	6,047,997	3½ cents.	211,679 90
June 30, 1864, refined	21,910	4 cents.	876 40
June 30, 1864, sugar candy	49,700	6 to 10 cents.	4,321 52
Total, 1864	532,631,141	....	‡13,538,161 51

The rates of duty on cane-molasses imported into the United States since 1856 have been as follows: From 1856 to 1858, 30 per cent. *ad valorem;* from 1858 to 1861, 24 per cent. *ad valorem.*

By the act of March 2, 1861, a duty of two cents per gallon was imposed on all imported molasses; by the act of August 5, 1861, the duty was advanced to five cents per gallon; by the act of December 24, 1861, to six cents per gallon; and by the act of June 30, 1864, the duty was still further advanced to eight cents per gallon, since when the rate has remained unchanged. On sirups and melado the present rate of duty is two and a half cents per pound.

	Gross imports.	Exports.	Consumption.	Duties accruing.
	Pounds.	*Pounds.*	*Pounds.*	
Sugars not above No. 12, Dutch standard	519,457,697	....	....	....
Sugars above No. 12, and not above No. 15, Dutch standard	75,738,169	....	....	....
Sugars above No. 15, and not above No. 20, Dutch standard	12,741,808	....	....	....
Total	607,937,674	28,155,268	579,782,406	$20,292,384

* For San Francisco, the returns are given only to the 30th of April, 1864.

† The rates of duty in 1862 varied from three-fourths of a cent to five cents, the average being one and three-fourth cents.

‡ After the above returns were prepared, the commission received from the department the following (doubtful) returns of the imports of sugar of different grades into the United States, and the duties accruing from the same for the fiscal year 1865:

The following table, prepared from returns furnished to the commission by the Treasury Department, shows the estimated quantities of molasses, sirups, &c., imported, and the duties received on the same for the five ports, Boston, New York, Philadelphia, Baltimore, and San Francisco,* during the years ending June 30, 1862, 1863, 1864, and 1865:

MOLASSES.

Year ending—	Quantity—gallons.	Rates.	Duties received.
June 30, 1862	7,257,716	2 cents	$145,154 32
June 30, 1862	3,025,250	5 cents	151,262 50
June 30, 1862	16,351,933	6 cents	981,115 98
Total, 1862	26,634,899		1,277,532 80
June 30, 1863	26,463,785	6 cents	1,587,827 10
June 30, 1864	22,832,102	6 cents	1,369,926 12
June 30, 1865	34,958,091	8 cents	2,796,647 28

SIRUPS, MELADO, ETC.

Year ending—	Pounds.	Rates.	Duties received.
June 30, 1862	7,389,189	¾ of a cent	$55,418 91
June 30, 1862	988,952	2 cents	19,779 04
June 30, 1862	312,215	2½ cents	7,805 37
Total, 1862	8,690,356		83,003 32
June 30, 1863	2,727,192	2 cents	54,543 84
June 30, 1864	5,524,102	2 cents	110,482 04
June 30, 1865	6,863,179	2½ cents	171,579 48

By the amended internal revenue act of March 3, 1865, the following rates of excise were levied on the production or manufacture of domestic cane sugars:

On sugars not above No. 12, Dutch standard, produced from the sugar-cane, and not from sorghum or imphee, other than those produced by the refiner, two and four-tenths cents per pound.

On sugars above No. 12, and not above No. 18, Dutch standard, produced directly from the sugar-cane, and not from sorghum or imphee, three cents per pound.

On sugars above No. 18, as above, four and two-tenths cents per pound.

On molasses produced from the sugar-cane, and not from sorghum or imphee six cents per gallon.

On sirups of molasses, or sugar-cane juice, concentrated molasses, or melado, and cistern-bottoms, one and a half cent per pound.

The following table shows the amount of internal revenue received from the excise on domestic cane sugars of the different varieties for the fiscal years ending June 30, 1863, 1864, and 1865:

* For San Francisco the returns are given only to the 30th of April, 1864.

		Revenue received. Currency.
1862–'63.	Total excise tax on domestic cane sugars, 1862–'63.	$261,044 58
1863–'64.	Total excise tax on domestic cane sugars, 1863–'64.	1,267,616 28
1864–'65.	Sugars not above No. 12, Dutch standard.........	86,464 76
	Sugars above No. 12, but not above No. 18..........	179,323 86
	Sugars above No. 18, Dutch standard	57,963 76
	Total excise tax on domestic cane sugars, 1864–'65.	323,752 38

For the fiscal year 1864–'65 the revenue obtained from the excise tax on domestic molasses produced from the sugar-cane, sirup of molasses, melado, and cistern-bottoms, was $54,971 78.

By the internal revenue act of June 30, 1864, an excise of two and a half per cent. *ad valorem* was levied on the gross amount of sales on sugar refiners. By the amended act of March 3, 1865, this excise was advanced to three per cent., the refiner being at the same time required to take out a license.

The following table shows the revenue received from the excise on the sales of sugar refiners, and the rates of excise for the fiscal years ending June 30, from 1863 to 1865, inclusive:

	Amount received Currency.
Year ending June 30, 1863, rate of excise 1½ per cent......	$93,418 09
Year ending June 30, 1864, rate of excise 1½ per cent......	873,139 85
Year ending June 30, 1865, { rate of excise 2½ per cent. ... rate of excise 3 per cent.... }	1,720,612 96

From the above tables it would therefore appear that the gross revenue received from the customs duties and excise on sugars of all kinds, and on the gross sales of sugar refiners, for the year ending June 30, 1865, has been as follows:

Customs duties on imported sugars, &c.............(gold)	$20,292,384 21
Customs duties on imported molasses...............(gold)	2,796,647 28
Sirups, melado, &c................................(gold)	171,579 48
Total receipts from customs (doubtful).........(gold)	23,260,610 97
Excise on domestic cane sugars ....(currency)	$323,752 38
Excise on sales of sugar refiners..............(currency)	1,720,612 96
Total receipts from excise ....(currency)	2,044,365 34

The commission, in this connexion, would direct special attention to the effect of the present excise tax on the gross sales of sugar refiners.

Previous to 1850 the raw material employed by the manufacturers of refined sugars in the United States consisted mainly of "Havana box," "clayed Manilla," and the better class of "Porto Rico" sugars; all containing a high percentage of cane sugar and a very small proportion of molasses and (other) impurities. The sirups resulting from the treatment of these varieties of the raw material, being all rich in sugar, were "worked back," as it is termed, in the refineries, and by secondary results tended to swell the product of the refined sugar.

Under these circumstances the average production of refined sugar, resulting from the treatment of the above varieties, was as follows:

	Per cent.	
Refined in various forms—crushed, pulverized, &c.	70.63	
A, white, wet	2.28	
First product		72.91
B and C, yellow, wet	12.40	
Molasses	11.18	
Second product		23.58
Total yield of merchantable product		96.49
Loss—impurities and moisture		3.51

About 1848 to 1850 the increasing competition of grocers for the grades of sugars heretofore used in refining compelled the refiners to seek their supplies in the lower grades of Muscovado sugars, from which, by the application of more perfect chemical processes and mechanical appliances, with rigid economy in expense, waste, and time, they were enabled to produce an article in all respects equal in quality to that previously made, but in largely diminished proportions of the higher class of refined sugars.

Since 1850 the average results of refineries in treating the last-mentioned varieties of raw cane sugars is reported to the commission as follows:

	Per cent.	
Refined in various forms—crushed, pulverized, &c.	37.49	
A, white, wet	13.12	
		50.61
B and C, yellow, wet	24.60	
Molasses, at 12 lbs. per gallon	17.81	
		42.41
Total yield of merchantable product		93.02
Loss—impurities and moisture		6.98

This last result is obtained by what is known as the "direct process," in which the resulting sirups from the first boiling, being poor in sugar, (from the low grade of sugars operated upon,) are boiled at once to make B and C (yellow) sugars and molasses, instead of being "worked back," as in the first process detailed. The obvious effect of the direct process is a largely reduced yield of refined sugars and a proportionate increase of yellow sugars and molasses; but in the calculations of the refiner this is compensated for by the largely increased quantity of raw sugars which they are enabled to melt and refine with the same machinery and labor, by the higher quality of the secondary products, and by the diminished cost of labor and working.

The business of refining sugar constitutes one of the largest branches of manufacturing industry followed in the United States, and as regards capital invested and number of men employed, probably ranks among the first of the special industries of the cities of Boston, New York, Philadelphia, Baltimore, Cincinnati, and St. Louis. Of the whole amount of raw cane-sugars imported into or produced in the United States, about *two-thirds* are estimated to pass through the refineries previous to final consumption.*

From the table above submitted it would appear that, by the processes now followed in American refineries, about *fifty* per cent. of *refined* sugars, by weight, are obtained from the raw sugars treated.

The absolute loss in refining sugar may be estimated at about seven per cent.

The estimated additional value given to the product of any given weight of sugar in refining, *less* the interest on capital invested in the business of refining, is also estimated at about *seven* per cent. at present prices of the raw material, (6.93.)

The raw sugars at present employed for refining, when imported, pay a specific duty of three cents per pound. Upon the sales of all the product of the refinery (refined sugars, yellow sugars, and molasses) there is at present imposed an excise of three per cent.

As has already been stated, the refiner obtains but about fifty per cent. of refined sugar from the raw product treated by him; the remaining fifty per cent. being represented by the secondary products of yellow sugars and molasses, with the *seven* per cent. loss (from impurities and moisture) before noticed. These secondary products the refiner is obliged to sell in direct competition with the foreign unrefined raw sugars and molasses, at corresponding prices, making all allowance for any superiority in quality or cost on the part of the former.

So far, therefore, as these grades of sugars are concerned, the excise of three per cent. levied on the refiners' sales is equivalent to a direct protection to the foreign producer; while the refiner, not being able, by reason of the foreign competition, to charge the three per cent. paid on the secondary products to the price at which he is obliged to dispose of them, adds it to the cost of his fifty per cent. refined product. The excise tax of three per cent. on the gross sales of sugar-refiners, therefore, in fact falls wholly on refined sugars; thus unduly enhancing their cost to the consumers, reducing their consumption, and under the present allowance for drawback, restricting their export. The excise tax of three per cent. upon the sales of all products of the refinery is thus made equivalent to about six per cent. on the sales of refined sugars, a tax nearly equal to the absolute value resulting from all the labor employed in the business of sugar-refining in the United States. That such a tax tends to diminish the consumption of refined sugars in the United States, and affect injuriously the domestic industry and commerce of the country, cannot be doubted.

The commission, therefore, recommend, *that the excise tax of three per cent. on the sales of sugar-refiners be repealed, and that in l eu thereof, the impost and excise on all foreign and domestic cane-sugars be advanced one-half cent per pound, and on all foreign and domestic molasses two cents per gallon.* The commission believe that by this method all the objections growing out of the present system, above described, will be removed, the refining interest of the country stimulated, and a largely increased revenue accrue to the government; an additional *one-half* cent on 600,000,000 of pounds of imported sugar will yield $3,000,000, or nearly one hundred per cent. more than the revenue derived, during the last fiscal year, from a tax of three per cent. on the sales of refiners.

If it be urged that this plan relieves the great industrial interest of sugar-refining from all direct taxation, we reply that this is the wish and aim of the

---

* In 1858 the quantity of brown sugar used by *nineteen* refineries in the city of New York was estimated to be at the rate of about 112,000 tons (250,880,000 pounds) per annum. In 1865, in twenty-nine refineries, the estimated consumption was about 25,000 hogsheads per month, or 30,600,000 pounds.

commission. The object of the government in arranging its revenue system, is not taxation merely, but revenue.*

We believe, further, that it is expedient, at least at present, in devising a national revenue system for this country, that the taxes should be made as indirect and as concrete as possible; that direct taxes upon the necessary industries should be avoided; and that, as rapidly as possible, the machinery of the excise should be reduced and simplified. In making the alterations proposed, these several ends will be attained, so far as one great industrial interest of the country is concerned

Furthermore, in advancing the customs and excise rates on foreign and domestic cane-sugars, *one-half* cent per pound, it is not certain that this advance will fall upon the consumer. Unlike coffee, the production of cane-sugar throughout the world continually tends to exceed the demand for consumption, and thus the additional one-half cent duty will fall mainly on the foreign producers, and only slightly on consumers.

The average annual production of sugar throughout the world for the *five* years, 1860–'64, is estimated at 3,729,000,000 pounds, while the estimated average annual demand for consumption for the same period is fixed at about 3,642,000,000 pounds; the average annual production being thus eighty-seven millions of pounds, or two and four-tenths per cent. larger than the average annual demand for consumption. The stock of sugar, therefore, in all the markets of the world, tends to accumulate; the stock in the principal ports of Europe, on the first of August, 1865, being 249,000 tons against 219,000 tons in 1864; an excess of 30,000 tons, or sixty-seven millions of pounds.

In this connexion the following tables, prepared by H. E. Moring, esq., of New York city, showing the estimated *distribution* throughout the world, of the production and of the consumption of sugars, distinguishing cane-sugars from those derived from the beet-root, may not be uninteresting.†

---

* If it be urged that this plan relieves the great industrial interest of sugar refining from all taxation, we reply: The case is peculiar, inasmuch as in this great interest alone, the raw material of the manufacturer, in the shape of raw sugar as imported, enters into direct competition in the consumption of the country; and the difference of three per cent. direct tax on the sales of the refiner is equal to one-third of a cent per pound on a sugar worth eleven cents, and proportionately more on the higher-priced sugars, which gives the competing grocer an advantage over the refiner of from one-third to one-half cent per pound, a difference always sufficient to determine that a given sample of sugar shall enter into consumption through the scales of the grocer, free from all taxation, rather than through the taxed processes of the refiner. Again, we hold that the rate of taxation, when measured by the increase of value placed upon the raw material, is in the case under consideration disproportionately great, as compared with any other great industrial interest in our country. In this case the increase of value thus placed on the raw material is found to be but about seven per cent. of the cost, whilst the tax is equal to nearly fifty per cent. of this increase in value.

Now, wool, cotton, iron, rags, hides, and all other raw materials which enter into the other various great industrial interests of the country, are not only wholly unfitted for the use of man and thus removed from the competition which the sugar-refiner must meet, but they also form, comparatively, a small proportion of the value of the articles manufactured therefrom.

The increased value placed upon these raw materials is so great, that the tax of three per cent. bears but a slight proportion to such increase; consequently is little felt. Were it proposed to tax these interests forty per cent. on the increased value placed upon their raw material, exorbitant as it might seem, they still would enjoy immunity from the competition of the raw material, which the sugar-refiner is subjected to.

† Since the above was written, the commission have learned that large shipments of refined sugar (including beet-root sugar) have been made or are about to be made from France to the United States. This is entirely a new enterprise, as regards the trade of the two countries, and under the present tariff was not supposed to be possible. The commission cannot reconcile the transaction with any object of present gain, unless there is a large bounty allowed by the imperial government, and as regards this they have no information.

Table showing the estimated distribution, throughout the world, of the production of sugars (both from the cane and from the beet-root,) for each of the six years, 1860 *to* 1865 *inclusive.*

	1860.	1861.	1862.	1863.	1864.	1865.
CANE-SUGARS.						
	Tons.	*Tons.*	*Tons.*	*Tons.*	*Tons.*	*Tons.*
Cuba	415,000	425,000	450,000	470,000	504,000	520,000
Porto Rico	50,000	65,000	67,000	70,000	50,000	60,000
Brazil	43,000	65,000	115,000	100,000	75,000	70,000
French colonies	117,000	122,000	111,000	120,000	75,000	90,000
Dutch West Indies	13,000	14,000	14,000	14,000	17,000	17,000
Danish West Indies	4,000	4,000	4,000	4,000	5,000	5,000
British West Indies	172,000	187,000	195,000	195,000	160,000	190,000
British East Indies	41,000	39,000	22,000	20,000	40,000	20,000
Mauritius	76,000	94,000	59,000	85,000	120,000	130,000
Java	99,000	110,000	99,000	85,000	130,000	120,000
Manilla, Siam, China	40,000	50,000	35,000	45,000	55,000	55,000
Total	1,070,000	1,175,000	1,171,000	1,208,000	1,231,000	1,277,000
Louisiana crop	114,000	117,400	235,900	53,000	28,000	3,500
Total	1,184,000	1,292,400	1,406,900	1,261,000	1,259,000	1,280,500
BEET-ROOT CROP.						
Germany	117,000	100,000	125,800	138,000	151,200	166,000
France*	125,000	100,000	146,400	193,700	108,500	146,100
Austria	45,000	50,000	54,400	76,200	58,400	84,600
Russia	40,000	40,000	48,500	30,300	34,200	42,500
Belgium	18,000	18,000	17,800	32,000	20,000	21,900
Poland and Sweden	10,000	10,000	10,000	10,000	10,900	11,500
Holland	1,500	1,500	1,500	1,900	2,500	2,500
Total	356,500	319,500	404,400	452,100	385,700	475,100
Grand total	1,540,500	1,611,900	1,811,300	1,713,100	1,644,700	1,755,500
Millions of pounds	3,451	3,611	4,057	3,838	3,684	3,932

* The yield of 1865 and 1866 in France is estimated at the unprecedented figure of 250,000 tons; and other countries, will probably also show an increase; which will tend to establish low prices in the cane-sugar producing countries.

Table showing the estimated distribution throughout the world of the consumption of sugars, for each of the five years, 1860 *to* 1864 *inclusive.*

	1860.	1861.	1862.	1863.	1864.
In Europe:	*Tons.*	*Tons.*	*Tons.*	*Tons.*	*Tons.*
Great Britain—Cane-sugars	441,100	476,200	486,200	497,300	479,300
France—Cane-sugars	178,000	204,300	213,200	237,500	213,200
Continent of Europe—Cane-sugar	194,200	212,600	239,500	230,100	190,700
Total cane-sugar	813,300	893,000	938,900	964,900	883,200
Beet-root crop	356,500	319,500	404,400	452,100	385,700
Total consumption of sugar in Europe	1,169,800	1,212,500	1,343,300	1,417,000	1,268,900
In the United States (cane-sugar)	415,300	363,800	432,411	284,300	220,000
Grand total, in tons	1,585,100	1,576,300	1,775,711	1,701,300	1,498,900
Grand total, millions of pounds	3,551	3,531	3,978	3,811	3,340

The following table compares the estimated production and consumption of sugars of all kinds, throughout the world, for each of the five calendar years, from 1860 to 1864, inclusive; and exhibiting the excess in each year (deficiency in 1860) of production over consumption.

	Production.	Consumption.	Excess of production over consumption.
1860	1,541,000 tons.	1,585,000 tons.	— 44,000 tons.
1861	1,612,000	1,576,000	+ 36,000
1862	1,811,000	1,776,000	+ 35,000
1863	1,713,000	1,701,000	+ 12,000
1864	1,645,000	1,491,000	+ 154,000
1865	1,756,000		
Average of the five years, 1860–'64	1,665,000 or 3,729 millions lbs.	1,626,000 or 3,642 millions lbs.	+ 39,600 or 87 millions lbs.

Of the extent to which sugars, molasses, &c., can be made available, as sources of revenue, under the present rates, and under the rates proposed by the commissioners for the fiscal year ending June 30, 1867, the commission present the following estimate:

CUSTOMS.

470 millions of pounds of sugar, (imported,) paying 3 cents per lb	$14,100,000
150 millions of pounds of sugar, (imported,) paying 3½ to 4 c. per lb	5,650,000
25 millions of gallons of molasses, paying 8 cents per gallon	2,000,000
Total receipts from customs	21,750,000

EXCISE.

50 millions of pounds domestic cane-sugars, 2 cents per lb	$1,000,000	
50 millions of pounds domestic cane-sugars, 2½ cents per lb	1,250,000	
10 millions of gallons of molasses, 6 cents per gallon	600,000	
Excise on sales of refined sugar, 3 per cent	1,800,000	
Total receipts from excise		4,650,000
Gross receipts, customs and excise		26,400,000

Rates proposed by the commission.

CUSTOM.

470 millions of pounds of sugar, (imported,) paying 3½ cents per lb.	$16,450,000
150 millions of pounds of sugar, (imported,) paying 4 to 4½ cents per lb	6,550,000
25 millions of gallons of molasses, paying 10 cents per gallon	2,500,000
Total receipts from customs	25,500,000

EXCISE.

50 millions of pounds of domestic cane-sugar, 2½ cents per lb	$1, 250, 000	
50 millions of pounds of domestic cane-sugar, 3 cents per lb	1, 500, 000	
10 millions of gallons of molasses, 8 cents per gallon	800, 000	
Total receipts from excise		3, 550, 000
Gross receipts, customs and excise		29, 050, 000

The above estimates of the immediate future consumption of cane-sugars in the United States have been prepared by the commission under the supervision of some of the best commercial authorities of the country, and are believed to be considerably less than what time and experience will demonstrate.* With continued prosperity on the part of the industrial interests of the country, we think an increment of at least ten per cent. on the above estimates for the fiscal years 1867 and 1868 may be reasonably anticipated, with necessarily a like proportional augmentation of the revenues. A reduction in the price of foreign sugar, consequent upon a decline in the price of gold, would also, in all probability, increase consumption to a degree even greater than that above indicated.

With the retention of the present rates of customs and excise upon sugars and molasses, the increase of revenue from this source for the fiscal year ending June 30, 1867, will, in the opinion of the commission, amount to $10,000,000, as compared with the receipts for the fiscal year 1863–'64, and nearly $3,000,000 as compared with the treasury estimates of receipts for the fiscal year 1864–'65.

With an advance in the rates as proposed by the commission, the increase of revenue may be estimated at $13,000,000, as compared with the treasury returns of the fiscal year 1863–'64, and of over $5,000,000 as compared with those of 1864–'65.

The commission fully indorse the conclusions heretofore arrived at by Congress, that it is not expedient to levy any excise upon maple-sugar, or upon the sirup or sugar produced from the sorghum or imphee, nor upon beet-root, which is likely at an early day to become, to an important extent, one of our products; and they would recommend that the present discrimination made between the duties on foreign sugars and the excise on domestic sugars be continued.

The commission would also call attention, in this connexion, to the method at present in use in the customs for estimating the duties on raw sugars of foreign production, as one demanding, at an early day, a careful consideration and revision on the part of the government. By the method referred to, raw sugars are now classified for the purpose of estimating the duty upon them according to color: sugars below a certain standard of color, known as No. 12 "Dutch standard," paying three cents per pound; while those of lighter colors, referred to a similar arbitrary standard, pay proportionately higher rates. This may, perhaps, be the easiest method of classification, but it certainly has no foundation in equity, inasmuch as color alone is not indicative of the true value of the article levied upon. There are certain shades of color and brilliancy of grain which give value to sugars by fitting them for direct consumption, and the trade of grocers; yet these sugars, while paying the higher duties, may contain less cane-sugar than others which grade below No. 12, and pay the lower duty. It

* By reference to the tables before given it will be seen that our estimate for 1866–'67 falls short of the consumption of cane-sugar in 1862 by over 240,000,000 pounds.

would seem obvious, "that the duty being made dependent on the color of sugar, yellow,' 'white,' or 'brown,' and left to the arbitration of a custom-house, officer, must necessarily lead to uncertainty, error, doubt, and contradiction. What is of one color in cloudy weather may be of another in sunshine; so that, besides that opening to fraud which such distinctions present, the importer can have no absolute certainty as to the rate which he will be charged." The simple process of drying may, alone, cause a difference of one or more grades in a sample of raw sugar.

By reference to the tables appended to this report (marked A,) submitted to the commission by one of the most experienced sugar refiners in the country, it will be seen that hogshead or muscovado sugars vary in value in cane-sugar from seventy-nine per cent. to eighty-six per cent., with molasses running from seventeen per cent. to eight per cent.; while the clayed Brazil, Manilla, and Cuba sugars range from eighty-three per cent. to ninety-two per cent., with proportionately less of moisture, molasses, and impurities. As a general rule the value of raw sugar (to the refiner) is proportionate to the amount of cane-sugar therein contained; while the color of sugar is of secondary importance to the refiner, as his agencies fully master all depths of color.

The attention of the government was given to this subject as early as 1843, and under the direction of the Treasury Department many crude experiments were made to determine the value of various sugars and molasses, furnished from the customs. The processes, however, reported were tedious and uncertain in result, and further effort in this direction was abandoned. In Europe, however, the demand for more exact methods for determining the value of sugars or sugar solutions, in the extensive beet-sugar works, has led to the application of *polarized light* as a saccharometer; and an instrument devised for this purpose (*Soleil's*) is now of universal use in European sugar refineries, and (we understand) in the French customs, to determine the exact value of sugar therein contained. This instrument is so simple and so admirably adapted to the end in view, that a *tyro* in chemical manipulation may, in a few minutes, measure to within one-half of one per cent. the amount of *cane* or crystallizable sugar and grape-sugar contained in any sample of sugar presented, and assess the duties accordingly.

The commission at present content themselves with merely calling attention to this subject, as one of importance; and should future opportunity be afforded them, they propose to give it more special attention.

At present the classification of sugars, under the customs and under the excise, are dissimilar. The commission would suggest the propriety of making the classification, in both departments of the revenue, to correspond.

Respectfully submitted to the commission.

DAVID A. WELLS, *Chairman*.

Hon. HUGH McCULLOCH,
Secretary of the Treasury.

APPENDIX A.—*Showing the varying value of different raw sugars.*

Examination: For sugar, by polarized light; for gum, by basic acetate of lead; for moisture, by evaporation; molasses being the remainder.

Commercial marks.	Water.	Gum-dirt.	Cane-sugar.	Molasses.	Remarks on color and condition.
	Per cent.	*Per cent.*	*Per cent.*	*Per cent.*	
Manilla, (clayed)	1. 80	1. 88	88. 00	8. 32	Dark brown, good quality.
Cuba, hhd., (La Josepha)	5. 72	1. 09	79. 00	14. 19	Brown, heavy, gummy.
Porto Rico, (La Vega)	3. 86	1. 05	78. 00	17. 09	Yellow, dry, acid.
Cuba, hhd., (average quality)	3. 94	1. 42	86. 00	8. 64	Yellow brown, dry, good grain.
Porto Rico	4. 84	1. 26	81. 00	12. 90	Brown, heavy, good grain.
Porto Rico	4. 96	1. 15	81. 00	12. 89	Light brown, seemed dry, good grain.
Porto Rico	5. 90	1. 21	82. 00	10. 89	Yellow brown, heavy, good grain.
Porto Rico	4. 74	1. 24	86. 00	8. 02	Yellow brown, free, good grain.
Brazil, (clayed)	1. 90	1. 43	83. 00	13. 67	Yellow brown, lumpy, fine grain, dry.
Havana, box, (clayed)	1. 48	. 85	87. 00	10. 67	Light yellow, stopped filter.
Havana, box, (clayed)	1. 24	1. 52	83. 00	14. 24	Light brown, filtered, free.
Havana, box, (clayed)	1. 34	1. 76	82. 00	14. 90	Brown, lumpy, dirty.
Havana, box, (clayed)	. 47	. 88	92. 00	6. 65	Low white.
Cuba, hhd., (Constance)	4. 64	1. 31	83. 00	11. 05	Yellow brown, fine grain.
Porto Rico, (Incarnation)	5. 88	1. 43	84. 00	8. 69	Brown, heavy, good grain, free.
Manilla, (Muscovado)			72. 00		Dark red brown, heavy, free.
Java, brown } English samples.			87. 00		Brown, fine powdery grain.
Java, good.. } English samples.			92. 00		Yellow brown.
Batavia, No. 14, Dutch standard			93. 00		Yellow, good hard grain, very free.
Batavia, No. 20, Dutch standard			96. 00		White, good grain, very free.
Batavia, No. 6, Dutch standard			89. 00		Dark brown, black lumps, sticky.
Bengal, brown			80. 00		Dark brown, gummy, heavy, free.
Bengal, yellow			91. 00		Yellow, fine grain, stopped three filters.
Bengal, good to fine			94. 00		Gray white, fine feathery grain.
Madras, brown			82. 00		Red brown, black lumps, heavy, sticky.
Madras, yellow			93. 00		Gray yellow, good grain, dry and clean.
Madras, fine			98. 00		Yellow white, fine grain, clean, free.
Mauritius, brown			86. 00		Yellow brown, fine grain, clean.
Mauritius, fine			95. 00		Light yellow, fine grain, clean.
Mauritius, yellow			92. 00		Yellow, fine grain, clean.

A BILL for an act relative to the excise on domestic sugar and molasses.

Be it enacted by the Senate and House of Representatives of the United States of America in Congress assembled, That, in lieu of the duties imposed on sugars and molasses, by the provisions of section ninety-four of the act entitled "An act to provide internal revenue to support the government, to pay interest on the public debt, and for other purposes," approved June 30, 1864, as amended March 3, 1865, there shall be levied, collected, and paid, on and after the first day of July, A. D. 1866, on all sugars and molasses produced or manufactured within the United States or its territories, (other than such as are produced by the refiner,) and sold or removed for consumption or sale, an excise tax, corresponding to the following rates; that is to say:

On all sugar not above number twelve, Dutch standard in color, produced from the sugar-cane and not from sorghum or imphee, two and one-half cents per pound.

On all sugar above number twelve and not above number fifteen, Dutch standard in color, produced directly from the sugar-cane and not from sorghum or imphee, three cents per pound.

On all sugar above number fifteen and not above number twenty, Dutch standard in color, produced directly from the sugar-cane and not from sorghum or imphee, three and one-half cents per pound.

On all sugars above number twenty, Dutch standard in color, produced directly from the sugar-cane, and not from sorghum or imphee, four cents per pound.

Provided, That the standard by which the color and grades of sugar are to be regulated shall be furnished to the collectors of internal revenue of such district as may be necessary, by the Secretary of the Treasury from time to time, and in such manner as he may deem expedient: *Provided further,* That all other provisions of law applicable to the manufacture and sale of sugars mentioned in said section ninety-four shall be applicable hereto.

On molasses produced from the sugar-cane, and not from sorghum or imphee, eight cents per gallon.

On sirup of molasses or sugar-cane juice when removed from the plantation, concentrated molasses or melado, and cistern bottoms of sugar produced from the sugar-cane, and not made from sorghum or imphee, two cents per pound.

SECTION —. *And be it further enacted,* That the provision in said section ninety-fonr, in relation to duty on sales of sugar refiners, and the proviso thereto, in the words following, to wit: "On the gross amount of the sales of sugar refiners, including all the products of their manufactories or refineries, a duty of two and a half of one per centum *ad valorem: Provided,* That every person shall be regarded as a sugar refiner, and pay the duties levied by law, whose business it is to advance the quality and value of sugar upon which a duty has been assessed and paid, by melting or recrystallization, or by liquoring, claying, or other washing process, or by any other chemical or mechanical means, or who shall advance the quality or value of molasses, concentrated molasses or melado, upon which a duty has been assessed and paid, by boiling or other process," is hereby repealed.

A BILL for an act relative to duties on imported sugar and molasses.

Be it enacted by the Senate and House of Representatives of the United States of America in Congress assembled, That in lieu of the duties imposed on imported sugars and molasses, by the provisions of the act entitled "An act to increase duties on imports and for other purposes," approved June 30, 1864, there shall be levied, collected, and paid, on and after the first day of July, A. D. 1866, on all sugars and molasses of the descriptions herein mentioned, when imported from foreign countries, the following duties and rates of duty; that is to say:

On all sugar not above number twelve Dutch, standard in color, *three and one-half* cents per pound.

On all sugar above number twelve and not above number fifteen, Dutch standard in color, *four* cents per pound.

On all sugar above number fifteen, not stove-dried, and not above number twenty, Dutch standard in color, *four and one-half* cents per pound.

On all refined sugar in the form of loaf, lump, crushed, powdered, pulverized, or granulated, and all stove-dried or other sugar above number twenty, Dutch standard, in color, *five and one-half* cents per pound: *Provided,* That the standard by which the color and grades of sugar are to be regulated be selected and furnished to the collectors of such ports of entry as may be necessary, by the Secretary of the Treasury, from time to time, and in such manner as he may deem expedient.

On molasses from sugar-cane, *ten* cents per gallon.

On sirup of sugar-cane juice, melado, concentrated melado, or concentrated molasses, *three* cents per pound: *Provided,* That all sirup of sugar or sugar-cane or sugar-cane juice, concentrated molasses, or concentrated melado, entered under the name of molasses, or any other name than sirup of sugar, or of sugar-cane, cane-juice, concentrated molasses, or concentrated melado, shall be liable to forfeiture to the United States, ——— and the same shall be forfeited.

A BILL for an act to reduce into one act and to amend the excise laws relating to the brewing, manufacturing, and dealing in fermented liquors, and to prevent frauds in respect to the same.

Be it enacted by the Senate and House of Representatives of the United States of America in Congress assembled, That every person, firm, or corporation, who manufactures fermented liquors of any name or description for sale from malt, wholly or in part, or from any substitute therefor, shall be deemed a brewer under this act.

SECTION 2. *And be it further enacted,* That every brewer shall file with the assessor of the assessment district, in which he shall design to carry on his business, an application in writing for a license, stating therein the name of the person, company, corporation, or firm, and the names of the members of any company or firm making such application, together with the place or places of residence of such person or persons, and a description of the premises on which the brewery is situated, and of his or their title thereto, and the name or names of the owner or owners thereof; and also the whole quantity of malt liquors annually made and sold at the brewery for which the license is sought for two years last preceding the date of such application.

SECTION 3. *And be it further enacted,* That every brewer shall obtain a license for each brewery carried on by him, and shall pay therefor one hundred dollars, and shall execute a bond to the United States, to be approved by the collector of the district, in a sum equal to twice the amount of duty which, in the opinion of the assessor, said brewer will be liable to pay during any one month, which bond shall be renewed on the first day of May in each year, and shall be conditioned that he will pay or cause to be paid, as herein provided, the excise tax required by law on all beer, lager-beer, ale, porter, and other fermented liquors aforesaid made by him, or for him, on the premises mentioned in such license, before the same is sold or removed for consumption or sale, except as hereinafter provided; and that he will keep, or cause to be kept, a book in the manner and for the purposes hereinafter specified, and which shall be opened to inspection by the proper officers as by law required, and that he will in all respects faithfully comply, without fraud or evasion, with all requirements of law relating to the manufacture and sale of any malt liquors before mentioned: *Provided,* That no brewer shall be required to obtain a license as a wholesale dealer by reason of selling at wholesale, at a place other than his brewery, malt liquors manufactured by him.

SECTION 4. *And be it further enacted,* That there shall be paid on all beer, lager-beer, ale, porter, and other similar fermented liquors, by whatever name such liquors may be called, an excise tax of one dollar for each and every barrel containing not more than thirty-one gallons; and at a like rate for any other quantity or fractional part of a barrel which shall be brewed or manufactured and sold, or removed for consumption or sale, within the United States or the Territories thereof, or within the District of Columbia; which duty shall be paid by the owner, agent, or superintendent of the brewery or premises in which such fermented liquors shall be made, in the manner and at the time hereinafter specified: *Provided,* That fractional parts of a barrel shall be halves, quarters, sixths, and eighths, and any fractional part of a barrel containing less than one-eighth shall be accounted one-eighth; more than one-eighth, and not more than one-sixth, shall be accounted one-sixth; more than one-sixth, and not more than one-quarter, shall be accounted one-quarter; more than one-quarter, and not more than one-half, shall be accounted one-half; more than one-half, and not more than one barrel, shall be accounted one barrel; and more than one barrel, and not more than sixty-three gallons, shall be accounted two barrels, or a hogshead.

SECTION 5. *And be it further enacted,* That every person owning or occupying any brewery or premises used, or intended to be used, for the purpose of brewing or making such fermented liquors, or who shall have such premises under his control or superintendence as agent for the owner or occupant, or shall have in his possession or custody any brewing materials, utensils, or apparatus, used or intended to be used on said premises in the manufacture of beer, lager-beer, ale, porter, or other similar fermented liquors, either as owner, agent, or otherwise, shall, from day to day, enter or cause to be entered, in a book to be kept by him for that purpose, the kind of such fermented liquors, the description of packages, and number of barrels and fractional parts of barrels of fermented liquors made, and also the quantity sold, or removed for consumption or sale, to whom sold and when delivered, keeping separate account of the several kinds and descriptions; and shall render to said assessor or assistant assessor, on the first day of each month, or within ten days thereafter, a true statement in writing, taken from his books, of the whole quantity or number of barrels and fractional parts of barrels of fermented liquors brewed and sold, or removed for consumption or sale, for one month last preceding said first day of the month; and shall verify, or cause to be verified, the said statement, and the facts therein set forth, by oath or affirmation, to be taken before the assessor or assistant assessor of the district, according to the form required by law; and shall immediately forward to the collector of the district a duplicate of said statement, duly certified by the assessor or assistant assessor. And said books shall be open at all times (Sundays excepted) between the rising and setting of the sun, for the inspection of any assessor, assistant assessor, collector, deputy collector, inspector, or revenue agent, who may take memorandums and transcripts therefrom.

SECTION 6. *And be it further enacted,* That the entries made in such books shall, on the first day of each month, or within ten days thereafter, be verified by the oath or affirmation of the person or persons by whom such entries shall have been made, which oath or affirmation shall be written in the book at the end of such entries, and be certified by the officer administering the same, and shall be in form as follows: "I do swear (or affirm) that the foregoing entries were made by me, and that they state truly, according to the best of my knowledge and belief, the whole quantity of fermented liquors either brewed, or brewed and sold, or removed from the brewery owned by   , in the county of   , amounting to   barrels. And further, that I have no knowledge of any matter or thing, required by law to be stated in said entries, which has been omitted therefrom." And the owner, agent, or superintendent aforesaid shall also, in case the original entries made in his books shall not have been made by himself, subjoin thereto the following oath or affirmation, to be taken in manner as aforesaid: "I do swear (or affirm) that, to the best of my knowledge and belief, the foregoing entries fully set forth all the matters therein required by law, and that the same are just and true, and that I have taken all the means in my power to make them so."

SECTION 7. *And be it further enacted,* That the owner, agent, or superintendent of any brewery, vessels, or utensils used in making fermented liquors on which an excise tax is payable by affixing stamps in manner required by law, who shall evade or attempt to evade the payment thereof, or fraudulently neglect or refuse to make true and exact entry and report of the same in the manner herein required, or to do or cause to be done any of the things by law required to be done by him as aforesaid, or who shall intentionally make false entry in said book or in said statement, or knowingly allow or procure the same to be done, shall forfeit, for every such offence, all the liquors made by him or for him, and all the vessels, utensils, and apparatus used in making the same, and be liable to a penalty of not less than five hundred nor more than one thousand dollars, to be recovered with costs of suit, and shall be deemed guilty of a misdemeanor, and shall be imprisoned for a term not exceeding one year; and said liquors, utensils, and apparatus may be seized and held by any collector or deputy collector until a decision shall be had thereon according to law: *Provided,* That proceedings to enforce said forfeiture shall be commenced by such collector within twenty days after the seizure thereof. And such proceedings shall be in the nature of a proceeding *in rem,* or in any proper form of action, in the circuit or district court of the United States for the district where such seizure is made, or in any other court of competent jurisdiction. And every person licensed as a brewer, who shall neglect or refuse to furnish the account and duplicate thereof as hereinbefore provided, or who shall refuse to permit the proper officer to examine the books in the manner provided when requested, shall, for every such refusal or neglect, forfeit and pay the sum of three hundred dollars.

SECTION 8. *And be it further enacted,* That the Commissioner of Internal Revenue shall cause to be prepared, for the payment of duty aforesaid, suitable stamps denoting the amount of duty herein required to be paid on the hogshead, barrels, and halves, quarters, sixths, and eighths of a barrel of such fermented liquors, and shall furnish the same to the collectors of internal revenue, who shall each be required to keep on hand, at all times, a supply equal in amount to two months' sales thereof, if there shall be any brewery in his district, and the same shall be sold by such collectors to the brewers of their districts, respectively; and such collectors shall keep an account of the number of values of the stamps sold by them to each of such brewers, respectively, and upon all sales of such stamps in sums of two hundred dollars or more. To one person, at one time, an allowance or deduction of seven and one-half per centum shall be made to the purchaser if he is a licensed brewer.

SECTION 9. *And be it further enacted,* That every brewer shall obtain, from the collector of the district in which his brewery or place of manufacture may be situated, and not otherwise, unless said collector shall fail to furnish the same upon application to him, the proper stamp or stamps; and shall affix upon the spigot-hole or tap (of which there shall be but one) of each and every hogshead, barrel, keg, or other receptacle, in which any fermented liquor shall be contained, when sold or removed from such brewery or place of manufacture, a stamp, denoting the amount of the duty herein required upon such fermented liquor, in such a way that the said stamp or stamps will be destroyed upon the withdrawal of the liquor from such hogshead, barrel, keg, or other receptacle, or upon the introduction of a faucet or other instrument for that purpose; and shall also, at the time of affixing such stamp or stamps as aforesaid, cancel the same by writing or imprinting thereon the name of the person, firm, or corporation by whom such liquor may have been made, or the initial letters thereof, and the date when cancelled. Every brewer, who shall refuse or neglect to affix and cancel the stamp or stamps herein required in the manner aforesaid, or who shall affix a false or fraudulent stamp thereto, or knowingly permit the same to be done, shall be liable to pay a penalty of one hundred dollars for each barrel or package on which such omission or fraud occurs, and shall be liable to imprisonment for not more than one year.

SECTION 10. *And be it further enacted,* That any brewer, carman, agent for transportation, or other person, who shall sell, remove, receive, or purchase, or in any way aid in the sale, removal, receipt, or purchase of any fermented liquor contained in any hogshead, barrel, keg, or other receptacle from any brewery, upon which the stamp herein required shall not have been affixed, or on which a false or fraudulent stamp is affixed, with knowledge that it is such, or on which a stamp once cancelled is used a second time; and any retail dealer or other person, who shall withdraw or aid in the withdrawal of any fermented liquor from any hogshead, barrel, keg, or other receptacle containing the same without destroying or defacing the stamp affixed upon the same, or shall withdraw or aid in the withdrawal of any fermented liquor from any hogshead, barrel, keg, or other receptacle, upon which the proper stamp shall not have been affixed, or on which a false or fraudulent stamp is affixed, as hereinbefore required, shall be liable to a fine of one hundred dollars, and to imprisonment not more than one year. Every person who shall make, sell, or use any false or counterfeit stamp or die for printing or making stamps which shall be in imitation of, or purport to be a lawful stamp or die of, the kind before mentioned, or who shall procure the same to be done, shall be guilty of a felony, and be imprisoned for the term of five years: *Provided*, That every brewer, who sells fermented liquor at retail at the brewery or other place where the same is made, shall affix and cancel the proper stamp or stamps upon the hogsheads, barrels, kegs, or other receptacles in which the same is contained, and shall keep an account of the quantity so sold by him, and of the number and size of the hogsheads, barrels, kegs, or other receptacles in which the same may have been contained, and shall make a report thereof, verified by oath, monthly to the assessor, and forward a duplicate of same to the collector of the district: *And provided further*, That brewers may remove malt liquors of their own manufacture from their breweries or other places of manufacture to a warehouse or other place of storage occupied by them within the same district in quantities of not less than six barrels in one receptacle without affixing the stamp or stamps herein required, but shall affix the proper stamp or stamps, as aforesaid, upon such liquor when sold or removed from such warehouse or other place of storage: *And provided further*, That, where fermented liquor has become sour or damaged, so as to be incapable of use as such, brewers may sell the same for manufacturing purposes, and may remove the same to places where it may be used for such purposes, in receptacles unlike those ordinarily used for fermented liquors, containing, respectively, not less than one barrel each, and having the nature of their contents branded upon them, respectively, without affixing thereon the stamp or stamps herein required.

SECTION 11. *And be it further enacted*, That every brewer shall brand, or cause to be branded, upon every hogshead, barrel, keg, or other receptacle containing the fermented liquor made by him, before it is sold or removed from the brewery or other place of manufacture, the name of the person, firm, or corporation by whom such liquor was manufactured and the place where the same shall have been made; and any person other than the owner thereof or his agent, who shall intentionally remove or deface such brand therefrom, shall be liable to a penalty of fifty dollars for each cask from which the brand is so removed or defaced.

SECTION 12. *And be it further enacted*, That every person, other than the purchaser or owner of any fermented liquor, or person acting on his behalf, or as his agent, who shall intentionally remove or deface the stamp affixed as herein required, upon the hogshead, barrel, keg, or other receptacle in which the same may be contained, shall be liable to a fine of fifty dollars for each cask from which the stamp is so removed or defaced, and to render compensation to such purchaser or owner for all damage or damages sustained by him therefrom.

SECTION 13. *And be it further enacted*, That the ownership or possession by any person of any fermented liquor after its sale or removal from the brewery, or other place where it was made, upon which the duty herein required shall not have been paid, shall render the same liable to seizure wherever found, and to forfeiture; and that the want of the proper stamp or stamps upon any hogshead, barrel, keg, or other receptacle in which fermented liquor may be contained after its sale or removal from the brewery or other place where the same was made, as aforesaid, shall be notice to all persons that the duty has not been paid thereon, and shall be *prima facie* evidence of the non-payment thereof.

SECTION 14. *And be it further enacted*, That every person who shall withdraw any fermented liquor from any hogshead, barrel, keg, or other receptacle upon which the proper stamp or stamps shall not have been affixed as herein required, for the purpose of bottling the same, or who shall carry on, or attempt to carry on, the business of bottling fermented liquor in any brewery or other place in which fermented liquor is made, or upon any premises having communication with such brewery or such other place, shall be liable to a fine of five hundred dollars, and the property used in such bottling or business shall be liable to forfeiture.

SECTION 15. *And be it further enacted,* That all suits or actions for fines, penalties, and forfeitures imposed upon, or which may be incurred by, any person or persons under the provisions of this act, may be commenced and prosecuted to judgment in any court of the United States having jurisdiction in the district where such fines, penalties, and forfeitures were incurred; and all offences of any kind under this act may in like manner be prosecuted, tried, and conviction had in such court. And all fines and forfeitures imposed or incurred by virtue of this act shall be sued for and recovered as herein provided, and one moiety thereof shall be for the use of the United States, and the other moiety thereof to the use of the person who shall first inform of the cause, matter, or thing whereby any such fine, penalty, or forfeiture was incurred. The Commissioner of Internal Revenue, subject to the approval of the Secretary of the Treasury, shall make, from time to time, all rules and regulations necessary to carry this act into effect.

SECTION 16. *And be it further enacted,* That all acts and parts of acts inconsistent with the provisions of this act are hereby repealed: *Provided,* That nothing herein contained shall be construed to apply to any liability incurred or obligation created, or duty accrued, or offence committed prior to the time when this act shall take effect, but the same shall be subject to the laws in force previous thereto, the same as if this act had not been passed.

SECTION 17. *And be it further enacted,* That this act shall be in force on and after the day of , A. D. 1866.

A BILL for an act amendatory of the laws relative to tax on legacies, distributive shares, and successions.

Be it enacted by the Senate and House of Representatives of the United States of America in Congress assembled, That an act entitled "An act to provide internal revenue to support the government, to pay interest on the public debt, and for other purposes," approved June 30, 1864, as amended by the act of March 3, 1865, is hereby amended as follows, to wit:

Section one hundred and twenty-four (124) of said act is amended by striking out the words "after the passage of this act," immediately after the word "passing," in the sixth line of said section. Also by inserting immediately after the words "duty or tax" in the thirteenth line of said section, the words following, to wit: "Whenever the party interested in such legacy, or distributive share, or property, or interest aforesaid, shall become entitled to the possession or enjoyment thereof, or to the beneficial interest in the profits accruing therefrom, such duty or tax."

Section one hundred and twenty-five (125) of same act is amended by inserting, immediately after the words "United States," in the fifth line of said section, the words following, to wit: "And every administrator, executor, or trustee, having in charge or trust any legacy or distributive share, as hereinbefore recited, shall give notice thereof in writing to the assessor or assistant assessor of the district where the deceased grantor or bargainer last resided, within thirty days after he shall have taken charge of such trust; and for refusal or neglect so to do, shall be liable to a penalty of five hundred dollars, to be recovered with costs of suit."

The proviso to section one hundred and thirty-three of same act is amended by inserting the words "husband or" immediately after the word "the" and before the word "wife" in the last line thereof.

Section one hundred and thirty-seven (137) of same act is amended by inserting the words following, to wit: "Shall be assessed in the collection district where the predecessor last resided, and" immediately after the word "act" and before the word "shall" in the second line thereof. Also, by adding at the close of said section 137 the following clause, to wit: "All duties imposed by this act upon successions, and all duties or taxes which are declared by this act to be liens of the real estate shall be deemed and held to be of record, when returne by the assessor on the lists furnished by him to the collector of the district, and a certificate under the hand and official seal of the collector or other officer with whom such lists may be properly filed, setting forth the fact that such recorh appears, shall be good and sufficient proof of such record for all legal purposes."

Section one hundred and thirty-eight (138) of said act is amended by adding thereto the following, to wit: "And every administrator, executor, or trustee, having in charge or trust any disposition of real estate or interest therein, subject to duty under this act, shall give notice thereof in writing to the assessor or assistant assessor of the district where the predecessor of the trust last resided, within thirty days from the time when he shall have taken charge of such trust, and prior to any distribution of said real estate, and for refusal or neglect so to do shall be liable to a penalty of five hundred dollars, to be recovered with costs of suit."

Section one hundred and forty-five (145) of same act is amended by inserting immediately after the word "years," in the fourth line, the words following, to wit: "from the time when such duty or tax became due and payable."

Respectfully submitted for the commission:

DAVID A. WELLS, *Chairman.*

A BILL for an act to regulate the tax on brokers' sales.

Be it enacted by the Senate and House of Representatives of the United States of America in Congress assembled, That in lieu of the duties heretofore imposed by law upon the sales hereinafter mentioned, there shall be paid on sales made by brokers, and bankers doing business as brokers, whether made for the benefit of others or on their own account, an excise tax in accordance with the following rates—that is to say:

On all sales and contracts for sales of stocks and bonds, at the rate of one cent for every hundred dollars of the par value thereof.

On all sales and contracts for the sale of foreign exchange, uncurrent money, promissory notes, or other securities not before mentioned, at the rate of one cent for every hundred dollars of the amount of such sales or contracts.

On all sales and contracts for the sale of gold and silver bullion and coin, at the rate of one cent for every hundred dollars of the amount of such sales or contracts: *Provided,* That on all sales and contracts for sale negotiated and made by any person, firm, or company not licensed as a broker or banker, of any gold or silver bullion, coin, foreign exchange, uncurrent money, promissory notes, stocks, bonds, or other securities, not *bona fide* at the time his or their own property, and actually on hand, in addition to all penalties provided in such cases, there shall be paid an excise tax at the rate of five cents for every hundred dollars of the amount of such sales or contracts.

SECTION 2. *And be it further enacted,* That on every sale and contract of sale mentioned in the foregoing section there shall be made and delivered by the seller to the buyer a bill or memorandum of such sale or contract, on which there shall be affixed and cancelled by the seller a lawful stamp or stamps in value equal to the amount of tax on such sale, to be determined by the rates of duty before mentioned: *Provided,* That in computing the amount of the stamp duty or tax in any case herein provided for, any sum less than one hundred dollars, or any fractional part of one hundred dollars of value or amount on which tax is computed, shall be accounted as one hundred dollars.

SECTION 3. *And be it further enacted,* That every bill or memorandum of sale or contract of sale, before mentioned, shall show the date thereof, the names of the parties thereto, the amount of the sale or contract, and the matter or thing to which it refers. And any person or persons liable to pay any tax as herein provided, or any one who acts in the matter as agent or broker for such person or persons, who shall make any such sale or contract, or who shall, in pursuance of any sale or contract, deliver any stocks, bonds, bullion, coin, uncurrent money, foreign exchange, promissory notes, or other securities, and shall not deliver a bill or memorandum thereof as herein required, or who shall deliver such bill or memorandum without having the proper stamps affixed thereto, shall forfeit and pay to the United States a penalty of five hundred dollars for each and every offence where the tax so evaded, or attempted to be evaded, does not exceed one hundred dollars, and a penalty of one thousand dollars when such tax shall exceed one hundred dollars, which may be recovered with costs of suit in any court of the United States of competent jurisdiction in the district, at any time within one year after the liability to such forfeiture shall have been incurred; and one-half of the forfeiture recovered shall be awarded by the court to the person or persons who, in the judgment of the court, shall have first given the information of the violation of the law for which recovery is had.

SECTION 4. *And be it further enacted,* That the Secretary of the Treasury shall prescribe the form and style of the several kinds of stamps necessary to carry into effect the foregoing provisions of this act, and the Commissioner of Internal Revenue shall provide the same for sale in the manner he may deem proper. And any person who shall make, or knowingly sell or use, or attempt to use, in payment of the tax herein imposed, any false, fraudulent, or counterfeit stamp in imitation of, or purporting to be a lawful stamp of the kinds herein provided for, or who shall knowingly cause, or aid, or procure the same to be done, or who shall make, or cause to be made, any false or counterfeit stamp or die, or any part thereof, whereby an impression can be made on vellum, parchment, paper, or other material, in imitation of, and intended to be sold or used as lawful stamps aforesaid, or who shall make or use any fraudulent device whatever whereby the stamp duty herein provided for, or any part thereof, shall be evaded, shall be guilty of a felony, and on conviction shall be imprisoned not less than two nor more than five years.

SECTION 5. *And be it further enacted,* That all acts and parts of acts inconsistent with the provisions of this act are hereby repealed.

SECTION 6. *And be it further enacted,* That this act shall take effect on the day of A. D. 1866.

Respectfully submitted for the commission:

DAVID A. WELLS, *Chairman.*

FORM OF AN ACT respecting the appointment of supervisors of the revenue.

Be it enacted by the Senate and House of Representatives of the United States of America in Congress assembled, That the Secretary of the Treasury shall appoint, in each State and Territory of the United States, respectively, and in the District of Columbia, at least one and not more than four officers, who shall be styled supervisors of the revenue, whose duty it shall be to see that all laws and regulations of the United States relating to the collection of internal revenue are faithfully executed and complied with, and to aid in the prevention, detection, and punishment of frauds on the revenue; and they shall have general powers to review and examine all the official acts of any officer of internal revenue in the respective collection districts, and the manner in which they severally perform their duties, and the manner in which all persons comply with the requirements of said laws. And for such purposes, said supervisors shall have power to examine all persons, books, papers, accounts, and premises, and to administer oaths, and to summon any person to produce books and papers, or to appear and testify under oath before them, and to compel a compliance with such summons, in the same manner as assessors by law may do in like cases; and they shall have the same powers, as collectors of internal revenue have, to make seizures of property or premises, and to institute suits and proceedings for the recovery of fines, forfeitures, and penalties, and for the punishment of offences.

SECTION 2. *And be it further enacted*, That it shall be the duty of every such supervisor to report, in writing, to the Secretary of the Treasury, any neglect of duty, incompetency, delinquency, or malfeasance in office of any officer of any collection district of which he may obtain knowledge, and the evidence showing the same; and he may also transfer any inspector from one distillery to another, or any inspector, weigher, or gauger, from one district to another; and may, by a notice in writing, suspend from duty any inspector, weigher or gauger, in any district within his jurisdiction; and shall in such cases immediately notify the collector of the district and the Commissioner of Internal Revenue, and, within three days thereafter, make report of his action, and his reasons therefor, in writing, to the Secretary of the Treasury; who shall thereupon take such further action in relation thereto as he may deem proper. The Commissioner of Internal Revenue, in his discretion, may temporarily assign any supervisor to special service or general duty in any other district or State, and such supervisor shall have the same authority to act therein as in the district to which he was originally appointed.

Supervisors of revenue shall perform such other duties, and be subject to such rules and regulations as the Secretary of the Treasury shall from time to time prescribe; and shall each receive for services, exclusive of expenses and disbursements, a salary not exceeding three thousand dollars per annum, as the Secretary of the Treasury may direct.

SECTION 3. *And be it further enacted*, That this act shall take effect immediately.

Respectfully submitted for the commission:

DAVID A. WELLS, *Chairman.*

A BILL for an act to facilitate the enforcement of the internal revenue laws, and the collection of the revenue.

Be it enacted by the Senate and House of Representatives of the United States of America in Congress assembled, That United States commissioners heretofore appointed by any circuit court of the United States, or who may hereafter be appointed in the manner provided by law, having judicial powers, are hereby authorized and empowered to hold commissioners' courts, which may hear, try, and determine any suit, action, and proceedings, instituted and prosecuted by or on behalf of the United States, and arising under any of the internal revenue laws thereof, for the recovery of any duty, tax, debt, penalty, fine, or for any forfeiture. And for such purposes said commissioners are hereby vested with original jurisdiction in such cases, in the respective districts for which they are appointed, and shall have the same power and authority to hear, try, and determine the same, and to render judgment therein, as is now vested in any of the district courts of the United States; and are authorized to issue any original process and orders necessary in such cases, and are empowered to enforce and compel the execution and observance of the same, and in such suits, actions, and proceedings, may adopt the forms and rules of practice established in the district or circuit courts of the United States, so far as the same may be applicable, and not inconsistent with the provisions of this act, and may make such other rules and regulations governing proceedings before them as may be requisite to carry into effect the practice of such commissioners' courts.

SECTION 2. *And be it further enacted,* That such commissioners are authorized and empowered to hear and determine any such action or proceeding of which they have cognizance, and to render judgment therein without a jury, in cases wherein trial by jury shall be waived. In cases wherein the defendant claims the right of trial by jury he shall do so by a notice in writing filed with such commissioner, at least three days before the time of trial, and in default thereof a trial by jury in such case shall be deemed to have been waived by said defendant. And said commissioners shall have authority to summon and impanel any jury for the trial of actions in such courts, in the same manner in the several States respectively, as provided by law for the courts thereof; but it shall not be necessary to summon a new panel of jurors for each case. And any party to the proceedings shall have the right of appeal from any judgment of such commissioners' court to the circuit court of the United States, in all cases where the claim of the plaintiff, or the judgment against the defendant, is for the recovery of money or property, exceeding in amount one hundred dollars. And if such appeal is by the defendant he shall execute a bond with one or more sureties, to be approved by such commissioner as sufficient security for such judgment and costs of appeal. And upon the approval of said bond all proceedings for the enforcement of said judgment shall be stayed during the time the appeal is pending. And such appeal may be heard in the circuit court at any time after the lapse of twenty days from the time of appeal.

SECTION 3. *And be it further enacted,* That all proceedings and judgments of said commissioner shall be entered in a book kept by him; and any appeal shall be perfected by filing notice thereof and the bond aforesaid, with said commissioner, within five days after the rendition of the judgment appealed from; whereupon said commissioner shall, within ten days thereafter, file the bond aforesaid and a certified copy of the judgment and all proceedings and testimony in the case, with the clerk of the circuit court; and the same proceedings shall thereupon be had as on appeals from district courts. In all cases of rendition of a judgment for the recovery of money, a transcript thereof shall immediately be forwarded by the commissioner to the clerk of the district court of the district, who shall enter the same in a docket to be kept for that purpose; and thereupon such judgment shall be deemed to be of record, and become a lien on the property of the defendant the same as if the judgment had been originally entered in said district court, but the filing of such transcript shall not remove such judgment from the jurisdiction of the commissioner, who shall retain jurisdiction for all purposes of enforcing collection thereof, until the same shall be satisfied.

SECTION 4. *And be it further enacted,* That said commissioners may convene such courts at any time, either at stated periods or otherwise, as they may deem necessary; but a defendant shall not be required to answer in any action for the recovery of money or property within less than six days from the time of service of process on him; except that in cases where he may be liable to arrest, he may be brought before the court on summary process, and be required to give bail to appear and answer therein at such time as the court may require, but not less than six days thereafter. Proceedings shall be instituted in such courts upon complaint made by the prosecuting attorney, or other duly authorized officer. No formal pleadings shall be necessary in such actions; but on the part of the plaintiff, a process or summons shall be served on the defendant, by leaving with him, or at his place of business or residence, a copy of the same, which shall specify the time and place at which he is to answer, the nature of the complaint, the particular section or sections of the law under which the proceedings are instituted, and the section or sections of the law which it is claimed have been violated, and the amount of judgment claimed. On the part of the defendant, the answer may be a general denial, or admission of the whole or any part of the plaintiff's allegations and claims, and a denial as to the remainder thereof.

SECTION 5. *And be it further enacted,* That a default in appearance on the part of the defendant shall be a waiver of jury trial, and of a right to appeal, but shall not be taken as an admission of the claim; which shall be proven, or expressly admitted, in all cases, to entitle plaintiff to a recovery. But in case of judgment by default, the commissioner before whom the proceedings were had may, within twenty days thereafter, hear an application, made upon notice to plaintiff, for leave to appear and answer; and if the default is, in his opinion, properly excused, he may order a new trial in such case; and pending the same the first judgment shall stand as security. And said commissioners are hereby vested with all the powers of a district court of the United States, to enforce any judgment or other determination before them; and the United States marshals are authorized and directed to serve orders and execute process issued from said courts, in the same manner as in district courts, and shall be entitled to the same fees therefor; and the fees of jurors and witnesses shall be the same, and be paid in the same manner, as in district courts of the United States. And said commissioners, in addition to fees now allowed them for services, shall be entitled to demand and receive the same fees as are allowed to clerks of the district or circuit courts of the United States, for like or similar services, and to such further allowance for office expenses and clerk-hire as the Secretary of the Treasury may in his discretion direct. No suit before said commissioners shall be compromised, or discontinued, except on application of the prosecuting attorney, with the consent of the Commissioner of Internal Revenue, or the Secretary of the Treasury.

SECTION 6. *And be it further enacted,* That this act shall take effect immediately.

Respectfully submitted for the commission:

DAVID A. WELLS, *Chairman.*

A BILL for an act to reduce into one act and to amend the excise laws relating to distilling, rectifying, manufacturing, and dealing in spirituous liquors, and to prevent frauds in respect to the same.

Be it enacted by the Senate and House of Representatives of the United States of America in Congress assembled, That distillers and rectifiers shall obtain, and have in force, a license, from the proper officer authorized to grant the same, according to law: *Provided,* That no license shall be required for any druggist or chemist who uses any still, or stills, or other apparatus for the recovery of alcohol, which has been used for pharmaceutical, chemical, or scientific purposes.

SECTION 2. *And be it further enacted,* That every person, firm, or corporation, who distils or manufactures spirits, or who brews or makes mash, wort, or wash, for distillation or the production of spirits, shall be deemed a distiller, under this act. And the making or keeping by any person, of grain, mash, wash, or beer, prepared or fit for distillation, together with the possession by such person of a still or other apparatus capable of use for distilling, upon the same premises, shall be deemed and taken as presumptive evidence that such person is a distiller within the meaning of this act.

SECTION 3. *And be it further enacted,* That every person, firm, or corporation, who rectifies, purifies, or refines spirituous liquors or wines by any process, or who, by mixing distilled spirits, whiskey, brandy, gin, or wine, with any materials, manufactures any spurious, imitation, or compound liquors, for sale, under the name of whiskey, brandy, gin, rum, wine, "spirits," or "wine bitters," or any other name, shall be regarded as a rectifier under this act.

SECTION 4. *And be it further enacted,* That if any person or persons shall carry on any business of distilling or rectifying without having taken out such license as may be in that behalf required, he or they shall, for every such offence, besides being liable to the payment of the tax upon the spirits distilled, also be liable to a penalty of one hundred per cent. in addition, to be assessed by the assessor, and shall each be subject, upon conviction, to imprisonment for a term not exceeding two years; and upon sufficient information of such offence, the collector, deputy collector, or other authorized officer of the district, in which the same shall be alleged to have been committed, may enter upon the premises of the person or persons by whom such offence is alleged to have been committed, using such force as may be necessary for that purpose, and may seize all spirits or spirituous liquors, and all materials for making or preparing the same respectively, and all vessels and utensils containing the same, and all stills or other apparatus capable of being used for distilling, and may hold the same. And the said collector, upon the assessment aforesaid having been made, and upon the conviction of the said person or persons, shall proceed to destroy such stills or apparatus, or render the same permanently unfit for the purpose of distilling. And in case of conviction, the said collector shall sell the materials of which the same was composed, and such liquors and other materials and vessels and utensils, so seized; and shall apply the proceeds in satisfaction of such assessment, and of the fine, if imposed; and the said assessment and fine, or such part thereof as shall not have been so satisfied, shall, until paid, be a lien in favor of the United States, from and after the time when such assessment is made, or such fine laid, upon all property and rights to property of the person by whom such offence shall have been committed, and upon his interest in the lands and premises in which it shall have been committed, and upon all his property therein at the time of its commission; and such lien may be enforced by levy and distraint by said collector, or by suit *in rem;* and when the personal property found shall not be sufficient to satisfy the same, such lands and premises may be seized, and upon the decree of the court the interest aforesaid sold, and proceeds applied in payment thereof. And the person or persons furnishing the information upon which such seizure shall have been made, or the officer who made such seizure, if having acted upon information obtained by himself, shall, upon the order of the Secretary of the Treasury, receive such part and in such proportions of a moiety of the said one hundred per cent. assessed penalty, and of a moiety of the said fine when recovered, as the Secretary of the Treasury shall determine.

SECTION 5. *And be it further enacted,* That every person, firm or corporation required by this act to be licensed, as a distiller, or as a rectifier, shall, before receiving such license, make and sign an application therefor in writing to the assessor of the district. Every such application shall state the name or style under which, the name or names and the place or places of residence of the person or persons by whom, and the place where, the business is to be carried on, and its nature. If the business is that of a distiller, the application shall also state the nature of stills or boilers to be used, and the capacity of each, and the name or names of the owner or owners of the land or premises on which the distillery is situated, and the nature of the title by which such premises will be held and occupied by said applicant or applicants. Any false and fraudulent representation in such application contained shall make void a license issued thereupon from its issue; and the person or persons making the same shall be liable to a fine of three hundred dollars, to be recovered with costs of suit.

SECTION 6. *And be it further enacted,* That no license shall be granted to any person or persons to engage in the business of making or distilling spirits or spirituous liquors until such person has, jointly and severally, with two or more good and sufficient sureties, to be approved by the collector within whose district the business for which such license is required is to be carried on, entered into a bond to the United States in such sum as shall be hereinafter specified; and such bond shall be accompanied with satisfactory affidavits of the sufficiency of the sureties executing the same, and such approval shall be indorsed on said bond by the collector, and the affidavits be attached thereto; and a new bond may be required by the collector whenever, during the term for which the license to which it relates is in force, either of the sureties shall die, become insolvent, or remove permanently out of the collection district; in any of which cases, the license shall be suspended from the time the party to whom it was granted is required by the collector, by a notice in writing, to enter into a new bond, until the time when such bond is given; during which time the party failing to enter into such new bond shall be held to be without a license. The bond shall be conditioned that, in case any still or stills, or other implements to be used for distilling, shall be erected or used by him, his agent or superintendent, he will, before using, or causing, or permitting the same to be used, report in writing to said assessor the capacity thereof, and give information from time to time of any change in the location, form, capacity, ownership, agency, or superintendence, which all or either of the said still or stills or other implements may undergo; that he will, from day to day, enter or cause to be entered in a book to be kept for that purpose the number of pounds or gallons of materials used, and the number of gallons of spirits that may be distilled by said still or stills, or other implements; that said book shall be open at all hours during the day (Sundays excepted) to the inspection of any assessor, assistant assessor, collector, deputy collector, revenue agent, or inspector, who may make any memorandums or transcripts therefrom; that he will render to said assessor or assistant assessor, on the first, eleventh, and twenty-first days of each and every month, or within five days thereafter, an exact account in writing of the number of pounds or gallons of material used for the purpose of producing spirits, and the number of gallons of spirits distilled, and also the number of gallons placed in warehouse; and that he will not sell, or permit to be sold, or removed for consumption or sale, any spirits distilled by him under and by virtue of said license, until the same shall have been gauged, inspected, proved, and deposited in the bonded warehouse, and the quantity thereof duly entered upon his books as aforesaid, with name and place of business of the party to whom such spirits may be sold: *Provided*, That such bond shall not be required for a greater amount than double the amount of duties on the spirits that can be distilled by such still or stills or other implements during a period of fifteen days; and shall be conditioned for the rendering of all accounts, and the payment of all duties and penalties which the party, to whom the license is to be granted, will become liable to render or pay under the laws of the United States; and that such party will faithfully comply with the requirements thereof, according to their true intent and meaning, as well with regard to such accounts, duties, and penalties, as to all other matters and things whatsoever; and such bond shall be executed before the said collector of internal revenue, who shall cause such sureties to justify as to their sufficiency before him by affidavit indorsed upon such bond; and the said bond shall be filed with the said collector of internal revenue, and a copy of the same shall be forthwith transmitted to the Commissioner of Internal Revenue at Washington; and the bond aforesaid shall remain in force until all the provisions and conditions of said bond and license have been fully complied with But whenever any new license is granted to any party, a new bond shall be likewise entered into with reference to such new license.

SECTION 7. *And be it further enacted*, That upon every application duly made, as herein provided, for a license to carry on the business of making, distilling, rectifying, or compounding spirits or spirituous liquors, and upon the payment of the license fees or duties imposed, and the due execution of the bond with sureties as herein required by law, and not before, the collector of internal revenue of the district shall issue a license to carry on the business, and to use the utensils, machinery and apparatus specified in the application, and in the place or premises therein specified, and in such place or premises only; and the license thus granted shall be issued in duplicate when required by the applicant; and every person, firm, or corporation, licensed as herein provided, shall place such license, during the continuance thereof, in some conspicuous place in the distillery or rectifying house, or in the office connected therewith, and a duplicate thereof in a conspicuous place in each and every office or place of business established elsewhere by the manufacturer for the sale of such spirits, which duplicate it shall be the duty of the collector to furnish on application therefor; and in case of neglect so to do, shall forfeit and pay a fine of one hundred dollars for each and every case of such neglect: *Provided*, That any collector may refuse to issue a license to any distiller when, in his judgment, the location of the distillery is such as would enable the distiller to defraud the government in respect to the revenue; and, in case of such refusal, the distiller may appeal to the Commissioner of Internal Revenue, whose decision in the matter shall be final. The burden of proof that any license required by this act has issued shall rest upon the person to whom such license is alleged to have been issued. Upon the expiration of every license issued under this act, the granting of a new license in lieu thereof shall be subject to the same restrictions and conditions as the granting of the original license was subject to.

SECTION 8. *And be it further enacted*, That every license which shall be taken out under and by authority of this act shall contain and set forth the purpose for which such license is granted, and the name and place of abode of the person or persons taking out the same; and if for a distiller, the number and capacity of the stills, boilers, or other vessels to be used, and the place where the business for which such license is granted is to be carried on: *Provided*, That a license granted under this act shall not authorize the person or persons, firm, company, or corporation, mentioned therein, to carry on the business specified in such license in any other place than that mentioned therein; but nothing herein contained shall prohibit the storage of goods, wares, or merchandise, other than spirits upon which the duty shall not have been paid, in other places than the place of business of the person or persons, firm, company, or corporation, to whom the above license is granted; nor shall the distiller or rectifier be required to take out any additional license for the sale of the spirits distilled or rectified by him, and sold at the place of manufacture or at the principal office or place of business of such distiller or rectifier, licensed as aforesaid; nor shall he sell at retail at his place of manufacture; but such distiller or rectifier shall, before he shall sell any goods, wares, or merchandise, other than of his own manufacture, and stored in his manufactory or principal office or place of business or elsewhere, obtain a license therefor as by law provided; and any person licensed to carry on the business of distilling or rectifying as aforesaid shall, on demand of any officer of internal revenue, produce such license, and unless he shall do so, he may be taken and deemed to have no license.

SECTION 9. *And be it further enacted*, That upon the death of any person or persons licensed under and by virtue of this act, and in case of the transfer and assignment of said business to any other person or upon the removal of any person or persons from the house or premises, at which the business mentioned in such license was authorized to be carried on, with the purpose of carrying on such business at some other place, it may and shall be lawful for the collector to authorize, by indorsement on such license, the executors or administrators, or the wife or child of such deceased person, or the assignee or assignees of such person or persons so transferring and assigning said business as aforesaid, to whom such license may be assigned, and who shall be possessed of and occupy the house and premises before used for such purpose as aforesaid, in like manner to exercise or carry on the same business mentioned in such license, in the same house or upon the same premises at which said person or persons as aforesaid deceased or removing as before mentioned, by virtue of such license before exercised or carried on such business, the person or persons so removing as aforesaid to any other place to carry on the business specified in such license at the place to which such person may have removed, for or during the residue of the term for which such license was originally granted, without taking out any other or new license until the expiration thereof: *Provided*, That, in case of the decease of the person or persons licensed, a new bond shall be executed by the representatives of such deceased person who carry on business under such license, for the remaining time: *Provided further*, That a fresh entry of the premises, at which such business shall continue to be carried on as aforesaid, shall thereupon be made by or in the name or names of the person or persons to whom such authority as aforesaid shall be granted.

SECTION 10. *And be it further enacted*, That no license shall be granted to any person, firm, or corporation, to use any still, boiler, or other vessel, for the purpose of distilling spirituous liquors in any building or on any premises where beer, lager-beer, ale, porter, or other fermented liquors, are manufactured; and no still, boiler, or other vessel, shall be used as aforesaid in any building or on any premises where beer, lager-beer, ale, porter, or other fermented liquors, vinegar, ether, or alcohol, are manufactured or produced, or where sugars or sirups are refined, or where liquors of any description are retailed, or any other business is carried on; and every person who shall use such still, boiler, or other vessel, for the purpose of distilling, as aforesaid, in any building or other premises where the above specified articles are manufactured, produced, or other business is carried on, or who shall procure the same to be done, shall forfeit such stills, boilers, or other vessels so used, and all the spirits distilled, and pay a fine of one thousand dollars, and be imprisoned for not less than six months nor more than one year, in the discretion of the court; and any person, firm, or corporation, who shall manufacture any still, boiler, or other vessel, to be used for the purpose of distilling, shall, before the same is removed from the place of manufacture, notify the collector where such still, boiler, or other vessel, is to be used or sent, of the intention to send or set up the same, and of its capacity, and the time when the same is to be sent or set up; and no such still, boiler, or other vessel, shall be set up without the permit in writing of the collector for that purpose; and any person, firm, or corporation, who shall set up such still, boiler, or other vessel, without first obtaining a permit from the collector of the district in which such still, boiler, or other vessel, is intended to be used, or who shall fail to give such notice, shall forfeit and pay in either case the sum of five hundred dollars, and in all the distilling apparatus thus manufactured or set up in violation of this statute: *Provided*, That saleratus may be made or manufactured in any building or on any premises where spirits are distilled: *Provided further*, That any boiler used in generating steam or heating water to be used in such distillery may be located in any other building or on any other premises to be connected with such still or boiling tubs, by suitable pipes or other apparatus, or the steam from such boiler in the distillery may be conveyed to other premises to be used for manufacturing or other purposes.

SECTION 11. *And be it further enacted*, That there shall be paid annually for each license granted, the sums herein stated respectively; that is to say, distillers shall pay five hundred dollars for each license; rectifiers shall pay two hundred and fifty dollars for each license; wholesale dealers in liquors, whose annual sales do not exceed fifty thousand dollars, shall pay fifty dollars for each license; and if exceeding fifty thousand, dollars for every additional one thousand dollars in excess of fifty thousand dollars, one dollar. Every person who shall sell or offer for sale any distilled spirits, fermented liquors, or wines, not manufactured by him, in quantities of more than three gallons at one time to the same purchaser, or whose annual sales, including sales of other merchandise, shall exceed twenty-five thousand dollars, shall be regarded as a wholesale dealer in liquors under this act. Retail dealers in liquors shall pay twenty-five dollars for each license. Every person who shall sell, or offer for sale, foreign or domestic liquors, wines, ale, beer, or other malt liquors, in quantities of three gallons or less, or whose annual sales, including all sales of other merchandise, do not exceed twenty-five thousand dollars, shall be regarded as a retail dealer under this act: *Provided*, That nothing in this act shall be construed to prevent apothecaries from dispensing, upon physician's prescription, without a retail dealer's license, the wines and spirits officinal in the United States and other national pharmacopœias, either simple or compounded, in quantities not exceeding half a pint of either at one time, nor exceeding in aggregate cost value the sum of three hundred dollars per annum. Nothing herein contained shall authorize the sale of spirits, wines, or malt liquors to be drunk on the premises; and no license granted to a distiller, rectifier, wholesale or retail dealer in liquors, shall authorize the carrying on of any other business, trade, or occupation, for which a license would otherwise be required. All rectifiers and wholesale dealers in distilled spirits and fermented liquors shall keep such record of purchases and sales, and make such return thereof, in time, manner, and form, as may be required by the Commissioner of Internal Revenue. Every rectifier shall mark, with stencil plate, on each package of five gallons or more, his name and place of business: *Provided*, That no license hereinbefore provided for shall, if granted, be held or construed to exempt any person carrying on the trade, business, or profession specified in said license from any penalty or punishment provided by the laws of any State for carrying on such trade, business, or profession, within such State, or in any manner to authorize the commencement or continuance of such trade, business, or profession, contrary to the laws of such state, or in places prohibited by municipal law; nor shall any such license be held or construed to prevent or prohibit any State from placing a duty or tax for State or other purposes on any trade, business, or profession for which a license is required by this act; nor shall any person carrying on any trade, business, or profession, for which a license is required by this act, be exempted from procuring such license, or from any penalty or punishment herein provided, by, or in consequence of, any State law either authorizing or prohibiting such trade, business, or profession.

SECTION 12. *And be it further enacted*, That the owner or owners of any distillery licensed as aforesaid shall provide, at his or their own expense, a warehouse suitable for the storage of bonded spirits, of their own manufacture only; or he or they may provide a secure room, in a suitable building, to be used as such warehouse; and no door, window or other opening, shall be made or permitted in the walls thereof, leading to any other room or building used for any other purpose, or into the distillery; and after a bond has been given, as hereinafter provided, such warehouse or room, when approved by the Commissioner of Internal Revenue, on report of the district collector, is hereby declared to be a bonded warehouse of the United States, and shall be used only for the storing of spirits manufactured by the owner, agent, or superintendent thereof, and shall be under the custody of the inspector as hereinafter provided; and shall be kept locked up by the proper officer in charge, at all times, except when he shall be in attendance; and the duty on the spirits stored in such warehouse shall be paid before it is removed from such warehouse, unless destroyed by fire or the elements, or removed in pursuance of law; and the collector shall not issue a distiller's license to any person or persons until he or they shall have provided for his or their distillery a proper warehouse or room with proper fastenings approved by the aforesaid collector; and the owner or owners of such warehouse shall execute a general bond to the United States with two or more sureties to be approved by the collector; and such bond shall be for double the amount of duties on the spirits to be covered thereby, and in such form, and containing such conditions, as shall be approved by the Commissioner of Internal Revenue; and may be changed from time to time by the collector in regard to the amount and sureties thereof.

SECTION 13. *And be it further enacted,* That general bonded warehouses, for the storage of spirits or other merchandise allowed by law to be placed in bond to secure the payment of the internal revenue tax thereon, or the exportation thereof, may be established under such rules and regulations and upon the execution of such bonds as the Commissioner of Internal Revenue may prescribe, and shall be in the immediate custody of storekeepers who shall be appointed for that purpose, whose compensation shall be paid monthly to the collector of the district by the owners or proprietors of such warehouse, and shall not exceed the rates which may be allowed to storekeepers of bonded warehouses established under the laws and regulations relating to the customs.

SECTION 14. *And be it further enacted,* That there shall be appointed by the Secretary of the Treasury an inspector for each and every distillery established according to law, who shall take an oath faithfully to perform his duties; and who shall take an account of all the meal and vegetable productions or other substances to be used for the purpose of producing spirits, when put into the mash tub or otherwise used; and shall inspect, gauge and prove all the spirits distilled, under such rules and regulations as may be prescribed by the Commissioner of Internal Revenue; and shall take charge of the bonded warehouse established for the distillery in conformity to law; and such warehouse shall be in the joint custody of such inspector and the owner thereof, his agent or superintendent; and when any spirits shall be placed in such warehouse, an entry therefor, in such form as shall be prescribed by regulations, shall immediately be made and signed by the owner of said spirits, and shall have indorsed thereon a certificate of the inspector that the spirits mentioned have been duly inspected and received in said warehouse, and such entry and certificate shall be filed with the collector of the district; and whenever such warehouse is within the limits of any port of entry where there shall be a superintendent of exports, a duplicate of such entry and certificate shall forthwith be filed in the office of such superintendent; and said inspector shall also certify to the returns to be made by the distiller to the assessor; and shall not engage in any other business while holding the office of inspector; and he shall be paid such compensation as the Secretary of the Treasury may deem just and reasonable, at a rate not exceeding $1,500 per annum, for the time during which he is engaged; and the amount of compensation thus paid for inspection shall be assessed by the assessor upon the distiller, and returned to the collector monthly; and in addition to the above compensation, such inspector shall receive one-eighth of one cent for each and every proof-gallon of distilled spirits inspected by him and removed to the bonded warehouse, which shall be paid by the distiller or owner of the spirits; but no compensation shall be allowed to such inspector for more than one inspection of such spirits. And in case the duties of such inspector shall be greater at any time than he can perform, upon the joint application of the inspector and owner of such distillery, the collector may appoint an assistant inspector, and upon the refusal of the distiller to join in such application the collector shall decide as to such necessity; and such assistant inspector shall qualify in the same manner and be subject to the same penalties as the inspector; and he shall be paid in the same manner as the inspector, at a rate not exceeding the sum of three dollars ($3) per day while so employed; and in case of disagreement as to the necessity of retaining the services of such assistant, between the owner of the distillery and the inspector, the collector shall decide as to such necessity, and his decision in the matter shall be final. And in case of absence by sickness, or from any other cause, of such inspector or assistant, the collector may appoint an officer to take temporary charge of such distillery and warehouse, who shall receive the same rate of pay as said inspector or assistant for the time he may be so employed, such amount to be deducted from the pay of the absent officer: *Provided*, That the owner, agent or superintendent of any distillery licensed as herein provided, who shall use, cause or permit to be used, any materials for the purpose of producing spirits, or shall distil and remove any spirits in the absence of the acting inspector or assistant, without permission granted by the collector of the district, shall forfeit and pay double the amount of duties on the spirits so produced, distilled or removed, and in addition thereto a fine of one thousand dollars, to be recovered in the manner provided for other penalties imposed by this act. *Provided further*, That any person who shall ship, transport or remove any spirituous or fermented liquors or wines, under any other than the proper name or brand known to the trade as designating the kind and quality of the contents of the casks or packages containing the same, or who shall cause the same to be done, shall forfeit the same, and shall, on conviction thereof, be subject to and pay a fine of five hundred dollars.

SECTION 15. *And be it further enacted*, That there shall be appointed by the Secretary of the Treasury, in every collection district where the same may be necessary, one or more general inspectors of spirits, who shall each take an oath faithfully to perform his duties, in such form as the Commissioner of Internal Revenue may prescribe, and who shall be entitled to receive one-quarter of one cent for each and every wine-gallon gauged and proved by him; and any owner, agent or superintendent of any distillery or bonded warehouse, who shall refuse to admit an inspector upon such premises, so far as it may be necessary for the performance of his duties, or who shall obstruct an inspector in the performance of his duties, shall forfeit and pay the sum of five hundred dollars, to be recovered in the manner provided for recovery of other penalties imposed by this act.

SECTION 16. *And be it further enacted*, That every person who shall be the owner of any still, boiler, or other vessel, used or intended to be used, for the purpose of distilling spirits, as hereinbefore provided, or who shall have such still, boiler, or other vessel, under his superintendence, either as agent for the owner or for his own account; and every person who shall use any still or other vessel as aforesaid, either as owner, agent, or otherwise, shall from day to day make true and exact entry, or cause to be entered, in a book, to be kept in such form as the Commissioner of Internal Revenue may prescribe for that purpose, the number of pounds or gallons of materials used for the purpose of producing spirits, and the number of gallons of spirits distilled, and also the number of gallons placed in warehouse and the proof thereof, which book shall always be open in the daytime (Sundays excepted) for the inspection of any assessor, assistant assessor, collector, deputy collector, supervisor, or inspector, who may take minutes, memorandums, or transcripts thereof; and shall render to the assessor or assistant assessor of the district, on the first, eleventh, and twenty-first days of each and every month in each year, or within five days thereafter, an account in duplicate, taken from his books, of the number of pounds and gallons of material used in producing spirits, the number of gallons of spirits distilled, and also the number of gallons removed to bonded warehouse and the proof thereof—which said account shall be verified by affidavit prescribed by law, and be certified to by the inspector—and shall immediately forward to the collector of the district one of said duplicate accounts, and shall pay to the collector the duties on the spirits so distilled before removing the same from the bonded warehouse, unless removed as herein provided.

SECTION 17. *And be it further enacted*, That the entries to be made in the books of the distiller, as aforesaid, shall, upon the days when the respective returns are to be made, as hereinafter provided, be verified by the signature in writing of the person or persons by whom such entries shall have been made, in the presence of the assessor or assistant assessor, or other proper officer, who shall append thereto his certificate of the execution of the same.

SECTION 18. *And be it further enacted,* That the owner, agent, or superintendent of any distillery aforesaid shall, in case the original entries required to be made in his books by this act shall not have been made by himself, subjoin to the certificate of the person by whom they were made, the following certificate: "I do certify that, to the best of my knowledge and belief, the foregoing entries are just and true, and that I have taken all the means in my power to make them so."

Any person licensed as aforesaid to distil spirits who shall neglect or refuse to furnish the account and duplicate thereof, as herein provided, or who shall refuse to permit the said assessor or assistant assessor, collector or deputy collector, or inspector, to examine the books in the manner herein provided for, when requested, shall, for every such refusal or neglect, forfeit and pay the sum of five hundred dollars.

SECTION 19. *And be it further enacted,* That, in addition to the duties payable for licenses herein provided, there shall be levied, collected, and paid on all spirits that may be distilled and removed from the bonded warehouse for consumption or sale, of first-proof, on and after the passage of this act, an excise tax or duty of ——— dollars on each and every proof gallon; and the said duties shall be a lien on the spirits distilled, and on the distillery used for distilling the same, with the stills, vessels, fixtures, and tools therein, and on the interest of said distiller in lot or tract of land whereon the said distillery is situated, until the said duties shall be paid: *Provided,* That the duty on all spirits shall be collected at no lower rate than the basis of first-proof, and shall be increased in proportion for any greater strength than the strength of first-proof: *Provided further,* That drawback shall not in any case be allowed of any excise tax paid on such spirits.

SECTION 20. *And be it further enacted,* That the term first-proof used in this act and in the laws of the United States shall be construed, and is hereby declared, to mean that proof of a liquor which corresponds to fifty degrees of Tralle's centesimal hydrometer, adopted by regulation of the Treasury Department of August twelfth, eighteen hundred and fifty, at the temperature of sixty degrees Fahrenheit's thermometer; and that the Secretary of the Treasury is hereby empowered to adopt and procure hydrometers, gauging instruments, and such other apparatus as he may deem necessary, and to cause their use for the protection of the revenue in securing uniform and correct return of spirits subject to tax. And in all sales of spirits hereafter made, where not otherwise specially agreed, a gallon shall be taken to be a gallon of first-proof, according to the standard set forth and declared for the inspection and gauging of spirits throughout the United States.

SECTION 21. *And be it further enacted,* That the owner, agent, or superintendent of any distillery established as hereinbefore provided, shall erect, in a room or building to be provided and used for that purpose, and for no other, two or more receiving cisterns, each to be at least of sufficient capacity to hold all the spirits distilled during the day of twenty-four hours, into one of which shall be conveyed each day all the spirits manufactured in said distillery during that day; and such cisterns shall be so constructed as to leave an open space of at least three feet between the tops thereof and the floor or roof above, and of not less than eighteen inches between the bottoms thereof and the floor below, and shall be separated in such a manner as will enable the inspector to pass around the same, and shall be connected with the stills, boilers, or other vessels used for distilling, at their outlet, by suitable pipes or other apparatus so constructed as always to be exposed to the view of the inspector; such cisterns and the room in which they are contained shall be in charge of and under the lock and seal of the inspector; and on the third day after the spirits are conveyed into such cisterns the same shall be drawn off into casks or other packages, under the supervision of the inspector, and shall be immediately inspected, gauged, proved, and the casks or packages marked, as herein provided, and be removed directly to the bonded warehouse before mentioned: *Provided,* That the spirits may be drawn off from said cisterns at any time previous to the third day aforesaid, if so desired by the owner, agent, or superintendent of such distillery; and all locks and seals required under this act shall be provided by the Secretary of the Treasury, at the expense of the owner of the distillery, and shall be combination locks and susceptible of at least ninety-six changes, and the bits of the keys thereof shall be changed at least once a week, and shall always be in the custody of the inspector or assistant inspector, or the officer having charge of the distillery and warehouse.

SECTION 22. *And be it further enacted,* That any person who shall knowingly and fraudulently use any false weights and measures in ascertaining, weighing, or measuring the quantities of grain, meal, or vegetable materials, molasses, or beer, or other substances to be used for distillation, or who shall fraudulently make false record of the same, or who shall destroy or tamper with any locks or seal which may be placed on any cistern, rooms, or buildings, by the duly authorized officers of the revenue, shall be guilty of a felony, and on conviction thereof shall be imprisoned for the term of two years, and pay a fine not exceeding one thousand dollars, in the discretion of the court; and any person who shall use any molasses, beer, or other substances, whether fermented on the premises or elsewhere, for the purpose of producing spirits, before an account of the same shall have been registered in the proper record book provided for this purpose, shall forfeit and pay the sum of one thousand dollars for each and every offence so committed.

SECTION 23. *And be it further enacted,* That any person who shall be licensed to use any still, boiler, or other vessel for the purpose of re-distilling or rectifying, or for the purpose of distilling spirits other than spirituous liquors, and who shall use, cause or permit, with intent to evade the law, such still, boiler, or other vessel, to be used for the purpose of producing spirituous liquors, shall forfeit all the spirits distilled or found on the premises, and shall also forfeit such st ll, boiler, or other vessel, and all the tools and implements used therein, and pay a fine of one thousand dollars, and be imprisoned for not more than two years, in the discretion of the court.

SECTION 24 *And be it further enacted,* That upon all wines manufactured from the juice of grapes grown within or upon the territory of the United States, there shall be levied and paid a duty of six cents per gallon, and upon all other still wines, or liquors known or denominated as wine, (not made from currants, rhubarb, or berries,) produced by being rectified or mixed with other spirits, or into which any matter whatever may be infused, or manufactured from grapes grown elsewhere than in the United States, to be sold as wine or under any other name, and not otherwise provided for in this act, a duty of ten cents per gallon: *Provided,* That the return, assessment, collection, and the time of collection, of the duties on such wines, and wine made from grapes, shall be subject to the regulations of the Commissioner of Internal Revenue; and any person who shall wilfully and knowingly sell or offer for sale any such wine made after the passage of this act, upon which the duty herein imposed has not been paid, or has been fraudulently evaded, shall forfeit all wines, materials and implements used in the manufacture thereof, and, upon conviction thereof, be subject to a fine of five hundred dollars, or to imprisonment not exceeding one year, at the discretion of the court.

SECTION 25. *And be it further enacted,* That on all wines, liquors, or compounds known or denominated as wine, made in imitation of sparkling wine or champagne, and put up in bottles under the label, name, designation, or similitude of any imported wine, or wine of foreign growth or manufacture, or with the appearance or pretence of being imported wine, or wine of foreign growth or manufacture, there shall be levied and paid a duty of six dollars per dozen bottles, each bottle containing more than one pint; or three dollars per dozen bottles, each bottle containing not more than one pint; and the returns, assessment, collection, and time of collection of the duties on such imitation wines as are herein and above designated, shall be subject to the regulations of the Commissioner of Internal Revenue. And any person who shall wilfully and knowingly sell or offer for sale any such wine made after the passage of this act, upon which the duty herein imposed has not been paid, or which has been fraudulently evaded, shall, upon conviction thereof, be subject to a penalty of one thousand dollars, or to imprisonment not exceeding one year, at the discretion of the court.

SECTION 26. *And be it further enacted*, That every person licensed under this act, and his agents, shall, at all times when required, supply any officer of excise with all assistance, lights, ladders, tools, staging, or other things necessary for inspecting the premises, stock, tools, and apparatus, belonging to such licensed person, and shall open all doors, and open for examination all boxes, packages, and all casks, barrels, and other vessels not under the control of the inspector, when required so to do by any duly authorized officer of excise, under a penalty of two hundred dollars for any refusal or neglect so to do.

SECTION 27. *And be it further enacted*, That all spirits distilled as aforesaid, by any person licensed as aforesaid, shall, before the same are removed to the bonded warehouse, be inspected, gauged, and proved by the inspector appointed for that purpose, after the same has been drawn into casks or packages, each of not less capacity than twenty gallons, wine measure, and said inspector shall mark, by cutting or branding, upon the cask or package containing such spirits, in a manner to be prescribed by the Commissioner of Internal Revenue, the quantity and proof of the contents of such cask or package, with the date of inspection, the collection district, the name of the inspector, and the name of the distiller, and also the number of each cask in progressive order, such progressive number, for every distiller, to begin with number one with the first cask or package inspected after this act, and subsequently with number one with the first cask inspected on or after the first day of January in each year, and no two or more casks warehoused in the same year by the same distiller shall be marked with the same number, and the officer in charge of the warehouse shall refuse to allow any cask of spirits to be taken out therefrom which has not cut or branded thereon all the several particulars aforesaid, and in the manner required by this act. And the inspector or other revenue officer in charge of each and every distillery shall make a prompt return of all spirits inspected by him in accordance with the provisions of this act, and the name of the distiller, to the collector, and a duplicate thereof to the assessor of the district; and any person who shall fraudulently evade or attempt fraudulently to evade the payment of the duties upon any spirits distilled as aforesaid, by changing any marks upon any such cask or package, or in any other manner whatever, or who shall fraudulently put into such cask or package spirits of greater strength than that inspected and certified to by the inspector, shall pay double the amount of duties on each proof gallon of the quantity of such spirits, and forfeit and pay as a penalty the additional sum of five hundred dollars for each cask or package so altered or changed, to be recovered as herein provided; and any inspector who shall knowingly put upon any such cask or package any false or fraudulent marks, shall, on conviction, be imprisoned one year, and be liable to a fine of five hundred dollars, in the discretion of the court; and any person who shall fraudulently use any cask or package bearing inspection marks, for the purpose of selling any other spirits than that so inspected, or for selling spirits of a quantity or quality different from that so inspected, shall be imprisoned for a term of six months, or shall pay a fine of one hundred dollars for each cask or package so used, in the discretion of the court; and any person who shall knowingly purchase or sell any empty cask or package with inspection marks thereon, which has contained distilled spirits, or who shall fraudulently omit to permanently erase or obliterate the inspection marks upon any such package or cask at the time of emptying the same, shall forfeit and pay the sum of fifty dollars for each and every cask so purchased or used, or on which the marks are not so obliterated. And any person who shall, with fraudulent intent, use any inspector's brands or plates upon any cask or package containing or purporting to contain distilled spirits, except in the employ of the inspector, or who shall knowingly make or use any counterfeit or spurious brand or plate upon any cask or package of distilled spirits, as aforesaid, shall be deemed guilty of a felony, and, on conviction thereof, shall forfeit the same and shall pay a fine of one thousand dollars, and be imprisoned for not less than two nor more than five years. And any inspector who shall permit any person not employed by him to use any of his brands or plates, or who shall negligently or wilfully leave such brands or plates where they can be used by any other person than those who may be in his employ, shall pay a fine not exceeding one thousand dollars, in the discretion of the court. And any inspector who shall employ any owner, agent, or superintendent of any distillery or warehouse under his supervision, or who shall employ any person in the service of such owner, agent, or superintendent, to use his plates or brands, or to discharge any of the duties imposed by this act upon such inspector, shall, for each offence so committed, be subject to the same fine last mentioned.

SECTION 28. *And be it further enacted,* That any person or persons who shal add, or cause to be added, any ingredients to any spirits either before or after the duties imposed by law shall have been paid thereon, for the purpose of creating a fictitious proof, shall, upon conviction, each be subject to a fine of one thousand dollars for each cask or package so adulterated, and be imprisoned for not more than two nor less than one year, in the discretion of the court.

SECTION 29. *And be it further enacted,* That any distilled spirits, upon which an excise duty is imposed by law, which has been inspected, gauged, proved, and marked by the inspector, according to the provisions of this act, may be removed without the payment of duty from the bonded warehouse owned by the distiller, under such rules and regulations, and upon the execution of such transportation bonds or other security, as the Secretary of the Treasury may prescribe, and may be transported to any general bonded warehouse used for the storage of distilled spirits, and established under the internal revenue laws and regulations, after having been branded as follows: "U. S. bonded warehouse, —— district, ——: for transport to —— district, ——" (inserting in each case the number of the district and name of the State;) and immediately after the arrival of such distilled spirits at the bonded warehouse within the district of the collector to which it has been transferred, it shall again be inspected andplaced in bond, and the transportation brand last mentioned obliterated; and the duty shall be assessed and paid on any deficiency or reduction of the number of proof gallons (except the actual loss, not exceeding five per cent. for leakage) received at the warehouse, from the number of proof gallons as stated in the bond given at the place of shipment; and no allowance shall be made, except for the actual loss as aforesaid, or for destruction by unavoidable accident, or by the elements; and any distilled spirits entered in a general bonded warehouse shall be subject to such rules and regulations as the Commissioner of Internal Revenue may prescribe, and be chargeable with the same costs and expenses, in all respects, to which imported goods deposited in public store or bonded warehouse may be subject, and shall be in charge of a storekeeper, to be appointed by the Secretary of the Treasury, who, with the owner and proprietor of the warehouse, shall have the joint custody of all the distilled spirits so stored in said warehouse, which shall be at the risk of the owner of the said spirits; and all labor on the same shall be performed by the owner or proprietor of the warehouse, under the supervision of the officer in charge of the same, and at the expense of said owner or proprietor. And the same fees shall be paid for execution of all papers, instruments, and documents relating to the exportation of any spirits or other merchandise, as are charged to exporters for like services in the custom-house; and all expense and services required in the removal, transfer, and shipment of the same for export shall be paid by the owner thereof: *Provided also*, That any distilled spirits may be withdrawn from a bonded warehouse, after having been inspected and gauged by the proper officer, and after the payment to the collector of internal revenue, for the district in which the warehouse is situated, of the duty imposed by law; and when so delivered, shall be branded "U. S. bonded warehouse, tax paid;" or may be removed without the payment of the duty for the purpose of being exported; or for the purpose of being rectified, or re-distilled, canned, or put into other packages for export, after the quantity and proof of the spirits to be removed has been ascertained and inspected, according to the provisions of law, under such rules and regulations, and the execution of such bonds or other security, as the Secretary of the Treasury may prescribe; but such withdrawal of bonded spirits for the purpose of being rectified, re-distilled, or put into other packages, shall be allowed but once on the same spirits; and any spirits so removed for re-distillation, rectification, or change of package, shall be returned to the same warehouse, and shall again be inspected; and the duty shall be paid to the said collector on any deficiency or reduction beyond three per cent. for re-distillation, rectification, or evaporation, to be allowed in the number of proof gallons received at the warehouse for the purpose of being exported as aforesaid; and upon any spirits removed under bond for the purpose of being re-distilled or rectified, or for change of package as aforesaid, and upon which an allowance shall have been made, as herein provided, the duty upon such allowance shall be paid, together with the duties imposed by law upon such spirits, in case such spirits shall be withdrawn from warehouse for consumption or sale, or for transportation without being exported; and nothing in this section shall be so construed as to prevent the manufacture in bond for exportation, without the payment of duties, of medicines, preparations, compositions, perfumery, cosmetics, cordials, and other liquors manufactured wholly or in part of domestic spirits, as provided by law.

SECTION 30. *And be it further enacted*, That any spirits or other merchandise may be removed from bonded warehouse, for the purpose of being exported, upon the order of the superintendent of exports for the port whence the spirits are to be removed; and such order shall state the port to which such spirits are to be shipped and at which they are to be landed, and the name of the vessel, and also the number of proof-gallons, and the marks of the packages or casks; which shall be taken from and shall agree with the return of said spirits made by the inspector of the warehouse; and such spirits or other merchandise shall be branded "U. S. bonded warehouse, for export," and shall be put on board of the vessel in or by which they are to be exported, by an officer under direction of the superintendent of exports, and placed under the supervision of an officer of the customs, after a bond shall have been given in such form as, and containing the conditions which the Commissioner of Internal Revenue may prescribe, with one or more sureties, to be approved, as to the sufficiency of the sureties, as the Commissioner of Internal Revenue may direct. And such bond shall be cancelled upon the presentation of the proper certificate that said spirits have been landed at the port named in said bond, or at any other port without the jurisdiction of the United States, or upon satisfactory proof that after shipment the spirits have been lost: *Provided*, That the superintendent of exports may, when he shall deem it proper, give permission in writing, indorsed on or attached to the bond, to change the name of the vessel mentioned in the export bond to that of any other vessel bound to the same port, and by which said spirits or other merchandise may be shipped by his direction; and such change shall not release the principals or sureties from the obligations imposed by said bond. At any port where there shall be no superintendent of exports, all the duties and services required of superintendents of exports and drawback shall devolve upon and be performed by the collector of internal revenue designated to have charge of exportations.

SECTION 31. *And be it further enacted*, That any person or persons who shall execute or sign any false or fraudulent bond, permit, entry, or other document, required by law or regulations; or who shall fraudulently procure the same to be executed; or who shall connive at the execution thereof, by which the payment of any internal revenue tax or duty shall be evaded, or attempted to be evaded, or which shall be executed, or purport to be executed, for the purpose of placing in, or withdrawing from, any bonded warehouse, any spirits or other merchandise for any purpose whatever, or which shall in any way be used or attempted to be used in fraud of the internal revenue laws and regulations, shall be deemed guilty of a felony, and on conviction thereof shall forfeit all right, title, and interest in and to such spirits or other merchandise to which such instrument relates, or purports to relate; and shall be imprisoned for a term not less than two nor more than five years, at the discretion of the court.

SECTION 32. *And be it further enacted*, That any person owning any distilled spirits intended for sale, manufactured prior to the time when this act takes effect, exceeding fifty gallons altogether, shall notify in writing the collector of the district wherein such spirits may be stored, held, or owned, within sixty days thereafter, to gauge and prove the same; and upon the receipt of said notice the collector shall cause said spirits to be gauged and proved, and the casks or packages containing the same to be marked by the inspector in the following manner:

Manufactured prior to
———— 186—.
———— Inspector
—— District.
Inspected ——, 186—.

And no spirits so manufactured, held, or owned, shall be gauged, proved, or marked, in any cistern or other stationary vessel, but shall be gauged, proved, and marked only in barrels, casks, or packages, in which the same shall have been placed; and the quantity held in leach-tubs shall be estimated by the inspector, and, when drawn off into packages, shall be gauged and marked as herein provided. Upon the receipt of the return the collector shall immediately forward to the Commissioner of Internal Revenue a copy thereof; and any person holding or owning such spirits, and refusing or neglecting to notify the collector, as herein provided, shall forfeit the same and pay the sum of five hundred dollars, to be collected in the manner provided for the collection of other penalties incurred under this act. No distilled spirits on which the tax or duty has been paid shall be stored or allowed to remain on any distillery premises, under the penalty of a forfeiture of all spirits so found.

SECTION 33. *And be it further enacted*, That all boilers, stills, or other vessels, tools, and implements, used in distilling or rectifying, and forfeited under any of the provisions of this act, shall, under the direction of the court in which the forfeiture is recovered, be immediately broken up or rendered permanently unfit for use; and all such condemned material, together with any engine, boiler, or other machinery connected therewith, and all empty barrels, and all grain or other material suitable for distillation, shall be sold at public auction, and the proceeds thereof, after deducting the expenses of sale, be disposed of according to law; and all fines and forfeitures incurred or imposed by virtue of this act shall be sued for and recovered as by law provided, with cost of suit, and one moiety of the fines, forfeitures, and assessed penalties recovered shall be for the use of the United States, and the other moiety thereof to the use of the person or persons, to be ascertained by the judgment of the court, who shall, according to the judgment of such court, be in fact the cause of any such fine, penalty, or forfeiture being adjudged or recovered. And all spirits or spirituous liquors which may be forfeited under the provisions of this act, unless herein otherwise provided, shall be disposed of by the Commissioner of Internal Revenue as the Secretary of the Treasury may direct. When two or more persons constitute a firm, company, or corporation, the act of any one or more of such persons shall be deemed the act of all, so far as it affects their right to or forfeiture of any property or right in which they have a joint interest. The term "person," as used in this act, shall be held to include persons, firm, body corporate, company, or association.

SECTION 34. *And be it further enacted*, That all offences against any of the provisions of this act and for which punishments are herein prescribed, by fines or imprisonment, except such as shall otherwise be denominated in this act, are hereby declared to be misdemeanors. And all fines and forfeitures, pains or penalties imposed by the provisions of this act, shall be construed to be in addition to any liability or recovery against any party, by reason of the obligations or penalties contained in any bond. And all suits or actions for fines, penalties, and forfeitures imposed, or which may be incurred by any person or persons, under the provisions of this act, may be commenced and prosecuted to judgment in any court of the United States having jurisdiction in the district where such fines, penalties, and forfeitures were incurred; and all offences of any kind under this act may in like manner be prosecuted, tried, and conviction had, in any court of competent jurisdiction in the district; and in no case shall there be any compromise of any such suit or action, nor shall any prosecution be stayed except with the concurrence and consent of the United States attorney, or other person authorized to prosecute such suits for such district or circuit, and the Commissioner of Internal Revenue; and all such suits, actions, and prosecutions shall have preference on the calendar of such courts over any other suits or proceedings pending therein.

SECTION 35. *And be it further enacted*, That it shall be the duty of the Secretary of the Treasury and the Commissioner of Internal Revenue, immediately upon the passage of this act, to prepare and issue in proper form to the proper officers appointed under the internal revenue act, all the rules, regulations, and instructions required by, and which may be necessary to carry into full effect the several provisions of this act.

SECTION 36. *And be it further enacted*, That all the provisions of law relating to distilling, rectifying, manufacturing, and dealing in spirituous liquors, contained in the act entitled "An act to provide internal revenue to support the government, to pay interest on the public debt, and for other purposes," approved June 30, 1864, and the amendments thereto, and all provisions of law inconsistent herewith, are hereby repealed: *Provided, however*, That no duty or tax imposed or liability created by any previous act, and remaining unpaid, which has become due, or been incurred, or of which return has been or ought to be made, and no fine, forfeiture, or penalty incurred, or offence committed, or action, or rights of action or of property, existing or accrued prior to the time when this act shall take effect, shall be remitted or released, increased or diminished, by anything in this act contained; but the same shall be enforced, collected, and paid, and such offences punished in same manner as heretofore provided; and all bonds taken and licenses granted, and all things done under the authority and in pursuance of any of the acts or parts of acts hereby repealed, shall be as valid and effectual as if this act had not been passed: *Provided further*, That all spirits in bonded warehouse, or in transit under transportation bonds, or in the possession of the distiller, and subject to an excise duty, upon the passage of this act, shall be subject only to the provisions of said act.

SECTION 37. *And be it further enacted*, That this act shall take effect from and after ———

Respectfully submitted for the commission.

DAVID A. WELLS, *Chairman*.

www.ingramcontent.com/pod-product-compliance
Lightning Source LLC
LaVergne TN
LVHW021417110826
845150LV00007B/1970

9781425509262